Sex in the Digital Age

**Edited by Paul G. Nixon and
Isabel K. Düsterhöft**

Routledge
Taylor & Francis Group

LONDON AND NEW YORK

First published 2018 by Routledge

2 Park Square, Milton Park, Abingdon, Oxfordshire OX14 4RN

52 Vanderbilt Avenue, New York, NY 10017

Routledge is an imprint of the Taylor & Francis Group, an informa business

First issued in paperback 2018

British Library Cataloguing-in-Publication Data
A catalogue record for this book is available from the British Library

Library of Congress Cataloging-in-Publication Data
Names: Nixon, Paul G., author. | Dèusterhèoft, Isabel K., author.
Title: Sex in the digital age / Paul G. Nixon and Isabel K. Dèusterhèoft.
Description: Abingdon, Oxon; New York, NY: Routledge is an imprint of the Taylor & Francis Group, an Informa Business, [2017] | Series: Sexualities in society | Includes bibliographical references and index.
Identifiers: LCCN 2017016765 | ISBN 9781138214316 (hbk) | ISBN 9781315446240 (ebk)
Subjects: LCSH: Sex instruction—Social aspects. | Sex—Social aspects. | Online social networks. | Internet—Social aspects.
Classification: LCC HQ56 .N59 2017 | DDC 306.7—dc23
LC record available at https://lccn.loc.gov/2017016765

ISBN: 978-1-138-21431-6 (hbk)
ISBN: 978-0-367-20811-0 (pbk)

Typeset in Times New Roman
by codeMantra

Sex in the Digital Age

Shifts in societal development resulting from economic and technological advancements have had an impact upon the development of human sexuality and behaviour, and with the expansion of developments such as the Internet and associated technologies, it is likely that further societal shifts will ensue. This book recognises the importance of new digital spaces for discourses surrounding sexuality, examining issues such as pornography; sex education and health; LGBTQ sexualities; polysexuality or polyamory; abstention; sexual abuse and violence; erotic online literature; sex therapy; teledildonics; sex and gaming; online dating; celebrity porn; young people and sexual media; and sexting and sextainment, all of which are prominently affected by the use of digital media.

With case studies drawn from the US, Europe and Australia, *Sex in the Digital Age* engages in discussion about the changing acceptance of sex in the 21st century and the part played in that by digital media, and considers the future of sex and sexuality in an increasingly digital age. It will therefore appeal to scholars across the social sciences with interests in gender and sexuality, new technologies and media and cultural studies.

Paul G. Nixon is Principal Lecturer in Political Science in European Studies and University Platform Co-ordinator (Europe) at The Hague University of Applied Sciences, The Netherlands. He is the co-editor of *Digital Media Usage Across the Lifecourse*; *Lobbying the European Union: Changing Minds, Changing Times*; *Politics and the Internet in Comparative Context: Views from the Cloud*; *Understanding E-Government in Europe: Issues and Challenges*; *E-Government in Europe*; *Cyberprotest*; and *Politics Parties and the Internet*, and editor of *Representations of Education in Literature*.

Isabel K. Düsterhöft is a Lecturer in International and European Law in the European Studies programme at The Hague University of Applied Sciences, The Netherlands. Her research and publications mainly focus on international criminal law, international humanitarian law and civil society's contribution to conflict transformation. She was the editor in chief of the newsletter of the Association of Defence Counsel Practising Before the International Criminal Tribunal for the Former Yugoslavia (ADC-ICTY) between 2013 and 2016 and has managed the editorial process of various publications for this Association.

Sexualities in Society

https://www.routledge.com/Sexualities-in-Society/book-series/ASHSER1428

Series editor:
Helen Hester, The University of West London, UK

Sexualities in Society offers a dedicated and much-needed space for the very best in interdisciplinary research on sex, sexualities, and twenty-first century society. Its contemporary focus, methodological inclusivity, and international scope will provide a distinctive vantage point in terms of surveying the social organization of sexuality. It critically addresses numerous aspects of sex and sexuality, from media representations, to embodied sexual practices, to the sometimes controversial issues surrounding consent, sexual fantasy, and identity politics. It represents a critically rigorous, theoretically informed, and genuinely interdisciplinary attempt to interrogate a complex nexus of ideas regarding the ways in which sexualities inform, and are informed by, the broader sociopolitical contexts in which they emerge.

Titles in this series

1 **Rethinking Misogyny**
   Men's Perceptions of Female Power in Dating Relationships
   Anna Arrowsmith

2 **Consumer Sexualities**
   Women and Sex Shopping
   Rachel Wood

3 **Radical Sex Between Men**
   Assembling Desiring-Machines
   Edited by Dave Holmes, Stuart J. Murray and Thomas Foth

This collection is dedicated to the late Kitty Triest, a dear friend and colleague, who was an inspiration and a constant source of support and creative criticism.

Contents

Figures and tables

Figures

Tables

Contributors

Abbi Bloedel is a student at Northern Illinois University, USA and a sex, gender, reproductive rights and radical consent activist. They campaign regularly around issues of sexual freedom and consent. Abbi has also hosted non-sexual touch 'cuddle parties'. Mx. Bloedel was recently awarded one of eight scholarships to attend the 2016 Creating Change Conference in Chicago.

Ashley ML Brown is an assistant professor at Entertainment Arts and Engineering, University of Utah. She is the author of *Sexuality in Role-Playing Games* (Routledge 2015) and an editor of *The Dark Side of Game Play* (Routledge 2015). She has published extensively on the topic of sex and role-playing games, which remains the focus of her research. When she is not teaching or researching, Ashley enjoys taming unicorns and fighting dragons.

Michelle Drouin is a Professor in the Department of Psychology at Indiana University-Purdue University Fort Wayne. She received her B.A. in psychology from Cornell University in 1996 and her Ph.D. in psychology (developmental) from the University of Oxford in 2004. Her research, both disciplinary and pedagogical, is focused on the ways in which technology affects development, communication and learning. She has written numerous papers and book chapters on topics related to development in the digital age, including sexting, mobile phone addiction and the impact of texting on literacy.

Isabel Düsterhöft is a Lecturer in International and European Law in the European Studies programme at The Hague University of Applied Sciences, The Netherlands. Her research and publications mainly focus on international criminal law, international humanitarian law and civil society's contribution to conflict transformation. She was the editor in chief of the newsletter of the Association of Defence Counsel Practising Before the International Criminal Tribunal for the Former Yugoslavia (ADC-ICTY) between 2013 and 2016 and has managed the editorial process of various publications for this Association.

Rob Gallagher is a postdoctoral researcher based at King's College London. His current project addresses the impact of new media forms on practices of self-representation and conceptions of identity. Rob's research interests include digital gaming, queer aesthetics, identity and time. His work has appeared in venues such as *Games and Culture, G|A|M|E, Media-N* and the edited collection *Rated M for Mature: Sex and Sexuality in Video Games.*

Justin R. Garcia is Ruth N. Halls Assistant Professor in the Department of Gender Studies and Associate Director for Research and Education at The Kinsey Institute, Indiana University, Bloomington. His research focuses on romantic and sexual relationships across the life course, with an emphasis on biocultural approaches to intimate and sexual behaviours.

David Gudelunas is a Professor of Communication at Fairfield University where he also serves as Director of the School of Communication, Arts and Media. He researches and teaches in the areas of critical and cultural studies, gender, sexuality and communication, media history and communication industries. He is the author of *"Confidential to America: Newspaper Advice Columns and Sexual Education"*, and is widely published in the areas of popular and consumer culture as well as the intersections of sexuality, communication and emerging media.

Jessica L. James is a researcher and lecturer at Texas State University in the School of Journalism and Mass Communication. Her research focuses on mobile dating applications and the differences in use between genders, specifically how the digital capacities of smartphone technologies affect user behaviour.

Cáel M. Keegan is Assistant Professor of Women, Gender and Sexuality Studies and Liberal Studies at Grand Valley State University. His research specialises in the analysis of transgender media, image production and aesthetics, and he has published multiple articles on the global circulation and contested meaning of queer and transgender popular images. His current book project, *Lana and Lilly Wachowski: Imaging Transgender* is the first to interrogate the directors' ground-breaking filmography from a transgender studies perspective, claiming that their work invented a new transgender aesthetics that now operates at the very centre of 21st century global popular culture. The book will be published by the University of Illinois Press.

Deb Levine founded Internet Sexuality Information Services, Inc., now YTH, in 2001. Deb led the organisation to push the boundaries of traditional health education by creating many of the nation's firsts, including an ecard service for STD partner notification (inSPOT); an online STD testing service (STDtest.org); and a text messaging service (SexINFO). Under her leadership, the organisation won numerous awards, including the Full Circle Fund Technology award, a Webby honouree, the Drucker Innovation award and first place in a White House and HHS Challenge, Apps Against Abuse. As a Pop!Tech social innovation fellow, she has worked tirelessly to include sexual and reproductive health issues in the tech and pop cultural forefront, changing the way young people access and engage with sexual and reproductive health services. She has lectured both at home and abroad and published in numerous peer-reviewed journals. You can reach Deb at levinedeb@gmail.com or on Twitter @DebLOakland.

Nora Madison, PhD, is an Assistant Professor of Communication and the Co-Coordinator of the Women's Studies minor at Chestnut Hill College in Philadelphia, USA. Her research examines the social and cultural impacts of technology on everyday activism and digital representation, focusing on the importance of digital technologies for bisexual spaces. Nora has presented her findings around the world, including an invited talk at Sweden's International Science Festival (Vetenskapsfestivalen.) You can follow her blog on noramadison.net or follow her on twitter @theoryofnora.

Jimmie Manning is Associate Professor in the Department of Communication, Northern Illinois University, USA. He is known in the communication discipline for his work exploring sexuality in relationships, his blending of interpersonal and media communication research, teaching practices that involve community engagement and service learning and for serving in many different leadership positions for professional academic organisations.

Alexa Marcotte is a doctoral candidate in the Department of Gender Studies at Indiana University, Bloomington and works with The Kinsey Institute for Research in Sex, Gender and Reproduction. Her research focuses on the boundaries of coercive sex as well as the representations of sex work and sex trafficking in the United States.

Alan McKee is Associate Dean (Research and Development) in the Faculty of Arts and Social Sciences at University of Technology Sydney, Australia. He is an expert on entertainment and healthy sexual development. He holds an ARC Linkage with Family Planning Queensland to investigate the use of vulgar comedy to reach young men with information about healthy sexual development and was co-editor of the *Girlfriend Guide to Life*. He has published on healthy sexual development, the effects of pornography on young people and entertainment education for healthy sexuality in journals including the *Archives of Sexual Behavior*, the *International Journal of Sexual Health*, the *Journal of Sex Research* and *Sex Education*.

Paul G. Nixon is Principal Lecturer in Political Science in European Studies and University Platform Co-ordinator (Europe) at The Hague University of Applied Sciences, The Netherlands. He is the co-editor of *Digital Media Usage Across the Lifecourse*; *Lobbying the European Union: Changing Minds, Changing Times*; *Politics and the Internet in Comparative Context: Views from the Cloud*; *Understanding E-Government in Europe: Issues and Challenges*; *E-Government in Europe*; *Cyberprotest*; and *Politics Parties and the Internet*, and editor of *Representations of Education in Literature*.

Abigail Oakley is a PhD student at Arizona State University in the Writing, Rhetorics, and Literacy program. Her research interests include online identity, gender, feminist pedagogy, digital pedagogy and digital literacies. She recently published "Disturbing Hegemonic Discourse: Nonbinary Gender and Sexual Orientation Labeling on Tumblr" in *Social Media + Society*, which examines subversive nonbinary gender and sexual orientation identity construction practices on Tumblr.

Susanna Paasonen is Professor of Media Studies at University of Turku, Finland. With an interest in studies of popular culture, affect and media theory, she is most recently the author of *Carnal Resonance: Affect and Online Pornography* (MITP 2011) as well as co-editor of *Working with Affect in Feminist Readings: Disturbing Differences* (Routledge 2010) and *Networked Affect* (MITP 2015). She is currently working on a book on #NSFW together with Kylie Jarrett and Ben Light.

Agata Pacho is a Ph.D. candidate in Sociology, Goldsmiths University of London. Previously, she received MA in Gender and Culture and MRes in Sociology, both from Goldsmiths. Her doctoral project is an ethnography of a London specialist HIV clinic. Her research interests include sexuality, sexual health and medicine more broadly. She is one of the founders and a member of the steering committee for Association for the Social Sciences and Humanities in HIV UK (ASSHH UK).

Rebecca S. Randall is a Masters student at the Queensland University of Technology, studying Information Science (Library and Information Practice). She completed her Honours thesis entitled *How Do Young Brisbane BDSM practitioners use online resources in the development of their sexual identities?*, and received Second Class A Honours. She submitted this thesis to the Australian Law Reform Commission, as a response to the Revision of the Classification Guidelines. She has contributed to ongoing research projects within the Entertainment Industries at QUT.

Tobias Raun is an associate professor of communication studies at Roskilde University and the editor of the "New Media" section of TSQ: Transgender Studies Quarterly. He has published extensively on trans and digital media, most recently (in 2016) a book with Routledge entitled *Out Online: Trans Self-Representation and Community Building on YouTube*. He is the co-editor of a forthcoming anthology (in 2017) *New Media New Intimacies: Connectivities, Relationalities, Proximities*, Routledge Studies in European Communication Research and Education Series. His current research interest explores on the one hand "mourning online" (coping with the death of a close relative through Facebook) and on the other "capitalizing intimacy" (affective labour and subcultural vlogging).

Cosimo Marco Scarcelli, PhD is vice-chair of the Gender and Communication section at ECREA. He is a post-doctoral researcher and teaching assistant in Sociology, Sociology of Mass Communication and Social Science Methods in the Department FISPPA of the University of Padova and he works as a digital media educator in collaboration with different institutions and NGOs. His research deals with youth studies, social construction of gender, sexuality and intimacy, the connection between sexuality, gender and media, Internet studies and digital literacy. He is particularly interested in qualitative and participatory research.

Allegra W. Smith is a PhD student in Rhetoric and Composition at Purdue University. A technical and professional writing teacher-scholar, her research focuses on how intersectional facets of our identity mediate our experiences with digital technologies, tools and interfaces. Her work on Internet pornography communities has been featured in *Communication Design Quarterly.*

Jesus Gregorio Smith is a PhD Candidate and Diversity Fellow at Texas A&M University (TAMU) in the Department of Sociology. His expertise centre on the intersections of race, gender and sexuality online, and how they contribute to health behaviours such as condom use and sexual risk activity. Jesus received his Bachelors in Psychology and Master's in Sociology at the University of Texas at El Paso (UTEP), where he worked for several years as the lead intern on LGBT affairs, including heading SpeakOUT UTEP, an LGBT speaker's bureau, managing Queer History Month on campus and creating and establishing UTEP's first ever Queer Leadership and Academic Development conference, which continues to this day.

Katrin Tiidenberg is splitting her time between Aarhus University in Denmark, where she works as a postdoctoral researcher focussing on digital research ethics, future making methodologies and visual culture; and Tallinn University in Estonia, where she holds a part-time position of Associate Professor of Social Media and Visual Culture at the Baltic Film, Media, Arts and Communication School. She has published extensively on selfie culture and her research interests focus on visual culture, sexuality, gender and normative ideologies.

Abbreviations

AHF	AIDS Healthcare Foundation
AI	Artificial Intelligence
AP-MTV	Associated Press – Music Television
AR	Augmented reality
AVEN	Asexual Visibility and Education Network
BDSM	Bondage and Discipline, Dominance and Submission, Sadism and Masochism
CPE	Community Priority Evaluation
DIY	Do It Yourself
DVD	Digital Versatile Disc
EVA	Education as a Vaccine
FAQ	Frequently Asked Question
F2F	Face-to-face
GPS	Global Positioning System
gTLD	Generic top-level domain
HBO	Home Box Office
HIV	Human Immuno-Deficiency Virus
ICANN	Internet Corporation for Assigned Names and Numbers
ICT	Information and Communications Technology
IRB	Institutional Review Board
LGBTQ(IAA)	Lesbian-Gay-Bisexual-Transgender-Queer/Questioning-Intersex-Asexual-Ally
MOOC	Massive Open Online Courses
MILF	Mother I'd Like to Fuck
MSA	Metropolitan Statistical Area
MSM	Men who have sex with men
NPC	Non-Player Character
NSFG	National Survey of Family Growth
NSFW	Not Safe For Work
PC	Personal Computer
PPFA	Planned Parenthood Federation of America
Q&A	Questions and Answers
RPG	Role-Playing Game

SFM	Source Filmmaker
SNS	Social networking site
SMS	Short message service
STD	Sexually Transmitted Disease
STI	Sexually Transmitted Infection
STS	Science and Technology Studies
U&G	Uses and Gratification
UK	United Kingdom
US	Untied States (of America)
USD	United States Dollar
VCR	Video Cassette Recorder
VHS	Video Home System
WAVPM	Women against Violence in Pornography and Media
3D	Three Dimensional

Introduction

Paul G. Nixon and Isabel Düsterhöft

Sex it would seem is much more open for discussion and available than it once was. The grip on the sexual lives of individuals by both church and state is much loosened in today's society. Although it would be wrong to say that the traditionalists have totally 'lost' the argument, there can be no doubt that as individuals we are much 'freer' than our great grandparents were. Sex has also become a more open issue in many different ways. For example, nowadays, we understand sexual health to be a much wider concept than that of being free of sexual diseases. We also recognise the part sex can play for many of us in our own mental wellbeing. Fetish (in all its forms) has finally lost its peripheral status, receiving widespread recognition as a matter of personal choice. We are also seeing the acceptance of differing sexualities being welcomed into the mainstream and enjoying equal rights, as the binary divide is challenged and the hetero-normative ascendancy is contested. It is much more acceptable to talk about sex in public with one's friends and to 'admit' to indulging in practices that were once considered socially taboo (note the mainstream acceptance of Bondage and Discipline, Dominance and Submission, Sadism and Masochism (BDSM), oral and anal sex etc.) or even subject to the criminal code. Of course the development of sexual freedoms alluded to relate to Western cultures. The sexual freedoms which we take for granted are not universally guaranteed, both in other cultures and even indeed within Western cultures. Variance from culturally accepted sexual norms can lead to repression, such as those presently experienced by transgender people, or even to death, either in the case of being driven to suicide or being killed due to one's sexual preferences.

In Western society we can chart a history of sexual development and a more open approach to sexual issues. The emergence of feminism into the mainstream in the 1960s questioned the patriarchal view of society and the sexual relations that underpinned it. We can also see technology playing a part in this development. Advances in contraception played a huge part in facilitating recreational heterosexual sex without the fear of procreation. In the 1980s we saw an attempt to restrict sexual freedoms, particularly during the rise of the AIDS crisis, where contraception again played a key role in changing behaviours and practices.

The debates have moved on through various stages to reveal sex as an integral part of adult lives. It is an act that has extreme significance for us but that significance varies greatly from person to person. Some cling to the traditional perceptions of sex as a sacred and private activity, to be enjoyed only as part of a married couple. For others there is a perception at least that sex is a leisure activity which is more acceptable, that everyone deserves to enjoy a fulfilling sex life and that no shame should be attached to those who engage in it regardless of their orientation or their marital status. Though we still have a myriad of definitions for what does or does not constitute sex, the debate rages on. Some say that only full intercourse counts and other activities such as mutual masturbation or oral sex does not count as actually having had sex.

Whatever opinions one holds on sex there can be no doubt that sex is seemingly everywhere. On our televisions, on billboards, on our computers, almost everywhere we look we are reminded that this is a sexual society. As we increasingly move towards a more digitally orientated society it should come as no surprise that sex is also developing online. The chapters below show different applications of digital technologies which facilitate human sexuality. Whilst the Freudian notion that everything we do or think of is driven by sexual motivation may be somewhat overstated, there can be no doubt that sex is an important part of our lives and in an increasingly sexualised society may become even more important. The shifting and often competing nature of sexual identities, beliefs, ideologies and discourses impact upon our sexual lives and thus, as we evolve in other spheres of human activity, so too do our responses to, and acceptance of, sexual activities. We can chart changes in kinship and family systems as having an impact upon sexual behaviour. Economic changes have also played their part as have the emancipation of women and the repeal of laws criminalising and seeking to prohibit certain sexual activities. These changes have been part of a slow process of human growth and this is certainly not a process anywhere near completion.

If past shifts in societal development due to economic and technological advancements have had an impact upon the development of human sexuality and behaviour, then it seems likely that the societal shifts facilitated by technological developments such as the Internet and associated technologies may also result in further changes. In more recent times we have seen the rise of the Internet as a social space where discourses thrive and it is no surprise to see this space being colonised for sexual purposes. As the contributions to this book show, we can already recognise the importance of these new spaces for discourse. This book examines a variety of issues all of which are being prominently affected by the use of digital media. One can only postulate that as such spaces develop so the activities and communities facilitated by them will also flourish and indeed mutate or morph into as yet unidentifiable areas of sexually oriented congress. Advancements in other digital potentialities such as robotics, augmented reality (AR) and artificial intelligence (AI) are already changing the ways in which we view sex. Combined with the increased portability of digital devices, this opens up a whole new world of possibilities. Just how those developments and possibilities will influence the future of sex is a matter for conjecture.

This book brings together contributions from academics and practitioners on the theme of sex in the digital age. It showcases the work of experienced and internationally renowned scholars as well as some fresh young voices. It aims to provide a thorough, yet accessible and enjoyable, discussion of many of the major themes pertinent to the pursuance of healthy sexual encounters in the 21st century. This publication encompasses a wide range of differing uses of digital media related to the field of sex. This breadth of digital engagement is further supported as the contributors draw on a range of international experiences from a number of countries and cultures. It encompasses theoretical underpinnings in a way that can be easily understood and elaborates upon practical case study experiences which focus upon means, tools and strategies employed in the domain of sex in the digital age. It brings forward insights into new forms of sexual conduct which are made possible by digital technologies and postulates how these may develop over time. By combining these elements this publication provides the reader with dual insights into key elements of sex and digital media and adds to the present state of research in this field.

Contents

As editors we wrestled with the idea of dividing the chapters into distinct sub sections but found that the various interconnections between chapters made this a very, very difficult task to accomplish. We therefore settled on the structure of the book that you see before you with chapters grouped around themes and perceived commonalities but of course there is still a huge level of interconnectedness between items which might appear to be primarily focussed specifically on visual elements or community building. We hope that our different approach makes the collection a vibrant, interesting and challenging read.

The collection commences with the first of two chapters that examine pornography from differing perspectives and also go some way towards illustrating the breadth of content available online today. This, as the reader will see, is a recurring theme throughout many of the chapters. Chapter 1 is Susanna Paasonen's examination of *Monster (Car)Toon Porn*, which builds upon Japanese hentai (pornographic manga and anime) and machinima (videos generated with the aid of game engines), Monster toon porn focuses on depictions of sexual encounters of the fantastic, impossible and improbable kind. It is a sub-genre of computer-generated pornography that sits outside the mainstream, combining porn, celebrity and gaming in a fascinating collage. Demons, zombies and hulk-like creatures copulate with elves, celebrity starlets and female game characters. On the one hand, these scenarios are markedly affective in their visceral attention to bodily detail and in the dynamics of disgust, amusement and sexual arousal that they knowingly aim to evoke. Alternatively, the monsters and their partners are notably affectless in their animated, mechanistic bodily movements, vacuous facial and verbal expressions. Paasonen's chapter explores the monstrosity of monster toon porn in terms of both the irregular embodiments it features and their uncanny lack of affect, and considers how its nonhuman displays of sexuality connect to sexual and gendered dynamics of control.

Continuing with the topic of porn, in Chapter 2, Allegra W. Smith demonstrates how the impassioned debate and criticism in feminist theory ("the porn wars") mainly examined the rhetoric *surrounding* pornography and not the rhetoric *of* pornography itself. Smith describes the results of her study of two Internet porn communities on reddit.com examining the visual, aural and symbolic rhetorical differences between pornography consumed by male audiences versus female audiences. By placing the study results in conversation with previous scholarship on the identities of early web "porntrepreneurs", she discusses the development of a participatory porn culture: new sexual representations that incorporate the desires and bodies of *female* fans into pornographic images and videos, wherein women's fantasies are articulated and then depicted on screen (rather than a more traditional pornographic representation of a male gaze).

Our next two chapters directly address the general topics of young people and digital media usage in sexual contexts. Firstly, in Chapter 3 Cosimo Marco Scarcelli uses the theoretical and conceptual tools of Sociology and Media Studies to describe the way young people in a climate of rapid societal change use emergent technologies to consume digital resources and/or perform activities of an intimate or sexual nature. This chapter examines young people's activities (in the continuum online-offline) and the sense they give to their actions and choices in the context of technology and digital content. From the research of information related to sexuality, to the consumption of pornography, through performance in social networking sites, cybersex and sexting, the chapter clarifies the role of digital media in the process of exploration of intimacy and construction of experience, social reality and gender roles.

Secondly, in Chapter 4 Deb Levine examines the role of new media in sex education. She notes that scare tactics are still commonplace tools to encourage young people to abstain from sex. Pleasure from sex was seldom discussed in the sex education classroom. However, societal changes and the freedom of access to information engendered by the Internet and associated technologies suggests that sex education in the digital age will become more sex positive in its outlook, although this does of course depend upon the social and often religious underpinnings of the institution involved. Many projects have sprung up from short message services (SMS), text messaging services to native mobile apps and Internet forums and high-tech Questions and Answers (Q&A). Showcasing a range of examples, the chapter investigates promising trends for the future of sexual health education.

The next series of chapters focus more on the differing opportunities offered by the plethora of activities and/or services enabled by platforms, and apps available in the digital environment. Often, though not exclusively, containing pictoral representations of the subject, the range of explicit content can vary from mild innuendo, through somewhat risqué to the outright pornographic. Often characterised as a new and worrying problem is the swapping of intimate pictures between young people much different to the old school idea of 'you show me yours and I will show you mine' that seems to indicate a gentler less abusive time. Clearly one of the counter arguments is that the digital images swapped today can be retained by the recipient and then shared with others and may indeed then spread virally far beyond the audience intended by the sender. We should also remember that whilst many of the spaces described are colonised by many young people it would be wrong to ignore the adoption of such affordances by people from all age groups. Jessica L. James explores the burgeoning growth of mobile dating applications in Chapter 5. Once only accessible via a desktop computer, online dating tools have become readily available thanks to the convenience of smartphone technology and mobile dating applications. Using Tinder as a case study, Jessica L. James interrogates the design implications of such apps. Users upload up to six pictures from their Facebook account and a 500-word bio. In this gamified context profiles are presented much like a deck of cards, with users accepting or rejecting others based largely on physical appearance. This had led to criticism of Tinder being a "hook-up app" as some users use the application to find casual sex, leading one to question if the design and technical features of Tinder can affect user behaviour.

Another relatively new activity 'Sexting', the exchange of sexually-explicit material via mobile phone technology, forms the topic of Chapter 6. Sexting has become integrated into adolescent and young adult sexuality, with high prevalence rates and increased reliance on mobile technology for relationship formation and maintenance. Nonetheless, there are risks associated with sexting (e.g., pictures are sometimes shared or forwarded), and these risks have often overshadowed potential relationship benefits in the research literature. Michelle Drouin, building upon the variety of previous research, incorporates insights from emergent research avenues in the field, including sexting among married couples, coerced sexting, a risk factor for polyvictimisation, and sexting as perceived consent for sex. In doing so she seeks to broaden our understanding of sexting.

One of the key elements often used in sexting is that of sending photos of yourself known as selfies that can be suggestive and/or explicit. Chapter 7 has Katrin Tiidenberg arguing that sexy selfies are out of the closet and no longer a marginal practice. As the chapter shows, 2014 brought us the celebrity photo hack (the Fappening) and the Snapchat hack (the Snappening). The practice is widespread and not confined to one area or segment of society. As well as the more foregrounded sexting-based interpretation of sexy selfies as a form of communication, foreplay or sex, research with a community of sexy selfie enthusiasts on tumblr.com has shown that taking and sharing sexy selfies can function as a practice of (re)claiming control over the aesthetic of what is and is not 'sexy'. The chapter constructs a narrative of sexual reawakening afforded entirely by taking and sharing of sexy selfies.

Chapter 8 continues on the theme of selfies as emphasising or delineating sexuality. Tobias Raun and Cáel M. Keegan's exploration of the portrayal of trans men investigates the dilemmas faced by trans men in order that they be viewed as male and as sexually desirable. Utilising a duo of stylised photos that seek to depict manliness, and contextualising this in the wider comprehensive selfie-practice of one subject on YouTube and Instagram, Raun and Keegan pose an important question. How do trans men become more manly without becoming more invisible as trans? As Raun and Keegan comment, "trans" and "man" sometimes seem to eradicate each other.

Having spent some time examining the ways in which digital technologies are used to transmit various types of sexual content, our next eight chapters capture the diversity of activities centred around the building of community identities. Abigail Oakley's research featured in Chapter 9 focuses on online communities on Tumblr where one may meet those who share one's collective identities and interests. Tumblr is a platform known for hosting those who champion social justice causes including Lesbian Gay Bisexual Transgender Queer/Questioning Intersex Asexual (LGBTQIA) rights. In order to be seen as a legitimate source of information on this topic, Tumblr bloggers establish their identities – through public labelling, post tagging and answers to 'asks' (where readers submit questions and short comments) – as a firm and active member of the LGBTQIA community. Thus, LGBTQIA bloggers build an educational ethos that encourages new and potential members of the community to participate in community discourse. Building on existing literature about online communities and counter publics, this chapter, via a case study of nonbinary Tumblr blogger "Daniel", exemplifies the community building possibilities of online discourse relating to interpersonal relationships, shared resources and support.

A community that is sometimes overlooked in terms of research, though this is now changing, is the focus of Agata Pacho's Chapter 10. Challenging the obsession with sex that often pervades sections of the media, this chapter opens a window onto the sometimes less publicised world of asexuality. With sexuality and sexual desire perceived as a crucial aspect of one's identity, asexuality questions the dominant notion of a universal innate sexual drive. She investigates how the virtual world facilitates the possibilities for creating and negotiating representations of asexual identity. The chapter examines the emergence of asexual community and the processes of formulating community politics. Looking at the successes as well as difficulties experienced by members of the world's largest asexual association, AVEN, attempting to raise awareness of asexuality and/or build an asexual community, the chapter raises the question of what kind/s of community the virtual may engender.

David Gudelunas, in Chapter 11, explores how gay men have used new media technologies and how these emergent media have in turn helped shape the contours of the gay community. Gudelunas traces the changing uses of digital technologies to both challenge and recreate notions of gay community in the offline environment. By providing an overview of the literature relating to gay men in the online environment, this chapter ultimately suggests that the widespread adoption of online technologies by gay audiences has significant effects for how we conceptualise offline gay communities and social movements. How these technologies and the online environment have served to unite gay men online is far more complicated than earlier utopian visions suggest. Building upon the preceding chapter, Jesus Gregorio Smith examines the issue of race and sexuality with specific reference to gay men in Chapter 12. Contributing to the discussion on cyber racism and Internet sexuality by examining the infrastructure of adam4adam.com (A4A), a site specifically for men who wish to have sex with other men, Smith shows how the new digital media is often affected by the same racism found in the offline world. A4A's homepage, which includes a plethora of Internet porn ads, creates a sexual space that is, Smith argues, drenched in systemic racism delineating what is sexually desirable and acceptable. Users, through the creation of profiles, are forced to identify themselves by race, gender and body type. Search engines then group these variables together in order to give the ideal of sexual stereotypes. Smith shows how black gay men are constantly confronted by a culture of two faced racism which re-enforces the idealised norm and often discriminates as a naturalised result of the history of wider systemic racism. Smith argues that this website and many others like it display the sexually racist stereotypes and desires crafted by a white supremacist society. Focusing on yet another identity community, the representation of bisexuality is Nora Madison's topic in Chapter 13. She examines the practices and techniques employed by bisexuals in digitally mediated spaces within a dominant Western system of sexual orientation. Her study, based on ethnographic participant-observation and social semiotics, illustrates the struggle for visibility that bisexuals encounter faced with the dominant binaries of heterosexuality and homosexuality in Western culture. The Internet, touted as a space of great potential for anonymity and exploration, where visibility could be masked and multiple identities explored, here becomes the place where users try to make their perceived invisibility 'visible' and culturally intelligible.

In Chapter 14 Abbi Bloedel and Jimmie Manning discuss the nature of polyamorous relationships which are often misunderstood by the wider community and in order to counter this they provide a basic review of common terms. The chapter examines differing forms of polyamory and how digital technologies have cultivated the evolving definition of polyamory and its practices. In common with other chapters they show how anonymity in digital space allows individuals to explore ideas and practices in a supportive environment. As such ideas are outside the original monogamy-normative belief systems, they are open to contestation and trolling as experienced in other spaces which do not conform to the norms of the majority.

In Chapter 15 we enter the world of BDSM which is slowly emerging from its former niche position and (almost) entering the mainstream. Rebecca S. Randall and Alan McKee provide insights from five young BDSMZ practitioners. Allowing the five to tell their own stories, similar to members of other queer minorities discussing the development of their identities, the authors highlight the role of online materials and communities in that process. Rather than displaying the traditional perspective of BDSM communities as places of implicit danger, they show how those spaces and communities can be used to ensure their safety.

Concluding the series of chapters centred around the topic of identity and community, Alexandra S. Marcotte and Justin R. Garcia, in Chapter 16, address an often overlooked gap in the literature, the online advertisements by women sex workers, specifically focusing on major US cities. The majority of research on sex workers' self-marketing has focused on male sex workers and to provide a broader and more complete perspective, the authors examine the "adult" section at backpage.com which had a reputation as a place to source sex, paid or otherwise. Since the chapter was written, ads of a sexual nature on Backpage.com have been shut down after pressure from US government agencies. This pressure was due to allegations that some ads were supporting criminal activities including the offering of child prostitutes. The ads are no longer accessible but this does not detract from the value of the research. Marcotte and Garcia explore that marketing, particularly in relation to identity, pleasure and sexual health, to give a fascinating insight into how such services are marketed and the pressures on the advertisers to conform to market expectations.

The next two chapters of this collection return to the sphere of play and imagination. Ashley M.L. Brown and Rob Gallagher in Chapter 17 lead us into the controversial realm of digital games and sexual activity. Gaming and online sexual play sometimes have an almost symbiotic relationship. They look at how sex has been designed into games. Addressing the (over) use of sex as a reward mechanic, they also articulate alternate ways that sex has been included in games' economies or gameplay. They then move on to discusses the ways in which sex and games intersect with groups of players. Looking at topics such as cybersex and erotic roleplay, they focus on how players use the medium of games to experiment or play with sexuality and sexual themes and topics. Brown and Gallagher examine studies of sex and single player games to see how sex is represented in such games and how sexual screen displays affect players.

Continuing the theme of play and coming almost full circle with the first chapter of this book, in Chapter 18 Paul G. Nixon expounds on the erstwhile taboo topic of the use of sex toys. Sex toys have a long history and this chapter takes us through that history into the present and near future, where sex toys are moving out into the open and onto the high street. The twin notions of play and imagination are recurring themes in this piece, just like its precedent chapter from Brown and Gallagher, and also Paasonen's opening chapter of the collection. The author postulates as to how that imagination might be stretched even further by future technological developments and, most crucially, the more widespread acceptance of technology into sexual everyday sexual activities. The chapter shows how advances in Teledildonics are helping to produce devices which can replicate the sexual functions of both sexes. The chapter then moves on to postulate on the future, a future that holds the promise of tantalising possibilities for sexual fulfilment on a level of which we can only dream at the moment!

This, then, is our collection. A wide ranging examination of digital sexual activities today which is also just the tip of the iceberg in terms of the range of sexual content and sexual activities empowered by using digital media. We have ranged from studies of pornography, thorough differing types of, mainly but not exclusively, visual, image based social media usage. We have examined community building between individuals who, by harnessing the bridging and bonding capacities afforded by the technologies, have sought to form communities and spaces linked to collective sexual identity. We have shown how that power can be harnessed to defend minorities and on a less confrontational level to provide safe spaces for discussion and questioning, centred around issues of sexual practices and identity. We have also seen how empowering the technology can be, affording spaces where people feel they can be their sexual selves. It will be of great importance to us all to see how far the technological shifts will shape our societies in general and our sexual identities, attitudes and activities in particular.

1 The affective and affectless bodies of monster toon porn

Susanna Paasonen

Monster (car)toon porn is a genre of three dimensional (3D) computer-generated pornography that focuses on depictions of sexual encounters of the impossible and improbable kind. In monster toon porn, demons, zombies and hulk-like creatures copulate with elves, Hollywood starlet look-alikes and female game characters, huge bodies penetrate tiny ones and human-like bodies sprout novel sexual organs. Broadly building on the combined traditions of Western cartoon porn, Japanese hentai and ero-manga (pornographic anime and comics) and machinima (3D videos generated in real time with game engines and, increasingly, with the aid of additional software), monster toon porn is often classified as hentai, independent of its factual geographical origins. Its imageries are characteristically fantastic and excessive in their displays of spectacularly incompatible bodies engaging in penetrative sex, in its scenarios of control and submission and in its displays of lust and disgust seemingly knowing no bounds. These images and videos originate from the efforts of amateur fans, commercial studios and crowdfunded non-profit enterprises alike.

This chapter explores monster toon porn in terms of both its irregular embodiments and their uncanny lack of affect, and considers how these nonhuman displays of sexualised and gendered dynamics of control connect to game culture. These considerations are tied in with a discussion on the specificities of digitally generated and distributed pornography in terms of media technology, labour and ethics. Specific focus will be given to the oeuvre of Studio FOW who specialise in crowdfunded Source Filmmaker (SFM) hentai monster videos set in game worlds.

The hyperboles of animated porn

The histories of modern pornography preceding photographic technologies hark back to the traditions of erotic literary fiction and the visual arts spanning engravings, graphic prints, drawings and paintings. In addition to attempting to sexually arouse their audiences, these have equally aimed at amusement through the means of exaggeration, mockery and excess. Some visual pornography – as in the format of paintings – was produced for the exclusive private amusement of wealthy male clientele whereas prints were in much broader circulation, especially after the introduction of inexpensive printing presses in the late 18th century. In visual pornography, penises, vaginas and various other body parts have set off on adventures, detached themselves from bodies, floated about, changed shape and copulated creatively for a number of centuries. In the early 20th century, this visual tradition expanded to sexually explicit comics, such as the 1930s *Tijuana Bibles* featuring pornographic variations of popular mainstream comic strips and celebrities (see Adelman, 1997; Pilcher, 2008; also Uidhir and Pratt, 2012). In animated film – an emergent art form characterised by visual simplification, surface, rhythm and repetition (Klein, 1998) – graphic pornography met the possibilities of moving image. Film scholar Constance Penley (2004, p. 318) identifies ribald humour, wanton penises, "hyperbolically exaggerated body parts and wildly impossible sexual positions" ubiquitous in these comics as equally standard elements of early animated pornographic film.

Among these, *Eveready Harton in Buried Treasure*, made in 1928–1929 and attributed to the production studio Climax Fables, was one of the very first. In the six-minute film, Eveready Harton's expansive penis escapes his body, hides behind rocks, functions as a third leg, gets attacked by a plate-sized crab louse during penetration, gets stuck in a man's anus, bends, is hurt by cacti and, in the film's happy end, gets licked by a cow. The film is rife with puns, bodily metamorphoses and hyperbolic body parts while the boundaries of the animate and the inanimate, human and animal, are in constant flux. As Jose B. Capino (2004, p. 59) points out,

> just as animals, plants and humans communicate and play with each other in mainstream animation, so also do the figures in animated pornography speak the same language of polysexual desire and perform more sexual roles than conventional human morality can tolerate.

In the German, undated Super 8 film loop most likely dating back to the late early 1970s, titled *Schwänzel und Gretel* (also known in English as *Dickzel and Gretel* and *Hans and Gretel in the Magic Forest*), trees and roofs of houses sprout human-like sexual organs, penises grow from the ground and people, squirrels, owls and pigs all engage in continuous orgies (also Capino, 2004, p. 57). This pornographic fantasyland is one of hyperbolic, excessive and even compulsive sexuality where ejaculate oozes from unsuspected outlets and lubricates the narrative action. The film is part of a broader cycle of German animated porn revisiting classic cartoons, from the Western adventures of *Puffalo Bill* to *Robert Keller und Dieter Hahn* where Max and Moritz play out some of their more adult tricks, *Rammel der Hase* featuring an amply endowed Bugs Bunny of sorts and *Schneeflittchen und die 7 Zwerge* where Snow White engages in group sex with the seven dwarfs and shoots pickles from her vagina. All these cartoons aim to titillate through their sexual explicitness but much more centrally to entertain through their surprising twists and turns, metamorphosing bodies and unequivocally smutty forms of humour.

Animated porn has since taken virtually endless shapes and forms, from parody versions of popular children's animation gone wild to fan-made machinima created out of The Sims and the 3D, high-resolution bodies approximating photorealistic aesthetics and representing the higher end in terms of production value. Alongside these, all kinds of pornographic comics and still images abound in resolutions high and low, in genres more and much less mainstream and in aesthetics ranging from the cartoonish to the photorealistic. Digital image manipulation and animation tools have grown increasingly accessible. At the same time, all kinds of pornographic animations are more readily available than ever on online video sharing platforms. These aggregate or tube sites enable the uploading, and hence the public archiving, of clips that were previously in much narrower circulation through screenings, Video Home Systems (VHS) and Digital Versatile Discs (DVD) compilations. The "affective processing of digital artifacts" (Gehl, 2011, p. 1230) on tube sites gives rise to heterogeneous archives of varying copyright statuses. Individual clips are detached from their original contexts of production and distribution, titled, described and tagged as users see fit (Gehl, 2009, pp. 46–47). This regularly results in an efficient erosion and loss of metadata, production data included. The titles of films may be missing or replaced with others while there is generally little information available on when the films were made, where and by whom. Given the diverse routes of circulation that online content takes across tube sites, paywall protected services and torrent platforms, the origins of individual clips can be hard to track.

In the horizontal space of tube archives, both those specialising in animated pornography and those catering to virtually all tastes, one may move from Pokémon hentai featuring some of Pikachu's more raunchy moments to porn variations of *Family Guy*, *Simpsons* and *Futurama*. In these, family members get it on with one another and the boundaries of species, as well as those of humans and machines, are overcome with gusto. Some tube sites feature all kinds of cartoon porn whereas others focus more exclusively on hentai, itself tagged under categories such as schoolgirls, tentacles, goblins, furries, futanari (inter-gender pornography where primary sexual characteristics of different genders are played with) and those familiar from other realms of pornography, such as 'anal', 'Bondage and Disciple, Dominance and Submission, Sadism and Masochism' (BDSM), 'blowjob' or 'gangbang'.

Rich and empty in affect

McLelland (2005) points out that in Japanese the term hentai refers only to sexual materials deemed unusual, extreme or abnormal. At the same time, Japanese pornographic anime more broadly involves narratives tied in with "the fantastic, the occult, or science fiction" and regularly privileges "the female body in pain" in scenes of sexual torture and mutilation (Napier, 2005, p. 64). This also applies to 'eroge', hentai computer games with their perennial – and perennially controversial – themes of incest and sexual violence that have grown part of global gaming cultures (Martinez and Manolovitz, 2010). For while some eroge remains relatively softcore, other releases veer firmly towards guro – that which Urban Dictionary defines as "grotesque pornography" involving "diarrhoea (*sic*) scat, necrophilia, amputee sex, skull-fucking and violent rape" (www.urbandictionary.com/define.php?term=guro; for a contemporary portfolio of eroge, see www.lewdgamer.com/).

Despite referring to sexual depictions of the more extraordinary and unlikely kind, in the Japanese context, hentai does not have a pejorative connotation similar to that of abnormality and perversion in Western *scientia sexualis* (McLelland, 2005; cf. Foucault, 1990; Foucault 2003). While hentai was considered too extreme or plain bizarre for Western pornographic DVD markets of the 1990s, it quickly gained ubiquitous recognisability on online platforms, followed by broad, multi-platform distribution (see Dahlqvist and Vigilant, 2004). Ortega-Bena (2009, p. 20) defines hentai through characteristics such as "substandard animation, ample dwelling on unconventional erotic practices, a fixation on rape and non-consensual sexual violence, and often preposterous scenarios", but also associates it with the grotesque and carnivalesque features of Japanese erotic fiction that veer towards the bizarre while making use of humour.

Building on the tradition of shunga, erotic woodblock prints, which peaked during the Edo period (1603–1868), hentai richly features many of its themes, such as "Massive genitalia, ingenious sexual aids, couplings of all kinds, a wide array of fetishes, bizarre viewpoints, physical anomalies, bawdy comedy, and satirical vignettes" (Ortega-Bena, 2009, p. 20). The influences of shunga remain evident in hentai, from exaggerated physical characteristics to humour and elaborate scenarios of tentacle rape (see Buckland, 2010; Gerstle and Clark, 2013; Kazutaka, 2013; Napier, 2005, p. 21; Screech, 2009). The uses of tentacles and other non-human phallic shapes owes partly to Japanese legislation banning the showing of genitalia without pixelation (see Hambleton, 2015; Napier, 2005, p. 79). The landscape of monster toon porn is populated by tentacle monsters owing to Hokusai's classic woodcut, *The Pearl Diver* (also known as *The Dream of the Fisherman's Wife*, 1814), as well as a vast range of giant worm-like creatures, demons, centaurs, elves, ogres, dragons, zombies and amalgamations of humans and bugs. The genre can be identified as post-human in a range of ways: due to its nonhuman and hybrid protagonists that often metamorphose from one shape to another, its computer-generated origins resulting from algorithmic functions and its affectless bodies engaging in mechanical sexual acts.

Like hentai, monster toons are rife with "demonic phallus incarnate": namely demonic characters that are "preternaturally huge, covered with rippling muscles, and inevitably equipped with an enormous penis (and often with phallic tentacles as well)" (Napier, 2005, pp. 65, 79). Be these monsters, insects, spiders, fish, slugs, extra-terrestrial creatures or demons, narrative action focuses firmly on vaginal, oral and anal penetrative sex that climaxes in money shots. Monsters of all kinds sport highly anthropomorphic penises, semen flows freely from all kinds of bodies and anthropomorphic female characters grow pregnant with bugs and demons alike.

The landscapes of action are mostly dungeons and simplified forests – spaces routinely featured in the games on which machinima builds – or other abstract spaces void of any excessive detail, let alone markers of everyday life. The sexual scenarios are overwhelmingly ones of domination and submission, often of the non-consensual sort. With the exception of futanari, it is generally the female bodies – young, fit, beautiful and firmly human-like as they tend to be – that are pushed to their boundaries of physical endurance by the sheer size of the penises, tentacles or objects inserted in their orifices. Monsters three times the size of elves slip excessively sized penises into mouths and vaginas while female bodies bend, flex and accommodate.

A search for 'monster toon' on Pornhub, the world's leading porn aggregate site, identifies five to six minute clips with titles such as 'Giant Monsters Take Hot Chick' and 'Monster Sex on Space Station'. In these, sex acts consist of the same motions repeated over and over again, accompanied by the same facial expressions and sounds, or the lack thereof. It is also more generally noteworthy that the bodies of monster toon porn move back and forth in their penetrative acts with notably little variation in gesture or motion. In sum, despite the unlimited possibilities that animation affords in imagining characters engaging in acts impossible for actual human bodies to accomplish, or even survive, the fantastic scenes of monster toon porn are recurrently tied up with highly predictable ways of imagining both sexual scenarios and gendered power dynamics. On the one hand, these scenarios are markedly affective in their visceral attention to (more or less fantastic) bodily detail and in the dynamics of disgust, amusement and sexual arousal that they aim to evoke. On the other hand, the monsters and their more or less human partners are regularly affectless in their animated, machinic bodily movements.

In terms of aesthetics, monster toon porn can be rather roughly divided into two main modes, namely high-resolution still images and cartoons aiming at full photorealism in the impossible bodies they depict and machinima videos of much lower technical execution. In both instances, female characters tend to resemble the Realdoll brand of sex dolls in their plastic, ultra-feminine human likeness and functional purpose alike. In still images, the details of bodies are carefully crafted towards a paradoxical sense of verisimilitude, from the pores of the skin to the gradations of the soft, hard and the liquid. The bodies of videos, for the most part, remain much more sketch-like. As is the case with Realdolls, the animated characters' facial expressions tend to be vacuous. Their verbal output remains limited to the repetitive loops of grunts, sighs, squeals and whimpers that are largely detached from the motion of bodies, mouths and faces. Like elsewhere in animated pornographic film, human voice is both an extension and displacement of the animated body (Capino, 2004, p. 64) that creates as much distance as it yields grains of proximity.

According to Ortega-Bena, hentai follows the more general trend of emotional inexpression, a visual blankness of sorts, in Japanese arts and film. There is little explicit or outward expression of emotion and animated bodies tend to be equally impassive. All this results in layers of spectacle and excess, blankness and inexpression that are deployed in conveying the markedly fantastic and out-of-the-ordinary (Ortega-Bena, 2009, pp. 20–21). Ortega-Bena (2009, p. 27) sees the bodies of hentai as constantly moving "between dichotomies of male, female; potent, impotent; demonic, human; oppressive, submissive; possessive, possessed; attacker, attacked; sadist, masochist". Although these categories are "ultimately fluid, can be shuffled around and are combined in a variety of ways" (Ortega-Bena, 2009, p. 27), in the realm of monster toon porn – independent of the centrality of non-human sexual partners – the positions of the submissive and the dominant tend to be clearly cut in gendered terms. While the boundaries of species are routinely crossed, bodies metamorphose from one form to another and novel incarnations are common, gendered lines of control remain much more tenacious and consistent.

Extending the game

3D monster toon porn largely builds on the expressive possibilities of machinima, both in its simpler game-engine based variations and those created with the aid of additional software, such as SFM, which encompasses a broad, and stylistically heterogeneous scene of amateur film practice. Independent of the specific forms it takes, machinima filmmaking is centrally derivative: "audiences look forward to familiar game locations, quests, items, and game-generated characters being reinterpreted by machinima filmmakers" (Falkenstein, 2011, p. 87). In other words, machinima involves a resampling and reimagining of game characters and events, and this is also where a central part of its attraction lies. To a degree, the practice of machinima resembles puppetry, of bending characters into new positions, scenes and motions (cf. Hancock, 2011, p. 32). In the sexually explicit extensions of in-game events, female characters, from Lara Croft to the female cast of Final Fantasy, appear in elaborate scenarios with nonhuman or semi-human partners originating both from within the game world and not. The key focus of machinima is firmly on the female characters while the details of the monsters are less of a concern. As Darkcrow of Studio FOW notes, "[o]nce you slap a dick on someone they're pretty much good to go!" (in Hernandez, 2015).

Shared online, machinima is part of a broader ecology of Do-It-Yourself (DIY) fan videos, mashups, remixes and parodies that results from both fan engagement with popular culture and the accessibility and increasing performance of digital production tools (Ito, 2011, p. 51):

> The socio-technical world of machinima embodies (...) the key characteristics of a thriving amateur creative scene: accessible tools, peer-based feedback and exchange, networked online distribution, spaces for participation for both beginners and experts, diverse exemplars (both creative work and people), and opportunities for competition, recognition and status.
>
> (Ito, 2011, p. 53)

Machinima is generally amateur-made and the rough, "a bit ugly" (Douglas, 2014, p. 333) aesthetic is part of its charm. While it is predominantly shared on YouTube, sexually explicit clips circulate on porn tubes – both ones specialising in cartoon porn, hentai and machinima and "general purpose" aggregate sites such as Pornhub and XVideos. On these sites, videos of drastically varying technical execution compete for viewer attention: from the rough-edged characters with repetitive, bouncy and jerky movements more suggestive of photorealism to the extensively worked, higher production value videos of Studio FOW. Protected by fair use copyright policies as parodies generated for non-profit purposes, these films can be freely downloaded and they reach an audience of millions across tube sites. Studio FOW's productions are enabled by fan contributions and their representatives interact actively with fans on Twitter and Tumblr. Their collaborators include "animators, voice actors, and artists, who have come together to work on video game porn movies as a hobby" (Hernandez, 2015). In terms of porn production, all this points to forms of voluntary participation and contribution, sharing and production particular to online platforms.

Studio FOW's 'born digital' films depict spectacular, violent 3D scenes of non-consensual sex between female game characters, monsters and demons, as well as human men. Their best-known film is the very first one, *Lara in Trouble* (2014), derived from the 2013 game featuring a controversial scene where Lara Croft manages to escape sexual violence on a deserted island. The film sets Lara in an alternative game event timeline where no escape occurs and she ends up being gang raped until, in the very end, trickster-like, Scout, a character of *Team Fortress 2,* appears and provides her with a gun (Hernandez, 2015). Hence, according to Studio FOW, "[a] survivor is born, and a studio is forged as the debut movie from two idiots screwing around in SFM comes to the digital big screen" (www.studiofow.com/movie/2).

The presence of Lara Croft in pornographic machinima is hardly surprising, given the character's remarkable popularity as 3D 'virtual celebrity', since the first launch of *Tomb Raider* in 1996 (e.g. Flanagan, 1999; Lancaster, 2004; Schleiner, 2001). Plenty of ink has been spilled on Lara's possible and impossible embodiments and the more general 'hypersexualisation' of female game characters (e.g. Burgess *et al.,* 2007; Stermer and Burkley, 2012). Studio FOW is far from being the only machinima maker that routinely places female game characters in scenarios of sexual humiliation and submission, even if their films do this in a more elaborate manner than most. In addition to featuring live-action cosplay with amateur and professional performers dressed up as Lara, tube sites offer animations with Lara Croft 'gangbanged brutally by monsters', 'destroyed by Ogres' and 'fucked by Demon' (www.xvideos.com), 'fucked in a tomb' and 'fucked by orcs' (www.pornhub.com). It is possible to see these scenarios as a response to the changes in the game character from the sexy fantasy model of the 1990s to the current, more fully clothed and physiologically viable incarnation (cf. Chess and Shaw, 2015, p. 216). As the game provides fans with less explicit titillation, they are generating their own sex clips. Given the number of futanari clips where Lara ('or Futa-Lara') sports a lengthy penis, these clips involve a range of fantasies and embodiments.

Pornographic Lara clips can also be associated with the intense, broad and highly public debates on toxic game culture, its patterns of male privilege and violent exclusion of women (see Consalvo, 2012). The misogynistic overtones of game culture have been rendered particularly explicit since the 2014 Gamergate controversy, which involved extensive harassment, shaming, threatening and silencing of women in game journalism, industry and scholarship (see Chess and Shaw, 2015; Massanari, 2015). As Cherie Todd (2015, p. 65) notes, these women all shared a "critical stance against how girls and women are typically portrayed in games (as submissive, sexualised and victimi[s]ed characters)" as well as a "stance against the cultural embeddedness of misogynist tendencies present within the gaming industry, in which the majority of employees are men". Framed in this vein, the appropriation of female game characters, no matter how strong and proactive they may be in their respective game worlds, in scenarios of non-consensual sex comes across as an extension of broader gendered dynamics of game culture.

As Hernandez (2015) notes, Studio FOW titles are brutal: "After sex scenes, women gush semen or vomit semen endlessly, from just about every orifice at once". Studio FOW's films derive their specific dynamics from game fan cultures, including those cutting through Gamergate. Equally centrally, the studio remains faithful to the conventions of hentai. According to Darkcrow, Studio FOW partly grew out from disillusionment "with the state of the Hentai scene in general, it has really stagnated in terms of the darker, more hardcore content over the past few years so we wanted to bring back a tiny slice of the glory days" (Hernandez, 2015). This fusion of machinima and hentai also has a solid female fan base, which suggests of a more complex entanglement of sexual fantasies, desires and identities than one allowed by a symptomatic reading of Studio FOW through Gamergate and misogyny alone. Sexual fantasies, be these computer-generated or not, often fail to conform to the principles of equalitarianism or good taste in ways that require more nuanced analytical attention.

Fantastic bodies

In addition to *Lara in Trouble*, the longer Studio FOW titles to date include *Kunoichi: Broken Princess* (2014) and *Kunoichi 2: Fall of the Shrinemaiden* (2015), featuring the ninja heroine Kasumi of the *Dead or Alive* and shrine maiden Momiji of *Ninja Gaiden* being both raped by and seeking the company of a series of demons, as well as *Bioshag: Trinity* (2015), Elizabeth from the first-person shooter game, *BioShock Infinite*, engaging in both consensual and non-consensual acts with both humans and nonhuman monsters. In addition, the studio releases monthly clips, based on different computer games as teasers of future action to be.

The demons in the two *Kunoichi* films come in varying sizes, from the pint-sized to the humongous. In the first film, Kasumi, appointed a demon cum dumpster, engages in a series of non-consensual scenes. Some acts occur on stage, some in industrial spaces and others in urban night scenery of apocalyptic Tokyo. As is standard in hentai, Kasumi stomach is shown stretching and bulging from the size of the penises pushed up to her ribcage. Driven to the edge of what her body can do, unable to bear the pain and sure of tearing apart, Kasumi is also driven to orgasm. It is with a demon with a penis the width of her own thigh and the length of her leg that she ultimately finds sexual abandon. Through this experience, she grows insatiable independent of the hordes of partners involved. In the second film, Kasumi initiates Mumji to a similar narrative procession from non-voluntary abasement to excessive lust.

In her discussion of the first film, Hernandez (2015) interprets Kasumi's sexual conversion as collapse into "mindbreak state" of voluntary submission. In a different interpretation, *Kunoichi* films show women gaining urgent carnal desires and pleasures through their extreme experiences and immersion in the liberally flowing demon seed. In this, they follow the more generic conventions of hentai in depicting female bodies as frightening, powerful, mysterious and "controllable only by demons" (Napier, 2005, p. 76). In the *Kunoichi* films, encounters with demons make the women grow ever stronger, the Kasumi of the second film being somewhat demonic herself.

In comparison, *Lara in Trouble* is much grittier and, given its focus on human characters, is devoid of the fantastic demons with penises in different shapes and hues. It is straightforwardly a film about sexual violence: Lara experiences no sexual conversion or revelation in the course of the repeated acts forced on her (even if she is shown vocally enjoying some of them). The narrative framing where she grows stronger as rape survivor remains disjointed in comparison to the preceding action. Despite the visual – both affective and representational – plane of sexual extremity, violence and risk, Studio FOW connects these films to work safety issues. Darkcrow emphasises the affordances of animation as a safe means to explore violent sexual scenarios:

This medium allows us to explore fetishes in a safe environment where 3D models are used instead of actual people [...] We aim to make movies for responsible adults [...] this medium bypasses the seedier facets of the pornography industry.

(in Hernandez, 2015.)

Since all the images are computer-generated, no actual bodies are involved. Contemporary animated porn is basically the work of algorithms and a means of exploring unlikely, fantastic and extreme scenarios impossible to physically act out without censure or bodily harm. Its spaces are ones of unlimited and unbridled sexual opulence that no mundane routines or chores disturb. Here, it resembles the tradition of literary pornography in particular (see Marcus, 1964).

Animation allows for constant metamorphoses of its "unreal, imaginary, fabricated, virtual" bodies (Capino, 2004, pp. 53–54) that are unburdened by gravity, causality or the limits of what physical human bodies can do, or be. In addition to bodies fantastically bulging without tearing, bursting or bleeding, their insides can be rendered visible. The motions of penises seen through a woman's body are a specific focus of interest in Studio FOW's titles, as they are in hentai more generally. These are occasionally visualised through small vignettes revealing the motions of the penis inside the body, under the woman's skin, flesh and muscle. In animated porn, the horizons of expressive and imaginary possibility of animation, such as exaggerated gestures, hypertrophied bodies and extreme doses of violence (Capino, 2004, p. 56), meet the excessive and hyperbolic features of pornography.

[A]nimated bodies can perform every desire and fantasy that the human body cannot utter. Relentlessly and with impunity, the animated body's plastic genitalia and invulnerable orifices grow and multiply, mutate and mutilate, probe or are penetrated by every imaginable object and animal. Sexual boundaries assume the solubility of water colors.

(Capino, 2004, p. 54.)

In hentai and ero manga (adult comics), human bodies are regularly pushed to the extremes, even to "the point at which it can be no longer recogni[s]ed as human" (Shamoon, 2004, p. 87). At the same time, these hyperbolic scenarios of excessive penetration, climax and lust involve plentiful instances of humour that are easily downplayed or even ignored when considering their gendered dynamics of submission and domination. Such instances may vary from the overall absurdity of the settings – winged creatures pounding tiny female bodies with their rainbow-hued penises that, impossibly, eventually do fit into the orifices where they are thrust – to the reflective exclamations such as Mumji's understated observation, "This is not normal", uttered during a particularly rough sex scene with a massive demon.

A laughing matter?

In the era of free tube sites, pornographic niches, fringes and specialities – in addition to web cams and live streaming – are exceptional as content that consumers are willing to pay for. Despite actors such as Studio FOW sharing their films for no fee, 3D monster toon sites are largely protected by paywalls or on sites requiring registration. Clips are made available on tube sites as teasers and advertisements. In addition, monster toon sites attract user attention with the now markedly vintage strategies of meta-sites (sites that function as directories to other web sites), link sites (sites consisting of external links with little original content) and click-throughs (links leading to endlessly new meta-sites and link sites). Widely in use before porn consumption began to centralise on aggregate sites – all of which emulate the operating principles of YouTube, launched in 2005 – these strategies for generating traffic, increasing click ratios and attracting users to pay, have since grown much more rare.

The members-only website, *Hellywood: Evil Invasion*, specialises in glossy, carefully rendered and hyperbolic 3D still images of female celebrities – from Jessica Alba to Lindsey Lohan, Jennifer Aniston and Katy Perry – engaging in elaborate sexual acts with monsters of all kinds. Hellywood promises its paying members access to several affiliate network sites similarly catering in 3D monster and evil forces in sexual play, from 'Evil Creatures Fucking Cute Girls' to 'World of Porncraft 3D', 'Fucked by Evil Creature 3D Video', '3D Evil Attack', 'Hell Fuckers', 'Fucked by Fiends' and 'Live-Action Taboo Tentacles'. These sites offer 3D monster toon as video, still images and comics complete with speech bubbles. These notably remediated aesthetics speak of the attraction that such visions hold: despite the abundant accessibility of free video, singular, specialised fantasy images retain their appeal. Monster toon porn features novelties, creatures and extreme acts never seen before. Characterised as a celebrity mansion where "total fucking madness gets a whole new meaning", Hellywood envisions:

> Shocking action-packed 3D hentai scenes of evil creatures from Hell fucking you (sic) favourite award-winning celebrities! Watch hottest women on Earth power-fucked by merciless invaders and gets (sic) orgasm from ugly cock fucking jaw-dropping hentai 3D fantasy scenes right now!
>
> (Hellywood)

The female celebrities' faces have been appropriated from mainstream media images – film shots, magazine poses and music video stills – and their expressions range from surprise to disgust, enthusiasm, startle, dismay, joy and panache. The heads often fail to match the bodies modelled for them, many of which come with hyperbolically tiny waists and huge breasts. A legion of computer-generated demons, aliens and other monstrous creatures in greys, greens, blues, blacks and browns is seen probing the celebrities with their perpetually hard penises.

It does not take a huge stretch of analytical imagination to associate the gaping orifices, phallic shapes and metamorphosing bodies of monster toon porn, or the hyperbolic landscape of Studio FOW and the tentacled glossy parallel universe of Hellywood more specifically, with the notion of the grotesque, as introduced by literary scholar Mikhail Bakhtin in his study of Rabelais. For Bahtin (1984, pp. 30–31, 317), grotesque represents the opposite of classic body ideas as limitlessness where the insides and outsides of bodies refuse to be confined within their regular boundaries. The aesthetics of the grotesque intermeshes with and immerses in bodily orifices, exaggerates and is resistant to moderation (Bahtin, 1984, pp. 303–304), hence breaking against any conventional notions of proper taste or appropriate demeanour. While carnivalesque excess and unruly laughter are, with Rabelais, connected to the undoing of cultural hierarchies and positions of power, such a symbolic reading is less readily achieved with monster toon porn. Grotesque aesthetics are in broad use and moments of dirty humour abound yet these do not add up to symbolic subversion of social hierarchies of power (see also Hester, 2014). All in all, monster toon porn – like pornography more broadly – remains resistant to most readings aiming to pin it neatly down as a cultural symbol or symptom (see Paasonen, 2011).

Humour has been elementary to the traditions of graphic pornography preceding film, pornographic animated film, comics as well as shunga and hentai that monster porn builds on. Ortega-Bena (2009) highlights the role of humour as adding to the pleasures of hentai and the sense of distance that its emotionally vacuous and expressionless characters contribute to. Much of this applies to Hellywood where facial expressions are frozen in still motion, recombined with computer-generated bodies, smoothed over and set in elaborate scenes of monster orgies. These images are colourful and high-definition, and a great deal of attention has been paid to detail. The resulting effect follows Capino's (2004, p. 56) more general account of animated porn's impossible, hyperbolic sexual activity as "multiplied in volume, exaggerated in magnitude – resulting in hyper-sexuality *par excellence*". The Hellywood effect is literally too much: tongue-in-cheek inasmuch as sexually explicit. The site is richly garnished with invitation to see 'Goblins, walking dead and disgusting creatures of ancient saga invade the Earth to nail every fuckable celeb in the area!' and 'Gape on tight celebrity pussies getting ripped by dreadful cocks and filled to the brim with hot infernal seed!'

Such enthusiasm towards evil creatures ripping and nailing hot chicks follows the vocabulary of hard-core porn that attaches unequivocally positive value to the dreadful, vile and disgusting as markers of no holds barred action (see Paasonen, 2011, pp. 57–59, 207–209). The huge monsters and tiny elves of monster porn also follow the guiding pornographic principles of spectacularly binary depiction of embodied differences, dynamics of submission and control. The rhetoric of hard-core porn draws firmly on the juxtaposition of the tiny and the colossal, the degenerate and the sweet while firmly amplifying differences in gender, age and ethnicity for the ultimate effect. (Capino, 2004, p. 56; Paasonen, 2011, pp. 126–128, 157) In monster toon porn, this hyperbolic modality grows highly literal as the tiny is truly miniscule and the colossal simply gargantuan.

In many ways, the dramatic, exaggerated and markedly unrealistic scenes and bodies of monster toon porn provide antitheses for amateur pornography, the popularity of which has been one of the major trends in online pornography for the last decade. If amateur porn draws its appeal from a sense of realness, recognisability, familiarity and authenticity, monster toons provide unreal, fantastic and alien scenarios. Meanwhile, its mechanical and machinic motions of bodies pushing back and forth without a great deal of expression, affective nuance or modulations in intensity come across as hyperbolic version of repetition, which has been seen as characteristic of pornography as a genre (e.g. Grosz, 2006, p. 197). Due to all this, monster toon porn remains resistant to literal interpretations based on the premises of realistic representation.

The heightened sense of fantastic, impossible unrealness, combined with the applications of photorealism, explains much of the appeal of 3D monster toon porn: its excessiveness is impossible to ignore. While immersion in its imageries is undoubtedly possible, a more literal identification with its emotionally vacuous and highly cartoon-like characters is more unlikely. Violent scenarios of submission and control are played out to the fullest, often on overdrive. The resonances that they afford are distinct from those of live-action pornography where the effects of bodies whipped, asphyxiated and stretched are bound up with indexicality – be this experienced as titillating, disturbing or both. In contrast, fantastic computer-generated bodies are endlessly pliable and resilient. The female bodies are perfectly symmetrical, smooth and fine-tuned as certain figures of fantasy. They stretch, bounce right back and never fail.

References

Adelman, B. (1997). *Tijuana Bibles: Art and Wit in America's Forbidden Funnies, 1930s–1950s.* New York: Simon & Schuster.

Bahtin, M. (1984/1965). *Rabelais and His World.* (H. Iswolsky, Trans.). Bloomington: Indiana University Press.

Buckland, R. (2010). *Shunga: Erotic Art in Japan.* London: British Museum Press.

Burgess, M. C. R., Stermer, S. P. and Burgess, S. R. (2007). Sex, Lies, and Video Games: The Portrayal of Male and Female Characters on Video Game Covers. *Sex Roles 57(5–6),* 419–433.

Capino, J. B. (2004). Filthy Funnies: Notes on the Body in Animated Pornography. *Animation Journal 1,* 53–71.

Chess, S. and Shaw, A. (2015). A Conspiracy of Fishes, or, How We Learned to Stop Worrying about #GamerGate and Embrace Hegemonic Masculinity. *Journal of Broadcasting & Electronic Media 59(1),* 208–220.

Clark, T., Gerstle C.A., Ishigami, A. and Yanno, A. (eds.) (2013). Shunga: Sex and Pleasure in Japanese Art. *The British Museum.*

Consalvo, M. (2012). Confronting Toxic Gamer Culture: A Challenge for Feminist Game Studies Scholars. *Ada: A Journal of Gender, New Media & Technology 1(1)* (online). Retrieved on 29 May 2017 on the ADA website: http://adanewmedia. org/2012/11/issue1-consalvo/.

Dahlqvist, J. P. and Vigilant, L. G. (2004). "Way Better than Real: Manga Sex to Tentacle Hentai". In Waskul, D. D. (ed.), *Net.seXXX: Readings of Sex, Pornography, and the Internet* (pp. 91–103). New York: Peter Lang.

Douglas, N. (2014). It's Supposed to Look like Shit: The Internet Ugly Aesthetic. *Journal of Visual Culture 13(3)*, 314–339.

Falkenstein, J. (2011). Machinima as a Viable Commercial Medium. *Journal of Visual Culture 10(1)*, 86–88.

Flanagan, M. (1999). Mobile Identities, Digital Stars, and Post-cinematic Selves. *Wide Angle 21(1)*, 77–93.

Foucault, M. (1990). *The History of Sexuality, Volume 1 – An Introduction*. (R. Hurley, Trans.). London: Penguin.

Foucault, M. (2003). "Abnormal: Lectures at the Collège de France, 1974–1975". In Marchetti, V. and Salomoni, A. (eds.), (G. Burchell, Trans.). New York: Picador.

Gehl, R. W. (2009). YouTube as Archive. Who Will Curate This Digital Wunderkammer? *International Journal of Cultural Studies 12(1)*, 43–60.

Gehl, R. W. (2011). The Archive and Processor: The Internal Logic of Web 2.0. *New Media & Society 13(8)*, 1228–1244.

Grosz, E. (2006). "Naked". In Smith, M. and Morra, J. (eds.) *The Prosthetic Impulse: From a Posthuman Present to a Biocultural Future* (pp. 187–202). Cambridge: MIT Press, 187–202.

Hambleton, A. (2015). When women watch: the subversive potential of female-friendly pornography in Japan. *Porn Studies*, published online before print 16 December 2015 doi: 10.1080/23268743.2015.1065203.

Hancock, H. (2011). Machinima: Limited, Ghettoized, and Spectacularly Promising. *Journal of Visual Culture 10(1)*, 31–37.

Hellywood. Retrieved on 20 September on the Hellywood website: http://hellywood3d. tumblr.com/.

Hernandez, P. (2015). "The People Who Make Brutal Video Porn". Retrieved on 11 March 2016 from the Kotaku website: http://kotaku.com/ the-people-who-make-brutal-video-game-porn-1690892332.

Hester, H. (2014). *Beyond Explicit. Pornography and the Displacement of Sex*. Albany: SUNY Press.

Ito, M. (2011). Machinima in a Fanvid Ecology. *Journal of Visual Culture 10(1)*, 51–54.

Kazutaka, H. (2013). No Laughing Matter: A Ghastly Shunga Illustration by Utagawa Toyokuni. *Japan Review 26*, 239–255.

Klein, N. M. (1993/1998). *7 Minutes: The Life and Death of the American Animated Cartoon*. London and New York: Verso.

Lancaster, K. (2004). Lara Croft: The Ultimate Young Adventure Girl: Or the Unending Media Desire for Models, Sex, and Fantasy. *PAJ: A Journal of Performance and Art 26(3)*, 87–97.

Marcus, S. (1964). *The Other Victorians: A Study of Sexuality and Pornography in Mid-Nineteenth Century England*. New Brunswick: Transaction Publishers.

Martinez, M. and Manolovitz, T. (2010). "Pornography in Gaming". In Riha, D. (ed.), *Videogame Cultures and the Future of Interactive Entertainment* (pp. 65–74). Oxford: Inter-Disciplinary Press.

Massanari, A. (2015). #Gamergate and The Fappening: How Reddit's algorithm, governance, and culture support toxic technocultures. *New Media & Society*, Published online before print 9 October 2015, doi:10.1177/1461444815608807.

McLelland, M. (July 2005). "A short history of 'hentai'". Paper presented at Sexualities, Genders and Rights in Asia: 1st International Conference of Asian Queer Studies. Bangkok, Thailand: AsiaPacifiQueer Network, Mahidol University; Australian National University. Retrieved on 6 June 2016 from the Australian National University website: http://hdl.handle.net/1885/8673.

Napier, S. J. (2005). *Anime from Akira to Howl's Moving Castle: Experiencing Contemporary Japanese Animation* (2nd ed.). New York: Palgrave.

Ortega-Brena, M. (2009), Peek-a-boo, I See You: Watching Japanese Hard-Core Animation. *Sexuality & Culture 13,* 17–31.

Paasonen, S. (2011). *Carnal Resonance: Affect and Online Pornography.* Cambridge: MIT Press.

Penley, C. (2004). "Crackers and Whackers: The White Trashing of Porn". In Williams, L. (ed.), *Porn Studies* (pp. 309–331). Durham: Duke University Press.

Pilcher, T. (2008), *Erotic Comics: A Graphic History from Tijuana Bibles to Underground Comix.* New York: Abrams.

Schleiner, A. (2001). Does Lara Croft Wear Fake Polygons? Gender and Gender-Role Subversion in Computer Adventure Games. *Leonardo 34(3),* 221–226.

Screech, T. (2009). *Sex and the Floating World: Erotic Images in Japan 1700–1820* (2nd ed.). London: Reaktion Books.

Shamoon, D. (2004). "Office Sluts and Rebel Flowers." In Williams, L. (ed.), *Porn Studies* (pp. 77–103). Durham: Duke University Press.

Stermer, P. S. and Burkley, M. (2012). Xbox or SeXbox? An Examination of Sexualized Content in Video Games. *Social and Personality Psychology Compass 6(7),* 525–535.

Todd, C. (2015). GamerGate and Resistance to the Diversification of Gaming Culture. *Women's Studies Journal 29(1),* 64–67.

Uidhir, C. M. and Pratt, H. J. (2012). "Pornography at the Edge: Depiction, Fiction, and Sexual Predilection." In Maes, H. and Levinson, J. (eds.), *Art & Pornography: Philosophical Essays* (pp. 137–157). Oxford: Oxford University Press.

2 Participatory porn culture

Feminist positions and oppositions in the internet pornosphere

Allegra W. Smith

Introductions: pornography, feminisms, and ongoing debate

Though first-wave feminists had engaged in debate and advocacy surrounding sexual knowledge and obscenity since the late-19th century (Horowitz, 2003), American advocates did not begin to address pornography as a feminist concern until the 1970s, ostensibly beginning with the formation of the activist group Women Against Violence in Pornography and Media (WAVPM) in 1978. WAVPM was a reactionary response to the mainstreaming of hard-core pornography in the wake of American sexual liberation, which many second wave feminists claimed "...encouraged rape and other acts of violence, threatening women's safety and establishing a climate of terror that silenced women and perpetuated their oppression... [thus helping] create and maintain women's subordinate status" (Bronstein, 2011, pp. 178–179).

The resulting 'porn wars' (or, more broadly, 'sex wars') of the 1980s and 1990s polarised second-and third-wave feminists into two camps: (1) anti-porn feminists, such as writer Andrea Dworkin (1981) and legal scholar Catharine MacKinnon (1984), who opposed the creation and distribution of pornographic images and videos on moral and political grounds; and (2) pro-porn or sex-positive feminists, such as anthropologist Gayle Rubin and feminist pornographer Candida Royalle, who advocated for freedom of sexual expression and representation. The rhetoric surrounding the social and cultural ills perpetuated by pornography was duly acrimonious, with one prominent feminist writing, "pornography is the theory, rape is the practice" (Morgan, 1978, p. 128).

Now, 40 years after the beginning of the 'porn wars', a similarly polarised debate still persists – criticising pornography and its purported role as an instrument of women's oppression, or framing it as a potential vehicle for women's empowerment. Simultaneously, media expansion, democratisation, and convergence has not only widened the reach of pornographic media, but also the scope and depth of the conversations surrounding it. The widespread adoption of VCRs and other home video technologies, followed by the proliferation of computers and high-speed Internet across the US, moved pornography from theatres and stag films into the homes of the private consumer. Digital porn communities such as fan sites and message boards enabled consumers to not only gather and share their interests about sexuality and also sexual imagery with the promise of relative anonymity, but also to establish visible erotic cultures and subcultures, chipping away at the stigma of pornography consumption, as well as sexuality writ large. This was especially true for women during Internet porn's initial heyday in the early 2000s, as noted by multiple authors in *The Feminist Porn Book* (2013); porn for women emerged as a counter-narrative to the adult films and images that galvanised second-wave feminists to begin the porn wars.

In *The Feminist Porn Book* (2013), as well as the *Porn Studies* journal that emerged at the same time, porn theorists and practitioners alike engaged in extensive theorising about what pornography created for women *could* or *should* look like, but limited empirical work on what the porn actually preferred by women *does* look like. What sets the porn consumed by women apart from the mainstream adult content consumed by men?

My research (Smith, 2015) has examined the content of two Internet porn communities on reddit.com, to delineate and quantify the differences between pornography preferred by male and female audiences. The results, excerpted here, illustrate the continued diversification of pornographic media, particularly with regard to the construction of a gendered 'gaze' that directs the filmic frame (Ms. Naughty, 2014; Mulvey, 1999). Perhaps the most striking visualisation of this shifting gaze is the development of what I have termed a women's 'participatory porn culture', wherein women's fantasies are articulated and then depicted on screen (rather than a more traditional pornographic representation of a male gaze), detailed in the last section of this chapter. I conclude with potential directions for future research, as well as a call for the application of an inclusive feminist sexual ethic to future research on pornography and other sexual representations.

Taking the pulse of the porn-watching public: digital communities as representative of erotic preferences and cultures

The social networking site reddit allows users ('redditors') to share and vote on content on message boards ('subreddits') that coalesce around particular themes – for example, r/gaming for videogames, or r/worldnews for global current events. Users then rank this content by giving 'upvotes' to posts they enjoy and 'downvotes' to posts they dislike, so that content with the highest number of upvotes appears at the top of the homepage for each subreddit and posts are organised sequentially in order of aggregate popularity.

In the case of pornography, reddit's peer-sourced and group-ranked information architecture offers researchers the opportunity to 'take the pulse' of the porn-viewing public at a given moment: the top videos on a not safe for work (NSFW) subreddit are indicative of the porn trends *du jour*. With over 8,400 NSFW subreddits as of April 2016, redditors and visitors can share, rank, and view pornographic content from the normative to the fetishistic (NSFW411, 2016). Much like the companies and websites that create this content, subreddits can offer a very broad range of porn (like on general boards such as r/nsfw, and r/Blowjobs), or very specific genres and niches (r/Russian girls, r/preggohentai, r/areolas, and r/GirlsHumpingThings, just to name a few) – giving users many options to find adult content that satisfies their particular "carnal resonance" (Paasonen, 2011).

PornVids, one of the largest porn subreddits (with 150,000 subscribers as of May 2016), is devoted to sharing pornography videos hosted on large free 'porn tube' websites such as PornVids, RedTube, and XVideos. ChickFlixxx has a smaller readership (39,000 subscribers) and is described as a board "for women, by women", designed to create a "female-oriented community" where "pro-porn women" can "share links to great sexual content and discuss porn" (r/ChickFlixx, 2016).

To obtain a representative sample for analysing the content of these networks, I downloaded and archived the top ten ranked videos from both subreddits at the time of data collection (October 2014). The twenty videos that compose the study sample represent the Internet pornography trends from both communities. Through reddit's peer-sourced and group-ranked information architecture, their landing pages are indicative of real-time user demand. They provide researchers with a finger on the pulse of porn trends of the moment.

These videos comprised nearly ten hours' worth of pornographic content: four hours, 43 minutes, and 40 seconds for the r/PornVids sample and five hours, four minutes, and eight seconds for the r/Chickflixxx sample, respectively. While this amount of content is certainly not indicative of the various norms and niches of the millions of pornographic files available online (Döring, 2009, p. 1092; Mazières *et al.*, 2014), these 20 videos provided a representative sample of the most popular content within two porn communities and their respective cultures: that of a more mainstream porn community, moderated by male users and dominated by a male viewership; and its emerging, female-focused counterpart.

After downloading and archiving the most popular content from these two communities, I then systematically analysed and coded the videos in the sample for both visual (Whose bodies are being shown? What acts are taking place?) and aural (What is being said? In what tone?) rhetoric, as well as for the presence (or absence) of a hegemonic male gaze.

Mobilising practitioner frameworks to codify the male gaze in porn

"Male gaze", as coined by feminist film scholar Laura Mulvey (1999) in her landmark essay *Visual Pleasure and Narrative Cinema*, describes the dominant heterosexual male perspective adopted in mainstream film that sexualises, commodifies, and subordinates the female body: empowering man as an active "bearer of the look" and rendering woman a passive "bearer of meaning" (Mulvey, 1999, pp. 842–843).

While Mulvey created her operationalisation of the male gaze to apply to mainline Hollywood cinema, the concept is magnified in pornography, where gender roles and sexual categories are amplified to titillate audiences – as noted by feminist pornographer Ms. Naughty (Louise Lush) in her 2014 video, *The Male Gaze in Porn (With Commentary by Doge)*. After a more than decade-long career creating content in the adult film industry as a writer, director, and critic, Ms. Naughty created the video to deconstruct the reasons why (in her experience) women do not enjoy watching mainstream porn, and to provide a name for those reasons: the male gaze. The framework that Ms. Naughty creates outlines eight different tenets of the male gaze in the construction of pornographic fantasies for men, by men – from phallocentric imagery ('the headless dick'), to synecdochic representations of the female body ('the woman is always looked *at*, she never *looks*'), to inauthentic portrayals of lesbian sex ('his fantasy'). Her critique uses clips from real porn videos, all comically censored using images from an Internet meme and accompanied by a kitschy backing track (Ms. Naughty, 2014).

I deployed six of these eight tenets as analytical criteria to determine and codify the presence of a male gaze in the porn videos from both reddit samples (For more information see Smith, 2015). The remaining two tenets explained the function of the male gaze in porn marketing (particularly DVD covers), and thus were not applicable to the Internet clips used for this project. The incorporation of this framework served two purposes. First, it generated data on the more latent and symbolic functions of the content being analysed, in relation to the performance and significance of gender as constructed by the visual and aural rhetorical actions of the filmmakers and performers. Second, mobilising Ms. Naughty's categories as analytical criteria continues the feminist tradition of recognising that there are theorists beyond the academy: that practitioners create and actualise theory in their work, just as scholars do in their publications. My inclusion of the theory of a working pornographer here is a deliberate rhetorical move to value and amplify the knowledge of practitioners alongside that of researchers in the field of porn studies.

Positions and oppositions: trends across mainstream and women's pornography

The results of this study shed light on the differences between the sexual cultures of r/PornVids and r/Chickflixxx, representative of a mainstream audience of mostly male porn consumers, and a more marginal audience largely comprised of female porn consumers, respectively.

Both qualitatively and quantitatively, the videos on the women's porn board demonstrated a greater diversity of sexual acts and practices than those on the mainstream porn board. The r/Chickflixxx sample included use of sex toys, while the mainstream sample did not. Interestingly enough, the woman-friendly sample was also the only one to include any anal sex, a practice typically thought – at least in a hetero-porn context – to be more appealing to men than to women. The video featuring anal sex also included the use of sex toys, and was the only clip in the sample directed by a woman.

Videos from the r/Chickflixxx sample included more kissing and foreplay than those from r/PornVids (6.42% of r/ChickFlixxx video content versus 4.59% of r/PornVids video content), as well as more cunnilingus and manual stimulation/fingering of female performers. However, much of the manual clitoral stimulation across the videos from both samples was performed not by male partners, but by female performers upon themselves. In spite of this, the 'male gaze scores' were radically different between the two samples: the ten r/PornVids clips met Ms. Naughty's (2014) male gaze criteria 44 times (out of a possible 60), while the ten r/Chickflixxx clips had less than half of that, with only 19 instances.

The most commonly met male gaze criteria across both datasets was the prioritisation of fellatio over cunnilingus; on this account, even the pornography selected and shared by women was still not entirely equitable, statistically speaking. Women on r/Chickflixxx often complained about the lack of cunnilingus in mainstream porn in particular, which led me to code specifically for the duration of oral sex acts across the study sample. The fellatio ratio – that is, the amount of male-receiving oral sex compared to the amount of female-receiving – spoke volumes, with the r/PornVids sample displaying 13.4 seconds of blowjob for every one second of cunnilingus, while the r/Chickflixxx sample showed 1.26 seconds of blowjob for every second of cunnilingus. Also contradicting the female redditors' claims of gender equity within the pornography they selected, both samples had the same number of videos depicting female orgasm (six videos out of ten on both r/Chickflixx and r/PornVids) – though it is worth noting that there were more instances of multiple female orgasms, thus a greater total female orgasm count, in the r/Chickflixxx videos. Visual representations of female orgasm are increasingly called for by feminist pornographers and porn theorists alike, particularly when the editors of the leading edited collection on feminist porn theory write that truly feminist pornography "depicts genuine female pleasure" (Taormino *et al.*, 2013, p. 12). If the videos in both samples depict more male orgasms than female ones, where is the gendered and sexual equity that these theorists and female fans envisioned?

While seemingly basic and admittedly a bit reductive, these simple numbers are indicative of greater trends across the visual rhetoric of pornography that value the pleasure of a man over the pleasure of a woman. These trends in turn influence the real life sexual practices of a generation that is increasingly porn educated, with reference to one study showing that more than half of UK students turn to pornography for their sex education (National Union of Students, 2015). Because of pornography's rising status as a sexual educator, the representation of a greater variety of sexual practices is increasingly important and impactful.

Participatory porn culture: creating new representations of women's sexuality

One commonality between both subreddits analysed for this project is their shared love of a particular male performer: 5'8" (1.72 cm), 30-year-old James Deen. Young women in particular enjoy Deen's performances because of his 'nonthreatening' appearance, 'boy-next-door' ethos and range of work – from softer, more intimate scenes, to hardcore gangbangs produced for websites like kink.com (Rosetti, 2012). The women of r/Chickflixxx devoted entire posts and threads to discussing Deen's work, and his videos were also frequently shared on r/PornVids.

Not only was James Deen especially popular on both porn subreddits analysed for this project, but a particular series of videos shot for his website were consistently among PornVids and Chickflixxx's highest rated. This group of similarly designed and edited videos, which I refer to as Deen's "civilian porn series", originated in 2013 and continue at the time of writing (summer 2016).

In September 2013, Deen had an afternoon off after his scheduled porn shoot was suddenly cancelled. He posted a (seemingly joking) request to his official Twitter account, asking if any female followers would be interested in shooting a scene with him (Deen, 2013a). The response to this informal casting call was so enthusiastic – with messages from hundreds of female fans, according to the still-open call for participants on Deen's website (Deen, 2013b) – that Deen is still shooting videos with applicants today, three years later. At press time for this collection, there are 84 videos listed under the 'amateur' tag on Deen's website (Deen, 2016); while not all of these videos were shot with 'true' amateurs (women with no previous experience in the adult film industry), two of them were among the top ten videos on r/Chickflixxx (and one on r/PornVids) at the time of data collection. These videos, which typically last for about an hour divided equally between Deen conversing with the women and having sex with them, exemplify the values of a growing participatory porn culture.

Participatory culture, as described by media and fan studies scholar Henry Jenkins and colleagues (2009), emphasises social connections between members of a culture maintained through active engagement, fostered through "low barriers to artistic expression and civic engagement", and where participants mentor each other and in so doing truly "believe that their contributions matter" (Jenkins *et al.*, 2016, p. 7). This is not the first time that the creations of porn fans have been valued alongside those of professional content creators in the adult film industry; homemade sex tapes (both of civilians and celebrities, such as Pamela Anderson and Tommy Lee – see Hillyer, 2004) have circulated on the Internet since the mid-to-late 1990s. Homemade sex tapes do appear among the top videos on r/PornVids and r/Chickflixxx, but have not been met with as enthusiastic a response as the videos from Deen's series, which not only feature the bodies and desires of 'real women', but do so in a way that connects fans with the object of their fandom – in an unprecedented participatory fashion that depicts and amplifies *women's* fantasies.

Unlike the amateur sex tape genre created by couples in their own home and intended largely for private consumption, this civilian porn series that Deen has created has no historical antecedent – at least not for women. Male fans have been tapped to star in adult videos alongside female porn stars to bring *their* fantasies to life, but female porn fans were not invited to engage with male performers in the same way. Women have self-published porn sites for their own personal and economic gain since the early days of the Internet, as noted by DeVoss (2002), but these women too were still creating images and videos that catered to a largely male gaze. Theirs was pornography created primarily for men to purchase and consume.

The creation of this particular series signifies a number of socio-cultural shifts. Firstly, Deen's popularity among women that built to create the series is demonstrative of shifting representations of masculinity in pornography and other sexual media; his 'nonthreatening' appearance created by a slim body and self-effacing ethos counters more traditional representations of hegemonic masculinity in adult media. Secondly, the continuation of Deen's series beyond the initial videos in the fall of 2013 remains a testament to the power of the female porn consumer.[1] Finally, and perhaps most pertinently for porn studies scholars, the popularity of videos featuring 'real woman' fans of pornography engaging in sexual activities with their favourite adult film star is representative of a move towards a more public and visible participatory porn culture, as the women shooting scenes with Deen are easily identifiable and occasionally even use their real names (see Tisdale, 2015).

Not only does this new amateur pornography series exemplify the values of participatory culture; it signifies a shift towards women's pornographic and erotic agency that distinctly contrasts with typical second-wave feminist accounts of porn demeaning and degrading women. The women in this participatory porn series, and the female fans who share and circulate the videos, are claiming agency: their ability to affect social change. Rhetoricians Carl Herndl and Adela Licona (2007) frame agency as radical, counterhegemonic action that changes or entirely dismantles social, institutional, and/or discursive practices. Couples have shot videos of themselves engaging in sexual acts since before the creation of porn websites, but never have women been provided such an opportunity to participate as an actress in the production of pornography made for them, by them – and in so doing, announce and affirm their status as porn consumers. These women, and their fans in communities like r/Chickflixxx that share and comment on the videos they star in, radically flip the pornographic gaze to create new sexual representations.

The women in this series claim a new erotic agency that has not been afforded to women previously: the ability to have public sex with a porn star who is an object of *female,* not male, desire. In turn, Deen and his female 'civilian' partners create a video that reflects that desire back into the Internet pornosphere through thousands of viewings by other porn consumers – of all genders. This reciprocal process redistributes the agency of the pornographic production more equitably between participants, in addition to involving fans in the creation of pornography so that sexual imagery reflects their practices and desires.

Conclusions: towards a feminist pornographic and sexual ethic for the digital age

When I began writing this chapter the release of the first film in the *Fifty Shades of Grey* trilogy was igniting feminist debate around subjects of fantasy, power, sexuality, and violence. Internet porn communities were similarly divided after James Deen was the subject of multiple allegations of sexual assault and misconduct from former partners and co-stars (Snow, 2015), creating conversation around working conditions for performers in the adult film industry, as well as the importance of seeking consent in all sexual encounters.

What perpetuates the continuing 'porn wars' between feminists and non-feminists alike, and what began my foray into rhetorical porn studies, is this paradoxical nature of pornography. Much as politicians claim that the government should not interfere in the private lives of citizens, yet seek to regulate those citizens' private activities behind bedroom doors, so too does pornography sit tenuously on the contested boundary of public rhetoric and private practice. Those who claim not to watch it aim to police its production and consumption, and those who do consume it are stigmatised into silence around their consumption.

Internet pornography uniquely demonstrates the symbols and manifestations of an erotic culture that is simultaneously public and private. In the 21st century, porn is always, already a part of our widely circulated norms of gender and sexuality, yet often relegated to the realm of impolite dinner conversation – a thing we do not speak of, despite its omnipresence in our media and culture.

While this work is not intended to be a definitive study on the effects or implications of all pornography – it would be foolhardy and reductive to attempt such sweeping generalisations in the first place – it does begin to unpack previous assertions by both academics and pundits alike that porn is a monolithic, violent discourse. It is clear that continued scholarship needs to engage with the multiplicity of sexual representations and cultures embodied through pornographic media, and that partnerships between scholars and adult industry practitioners – such as *The Feminist Porn Book* (2013) and the *Porn Studies* journal – can help to facilitate academic work that more faithfully represents this multiplicity.

Finally, in order to continue affirming the sexual agency of *all genders*, the crucial nature of consent must be emphasised within pornography and in sexual media writ large. It is clear that continued conversations are needed around not only the multiplicity of sexual practices and bodies, but also the consent required to maintain a feminist sexual ethic that acknowledges and honours bodily autonomy and integrity, in addition to desire.

Note

1 Also a testament to the power of the female porn consumer, however, is the decline in Deen's popularity after he was the subject of multiple allegations of sexual assault in November 2015, after a tweet from fellow porn-performer and Deen's former partner, Stoya, claimed that he had ignored her safe word and raped her during their relationship. I cannot fully address Deen's alleged misconduct here, due to constraints of this anthology; however, it would be remiss not to acknowledge these events and their resulting discourse, both inside and outside of the porn community, on consent and the negotiation of power during sexual activity, particularly that which involves BDSM or other power play. The theorising and reflection on James Deen's participatory pornography here should be taken as what it is – scholarship – rather than an endorsement of his actions or character.

References

Bronstein, C. (2011). *Battling Pornography: The American Feminist Anti-Pornography Movement, 1976–1986*. New York: Cambridge University Press.

Deen, J. [JamesDeen] (a). (5 September 2013). My scene got cancelled today:-(i guess i could shoot amateur porn for http://jamesdeen.com … anyone want to shoot a porno with me? [Tweet]. Retrieved on 5 July 2016 from Twitter: https://twitter.com/jamesdeen/status/375670052973862912.

Deen, J. [JamesDeen] (b). (2013). Do a scene with James [Web]. Retrieved on 5 July 2016 from Twitter http://www.jamesdeen.com/models.php.

Deen, J. [JamesDeen]. Amateur page 1 at JamesDeen.com. Retrieved on 7 June 2016 from Twitter http://jamesdeen.com/categories/43/amateur/page1.html.

DeVoss, D.N. (2002). Women's porn sites—Spaces of fissure and eruption or "I'm a little bit of everything." *Sexuality & Culture* 6(3), 75–94.

Döring, N.M. (2009). The Internet's Impact on Sexuality: A Critical Review of 15 Years of Research. *Computers in Human Behavior 25*, 1089–1101.

Dworkin, A. (26 May 1981). Pornography's Part in Sexual Violence. *The Los Angeles Times*. Los Angeles, CA.

Herndl, C.G., and Licona, A.C. (2007). Shifting Agency: Agency, Kairos, and the Possibilities of Social Action. In Zachry, M. and Thralls, C. (eds.), *Communicative Practices in Workplaces and the Professions* (pp. 133–153). Amityville: Baywood Publishing Company, Inc.

Hillyer, M. (2004). Sex in the Suburban: Porn, Home Movies, and the Live Action Performance of Love in *Pam and Tommy Lee: Hardcore and Uncensored*. In Williams, L. (ed.), *Porn Studies* (pp. 50–76). Durham: Duke University Press.

Horowitz, H.L. (2003). *Rereading Sex: Battles over Sexual Knowledge and Suppression in Nineteenth Century America*. New York: Vintage.

Jenkins, H., Purushotma, R., Weigel, M., Clinton, K., and Robison, A.J. (2009). *Confronting the Challenges of Participatory Culture: Media Education for the 21st Century* (The John D. and Catherine T. MacArthur Foundation Reports on Digital Media and Learning). Cambridge: Massachusetts Institute of Technology.

MacKinnon, C.A. (1984). Not a Moral Issue. *Yale Law & Policy Review 2*(2), 321–345.

Mazières, A., Trachman, M., Cointet, J.-P., and Coulmont, B. (2014). Deep Tags: Toward a Quantitative Analysis of Online Pornography. *Porn Studies 1*(1–2), 80–95.

Morgan, R. (1978). *Going Too Far: The Personal Chronicle of a Feminist*. New York: Vintage Books.

Ms. Naughty (Louise Lush). (2014). The male gaze in porn (With commentary by Doge) [Vimeo video]. Retrieved on 5 July 2016 from Vimeo: http://vimeo.com/85876551.

Mulvey, L. (1999). Visual Pleasure and Narrative Cinema. In Braudy, L. and Cohen, M. (eds.), *Film Theory and Criticism: Introductory Readings* (pp. 833–844). New York: Oxford University Press.

National Union of Students. (29 January 2015). Students turn to porn to fill the gaps in their sex education. Retrieved on 12 March 2015 from the National Union of Students websites: www.nus.org.uk/en/news/students-turn-to-porn-to-fill-the-gaps-in-their-sex-education/.

NSFW411. (April 2016). Fulllist1 (NSFW Subreddit Listing). Retrieved on 31 May 2016 from Reddit: www.reddit.com/r/NSFW411/wiki/fulllist4.

Paasonen, S. (2011). *Carnal Resonance: Affect and Online Pornography*. Cambridge: MIT University Press.

r/Chickflixxx. (31 May 2016). A place for women to confer about and share porn/erotica. Retrieved on 31 May 2016 from the Chickflixx website: https://m.reddit.com/r/chickflixxx.

Rosetti, C. (1 July 2012). James Deen, the "Prince Charming of Porn" for better or worse? Retrieved on 10 June 2016 from the Broad Recognition (Yale) website: www.broadrecognitionyale.com/2012/07/01/james-deen-the-prince-charming-of-porn-for-better-or-worse/.

Smith, A.W. (2015). *Whose Porn is it Anyway: Exploring the Differences between Feminist and Mainstream Internet Pornography*. M.A. Thesis submitted at Michigan State University, East Lansing, MI.

Snow, A. (30 November 2015). James Deen, the bill cosby of porn? A third accuser comes forward. Retrieved on 10 June 2016 from the Daily Beast website: www.thedailybeast.com/articles/2015/11/30/james-deen-the-bill-cosby-of-porn.html.

Taormino, T., Penley, C., Shimizu, C.P., and Miller-Young, M. (eds.). (2013). *The Feminist Porn Book: The Politics of Producing Pleasure*. New York: The Feminist Press at the City University of New York.

Tisdale, J. (30 November 2015). This one time: My amateur porn date with James Deen [Updated]. Retrieved on 3 June 2016 from the Jezebel website: http://jezebel.com/this-one-time-my-amateur-porn-date-with-james-deen-1456809112.

3 Young people and sexual media

Cosimo Marco Scarcelli

Introduction

For many young people, thanks to converging mobile media (Mascheroni and Ólafsson, 2014), the Internet represents an important part of their everyday life (boyd, 2014; Livingstone *et al.*, 2011) that is becoming even more mediated with a consequent merge between online and offline experiences (Livingstone and Helsper, 2010). These mutations interlace the transformations of intimacy in late modernity (Giddens, 1992) and the intertwining of intimate lives with the public arena (Plummer, 2003; Weeks, 1995). The Internet is an essential source of information and entertainment, and an important tool that permits them to communicate with others, mainly friends, and offering potential new ways to consume digital resources anonymously, often with free access, and of performing activities of an intimate or sexual nature. Technological and social changes touch intimate aspects of our lives (Döring, 2009; Mowlabocus, 2010). In particular, the Internet, considered as a highly sexualised environment (Peter and Valkenburg, 2006), permits an ample range of activities connected to sexuality, not just limited to finding information but concerning also interaction, access to explicit material and forms of self-expression "characterized by more casual and personal forms of public communication" (Ito *et al.*, 2010, p. 147).

Since 2000, the research on sexuality and the Internet has increased but has maintained a focus on the effects, polarising positive or (overwhelmingly) negative aspects (Döring, 2009), particularly when they focus on minors. Both in mainstream media (Haddon and Stald, 2009) and in public discourses, young people's sexual cultures and their connection with technology are frequently treated as a problematic issue (Livingstone and Bober, 2005), frequently triggering moral panic (Thiel-Stern, 2009). Despite that, the study of young people's engagements with sexual issues remains a relatively unexplored area due both to cultural taboos and to ethical and methodological hurdles.

To better illuminate the field of media, young people and sexuality, following the suggestion of media and cultural studies, I want to abandon a deterministic vision of technology, the child of media effects research, which implicitly assumes that correlation is evidence of causality (Buckingham and Bragg, 2004). Instead I view, and explain, the different processes in social terms, moving beyond the reductive question of whether sex and the media is good or bad. Examining how youths use the Internet's resources in the context of intimacy and sexuality, considering young people as active users of media and concentrating on the ways in which they understand and make judgements about their choices, I will focus on media practices (Couldry, 2004) that are shaped through making sense of media cultures, described as the "collections of sense-making practices whose main resources of meaning are media" (Couldry, 2012, p. 160). So I will consider media culture and, following Attwood and Smith (2011), sexual cultures as: "a particular way of life, which expresses certain meanings and values" (Williams, 1961, p. 57) and which is evident "not only in art and learning but also in institutions and ordinary behaviour" (ibid).

Starting from these assumptions, this chapter will focus on the main topics relating to young people's sexual culture and digital media, beginning with discussing searching for information about sexuality, then dealing with performance of sexuality, mainly on social network sites (SNS), with the consumption of pornography, and finally, focusing on sexual interaction through cybersex.

Sexual information

Empirical evidence shows that although the Internet is not the first source of information about sexuality among young people (González-Ortega *et al.*, 2015), it is an important reference that is increasing its relevance (Lou *et al.*, 2012; Powell, 2008). Writing about electronic media, Meyrowitz (1985) underlined the possibility of going beyond the boundaries that in the past separated experts from common people, men from women, adults from youths. Today this process is amplified by digital media that allow access to resources with a large number of up-to-date data about sexuality and sex. Compared to the past, information about sex has to become accessible to a larger number of people without distinction of class, race or age, but with important differences related to technological limits and digital literacy.

Young people often combine different sources of information and the importance of the Internet is situated within a complex equilibrium between peer group, school and family. Usually children and youth are very critical of sex education they have received in school because they consider it moralistic and more focused on biological issues than on experiences and matters closer to their everyday life (Buckingham and Bragg, 2004; Scarcelli, 2014). Especially when the family and the peer group close the communicative flow about sexuality, the Internet's platforms become useful to escape parents' control and peers' symbolic sanctions. The Internet comes up along with other traditional socialisation agents in a complementary way and young people undertake a continuous work of bricolage, trying to cope with anxiety and insecurities connected to their sexual 'first times'.

The Internet is a meta-experience that helps young people to cope with the fear of failure or of having a 'bad performance' during intercourse (see also Morrison *et al.*, 2004), but digital platforms are not the solution to every adolescent's doubts. According to my previous research (Scarcelli, 2014, 2015), there are gender differences evident in the request for information. Boys are more inclined to look for information relating to performance (e.g. average length of penis, average duration of intercourse, how to touch a girl, etc.); meanwhile girls seem to prefer to look for information relating to their own body and health. Gender seems to be one of the most important variables in relation to the behaviour connected to the research of sexual information (see also Gonzáles-Ortega *et al.*, 2015). Usually girls prefer a knowledge process that they construct during the relationship with the partner or in comparison with their friends' experiences rather than an instruction book that could explain everything immediately. On the other hand, for the boys the Internet represents an important expedient to help avoid or reduce the possibility of *défaillance* and to show themselves to others as 'great lovers'. Everything is connected to specific characteristics of the Internet that allow them to construct an experiential baggage of vast dimensions, anonymously and without risking too much in terms of reputation.

According to Simon and Daneback (2013), the most important characteristics that push young people to use the Internet to look for information about sex are connected on the one hand to the rapidity with which it is possible to find information and, on the other hand, to anonymity. The latter permits them to avoid the embarrassment of speaking to parents who have closed the communicative flow about sexuality and with friends who could be starting to mock. The Internet represents a space where they can find a sort of 'enlarged peer group' (Scarcelli, 2014) that is formed by other people of probably the same age. This group helps to relieve the tension that can exist when they speak about sex and sexuality.

To search for information, young people prefer to use platforms that allow them to enter into the enlarged peer group (such as forums). They do not like to use experts' forums because those who manage this kind of forum are adults who frequently suggest going to the doctor to make further checks and have, sometimes, a thinly disguised moral dimension (Hayez, 2009). It is also important to underline that a significant portion of young Internet users prefer not to access online sexual information because they believe that the Internet cannot help them as it contains only pornography and unreliable information.

Performing sexuality

One of the most important changes regarding the Internet and social interaction is the one related to the possibility for people to take part, quickly and simply, in the communication flow, thanks to what generally is called Web 2.0. Many platforms, such as blogs, social networks, instant messaging applications, etc., permit users to share images, to comment, to take part in a discussion and also to have opportunities to self-represent their intimacies to an extended audience that can only be imagined (Litt, 2012; Marwick and boyd, 2011). Young people use social media intensively and they "are part of a significant shift in how intimate communication and relationships are structured, expressed, and publicized" (Ito *et al.*, 2010, p. 147).

Within social media we can observe the production of intimate storytelling: "a concrete human action in which social media are used to create self-representations that give meaning to gender, sexuality, relationships, and desires" (de Ridder and Van Bauwel, 2013, p. 320). De Ridder (2015) describes intimate storytelling as a reflexive and everyday life practice. From a sociological point of view it is important to focus the attention on the complexity behind this practice that defines and reproduces normative frameworks and the social structure that regulates intimacy and gender relations in everyday life (Scarcelli, 2015), such as heteronormativity (Butler, 1990). To observe these practices that are shaped through making sense of media cultures (Couldry, 2012) we have to go beyond the incorporation/resistance paradigm, considering instead intimate stories as media production (de Ridder, 2015; Hasinoff, 2013). Observing the transformation of intimacy in symbolic content means considering audiences and media institutions as important actors (Silverstone, 1994).

Social networks represent spaces for identity construction and performance (boyd, 2007; Livingstone 2008) and a form of public display of sociality (Ellison and boyd, 2013). Romance practices are central in youths' construction of their social world and their use of digital media (Pascoe, 2011). Every day young people, organise socially and they culturally gender sexuality and desire through new media (Scarcelli, 2016). The use of digital media in relation to intimate practices is strictly connected with the definition of public and private. Using digital media intimate practices becomes "simultaneously more public and more private" (Ito *et al.*, 2010, p. 145).

Young people consider online spaces such as social networks important for their performance of intimacy but they continuously have to evaluate them to maintain material as public or private specific. Even if talk about intimacies is more explicit (Ito *et al.*, 2010) young people prefer not to make some information about their intimate life public because they believe that sentiment is trivialised if something becomes excessively public. As de Ridder and van Bauwel note, "[i]ntimate storytelling as a self-representational media practice is about performing, and entertaining, which creativity, aesthetics, and popular culture are important" (2015, p. 325). These practices come in a context based on a celebritised popular culture (Bailey *et al.*, 2013) where the objective of young people is to portray themselves in a positive way. As Livingstone (2008) also notes, we do not have to think that all intimate self-representation has to be considered as a meaningful self-disclosure. Even so, in this public exposure for young people it is important to search for realness, coherence, authenticity and privacy. Even in spaces that permit anonymity, more open to experimentation and contestation, young people underline that it is important to remain coherent with the self in everyday life.

Cybersex

Cybersex is defined as

> a real-time communication with another person that occurs through a device connected with the Internet [...] in which one or both of you describe or share in other ways sexual activities, sexual behaviours, sexual fantasies, or sexual desires that may lead to feelings of sexual pleasure or physical intimacy
>
> (Shaughnessy *et al.*, 2014, p. 87)

Rarely has research focused on this practice (mainly concerning young people) in terms of media practices, cultural interest or from the point of view of those who have it. The interest of the research remains on pathological and problematic issues (see Griffith, 2012).

In general, we can affirm that thanks to the potential for anonymity and its mediated nature, this practice tends to decrease inhibition and help a more open communication (Döring, 2009). If we do not consider 'sexting' as a form of cybersex, usually young people, especially the youngest, deny engaging in this practice. According to the research done with adolescents from 14 to 16 years old in Italy (Scarcelli, 2015), generally young people described cybersex as something that they were not interested in. The motivations for this refusal have different typologies. Physical contact maintains its importance for young people, who retain cybersex just as a surrogate of the relationship to use only in case of it being impossible to meet the partner for a while. Without contact they assume that there is no real sexual intercourse (this view changes when we speak with young adults). This point of view becomes stronger when the person who is on the other side of the screen is a stranger, a subject with whom they have not shared emotions and sensations before.

Another preoccupation of young people is the loss of face. Cybersex is seen as something that could expose them to the risk of defamation or humiliation that could undermine their public image. The youngest people in particular frequently believe that at the base of cybersex there is a sort of perversion connected to the necessity to appear and to bring on stage intimacy and sexuality. Furthermore, the anonymity in this case is not relevant because the use of a webcam could open physical and symbolic windows on intimacy. For example, showing their bedroom to a stranger is perceived as letting an unknown into their own home and into the intimate sphere.

Cybersex with unknown people is defined negatively (Eurispes and Telefono Azzurro, 2010). Boys' and girls' ideas looked different when they speak about cybersex with their existing partner. In this case, some define cybersex as a surrogate of sex because it represents an inchoate interaction. Others contemplate cybersex as an opportunity that does not have to last for a long time. For young people, intimacy is something that has to be connected as much as possible to the direct experience, to physicality and to face-to-face interaction.

Pornography

Many studies (such as Hammarén and Johansson, 2007) have showed that, due to the Internet, pornography has become part of the everyday lives of young people, for whom searching for pornographic material is a normal activity. Even with the differences between boys and girls (Stack *et al.*, 2004), the majority of adolescents who have an Internet connection have had contact with pornography (Livingstone and Helsper, 2010; Peter and Valkenburg 2006). Differences between girls and boys persist (McKee *et al.*, 2008) due to cultural context (Gagnon and Simon, 1973); it is more socially acceptable in Western society for men to use pornography than it is for women. The Internet increases the availability of sexually explicit material and, with mobile media, amplifies the domestication of pornography (Juffer, 1998). It enters into adolescents' everyday lives, going outside their house walls or bedroom walls, moving into adolescent discourse enriched by digital technology that can transform the narrative and the interactions within their peer group (for example, when a boy shows his friend a pornographic video through his own smartphone).

According to Attwood (2005) pornography "become[s] resources that are used as part of the performance of gender identities within peer groups. Here, the media functions to provide resources for the different ways in which girls and boys perform and display gender" (p. 80). This is amplified by the Internet and mobile media that become important in 'border games' (Scarcelli, 2015): a set of cultural and media practices that permit both boys and girls to define, to redefine, to experience and to pass through gender boundaries. To do that adolescents take advantage of the Internet's characteristics, primarily anonymity. The possibility to have anonymous access to sexually explicit material seems to be one of the most important motivations that push young people to use Internet pornography rather than other forms of explicit material. Remaining anonymous allows adolescents not to submit to the norm that prohibits the consumption of pornography to the underaged.

Anonymity also avoids the ritual of buying pornographic material and coping with the interaction with a seller who personifies the normative look of the adult world and the prohibitions that it carries. It is more significant for the girls who are forced to submit to a double stigma that sees it as doubly socially improper for them to gain access to pornographic material (Scarcelli, 2015). On the one hand, they are young, a portion of the population that has to be kept away from pornography, and, on the other hand, they are women, subjects who, in the social and cultural construction, should not be interested in pornography. The Internet allows girls to have a simpler access to pornographic material because, thanks to anonymity, it allows them to avoid exposure to symbolic sanctions that otherwise could damage adolescents. Another important Internet characteristic for young people is the possibility to have free access to sexually explicit material (free in terms of both money and time). This is relevant at this moment of their lives where economically the individuals depend completely on their parents.

Young people prefer to consume pornography via mobile media to avoid parental control connected to the possibility of leaving digital footprints in the case of the use of a shared computer. In relation to pornography mobile media are used (mainly by boys) also in-group interaction to define and redefine gender roles. If viewed with a classmate or friend a porn video is used to perform masculinity (with other men), it sometimes happens that they play with gender definition also by showing the video to girls who, usually, have a disappointed reaction. When boys introduce girls to pornography this practice confirms that boys are viewed as symbolic gatekeepers of sexual knowledge. There is also a homosocial reinforcement of masculinity (Gagnon and Simon, 1973). This relates to the management of who is a member of a group and who is an outsider. To show a video, to reject the viewing of it, to mock, etc., is the *mise-en-scène* of a symbolic and ritual conflict that contributes to maintaining the boundaries between girls and boys and increasing internal cohesion.

Conclusion

Adolescents use the Internet's resources for a wide set of activities connected to sex and intimacy: from looking for information to performing intimate storytelling, watching pornography and sexually interacting with other people. Digital practices related to sexuality confirm that digital spaces are "materially real, socially regulated, and discursively constructed" (Hayles, 1999, p. 291). As we saw in the previous pages, online platforms represent important spaces where young people work on social construction of gender, sexuality and desire.

Focusing on young digital practices and sexual cultures, we can affirm that the Internet does not represent a parallel reality but rather a catalyst of adolescents' desires and curiosities. 'Offline' life continues to be fundamental for the adolescents and the Internet adds online interaction to existing social relationships. Young people, daily, work on their identity through digital resources (Daneback, 2006), in a continuous tension between their own vision of themselves and others' vision of them. Also in digital spaces the priority of young people seems to be acceptance by a peer group (Allen and Land, 1999) that, on the Internet, could be related to friends or to what I have defined as an enlarged peer group. The Internet plays an important role in this process, permitting putting identity on probation and responding to questions about sexuality and intimacy that sometimes those who are physically near them could not answer.

Thanks to the Internet young people frequently try to give a definition of what is considered 'sexual normality' (Harvey *et al.*, 2007), performing their intimate storytelling and understanding what the peers think about sexuality and gender relations. As happens outside the digital space, frequently the idea of 'normal' sexuality and of gender (Butler, 1990) is constructed by the impulse of exclusion and negation of what is considered abnormal. Mainly during adolescence, the definition of masculinity is characterised by homophobic insults and tests (Pascoe, 2005; Plummer, 2001).

Abandoning a deterministic point of view that looks at mediated content as something that can directly influence young people's behaviour, what my analysis makes evident is the importance of looking at the relationship between young people, media and sexuality with a different perspective. Following the suggestion of Hasinoff (2013) and de Ridder (2015) we need to look at the young people's practices as media practices, remembering to frame the different actions within the media in the broader context of media cultures and intertwining this with the frame of sexual cultures (Attwood and Smith, 2011). Only from this point of view can we understand young people's practices without falling into the effect paradigm, understanding that the effects are more complex and need to be understood through an approach able to embrace and analyse this complexity.

References

Attwood, F. (2005). What do people with porn? Qualitative research into the consumption, use and experience of pornography and other sexually explicit media. *Sexuality and Culture 9*(2), 65–86.

Attwood, F. and Smith, C. (2011). Investigating young people's sexual cultures: An introduction. *Sex Education 11*(3), 235–242.

Bailey, J., Steeves, V., Burkell, J. and Regan, P. (2013). Negotiating with gender stereotypes on social networking sites: From "bicycle face" to Facebook. *Journal of Communication Inquiry 37*(2), 91–112.

boyd, d. (2007). Why youth (heart) social network sites: The role of networked publics in teenage social live. In Buckingham, D. (ed.), *Youth, identity and digital media* (119–142). Cambridge: MIT Press.

boyd, d. (2014). *It's complicated: The Social lives of networked teens.* New Haven: Yale University Press.

Buckingham, D. and Bragg, S. (2004). *Young people, sex and the media: The facts of life?* New York: Palgrave Macmillan.

Butler, J. (1990). *Gender trouble.* London: Routledge.

Couldry, N. (2004). Theorising media as practice. *Social Semiotics 14*(2), 115–132.

Couldry, N. (2012). *Media, society, world: Social theory and digital media practice.* Malden: Polity Press.

Daneback, K., Ross, M.W., and Mansson, S.A. (2006). Characteristics and behaviors of sexual compulsives who use the Internet for sexual purposes. *Sexual Addiction and Compulsivity 13*(1), 53–67.

De Ridder, S. (2015). Are digital media institutions shaping youth's intimate stories? Strategies and tactics in the social networking site Netlog. *New Media and Society 17*(3), 356–374.

De Ridder, S. and Van Bauwel, S. (2013). Commenting on pictures: Teens negotiating gender and sexualities on social networking sites. *Sexualities 16*(5–6), 565–586.

Döring, N. M. (2009). The Internet's impact on sexuality: A critical review of 15 years of research. *Computer in Human Behaviour 25*, 1089–1101.

Ellison, N. B. and boyd, d. (2013). Sociality through social network sites. In Dutton, W. H. (ed.), *The Oxford handbook of internet studies* (151–171). Oxford: Oxford University Press.

EURISPES and Telefono Azzurro (2010). *Indagine conoscitiva sulle condizione dell'infanzia e dell'adolescenza in Italia 2010*. Documento di Sintesi. Retrieved 26 May 2017 from the Telefono Azzurro website: http://www.azzurro.it/sites/default/files/Materiali/InfoConsigli/Ricerche%20e%20indagini/sintesi_eurispestelefono_azzurro_2010.pdf

Gagnon, J. H. and Simon, W. (1973). *Sexual conduct: The social sources of human sexuality*. Chicago: Aldine.

Giddens, A. (1992). *The transformations of intimacy*. Cambridge: Polity.

González-Ortega, E., Vicario-Molina, I., Martínez, J. L. and Orgaz, B. (2015). The internet as a source of sexual information in a sample of Spanish adolescents: Associations with sexual behavior. *Sexuality Research and Social Policy 12*(4), 290–300.

Haddon, L. and Stald, G. (2009). A comparative analysis of European press coverage of children and the Internet. *Journal of Children and Media 3*(4), 379–393.

Hammarén, N. and Johansson, T. (2007). Pornotopia: Theoretical considerations and young pornographers. In Knudsen, S. V., L. Löfgren-Mårtenson and S. Månsson (eds.), *Generation P? Youth, Gender and Pornography* (33–46). Copenhagen: Danish School of Education Press.

Harvey, K. J., Brown, B., Crawford, P., Macfarlane, A. and McPherson, A. (2007). 'Am I normal?'. Teenagers, sexual health and the Internet. *Social Science and Medicine 65*, 771–781.

Hasinoff, A. A. (2013). Sexting as media production: Rethinking social media and sexuality. *New Media and Society 15*(4), 449–465.

Hayez, J. (2009). Pratiques et intérêts sexuels des jeunes 'normaux' sut Internet. *Neuropsychiatrie de l'enfance et de l'adolescence 57*(3), 231–239.

Hayles, N. K. (1999). *How we became posthuman. Virtual bodies in cybernetics, literature, and informatics*. Chicago: University of Chicago Press.

Ito, M., Baumer, S., Bittanti, M., boyd, d., Cody, R., Herr-Stephenson, B. and Ripp, L. (2010). *Hanging out, messing around, and geeking out. Kids living and learning with new media*. Cambridge: MIT Press.

Juffer, J. (1998). *At home with pornography: Women, sex, and everyday life*. New York: NYU Press.

Litt, E. (2012). Knock, knock. Who's there? The imagined audience. *Journal of Broadcasting and Electronic Media 56*(3), 330–345.

Livingstone, S. (2008). Taking risky opportunities in youthful content creation: Teenagers' use of social networking sites for intimacy, privacy and self-expression. *New Media and Society 10*(3), 393–411.

Livingstone, S. and Bober, M. (2005). *UK children go online: Final report of key project findings*. London: LSE.

Livingstone, S. and Helsper, E. (2010). Balancing opportunities and risks in teenagers' use of the internet: The role of online skills and internet self-efficacy. *New Media and Society 12*(2), 309–329.

Livingstone, S., Haddon, L., Göriz, A. and Ólafsson, K. (2011). *EU kids on-line. Final report*. London: LSE.

Lou, L.L., Yan. Z., Nickerson, A. and McMorris, R. (2012). An examination of the reciprocal relationship of loneliness and Facebook use among first-year college students. *Journal of Educational Computing Research 46*(1), 105–117.

Marwick, A. E. and boyd, d. (2011). I tweet honestly, I tweet passionately: Twitter users, context collapse, and the imagined audience. *New Media and Society 13*(1), 114–133.

Mascheroni, G. and Ólafsson, K. (2014). *Net children go mobile: Risks and opportunities*. Milano: Educatt.

McKee, A., Albury, K. and Lumby, C. (2008). *The porn report*. Carlton: Melbourne University Press.

Meyrowitz, J. (1985). *No sense of place. The impact of electronic media on social behavior*. Oxford: Oxford University Press.

Morrison, T. G., Harriman, R., Morrison, M. A., Bearden, A. and Ellis, S. R. (2004). Correlates of exposure to sexuality explicit material among Canadian post-secolary students. *Canadian Journal of Human Sexuality 13*, 143–156.

Mowlabocus, S. (2010). Porn 2.0? Technology, social practice, and the new online porn industry. In Atwood, F. (ed.), *porn.com. Making sense of online pornography* (69–87). New York: Peter Lang.

Pascoe, C. J. (2005). 'Dude, you're a fag'. Adolescent masculinity and the fag discourse. *Sexualities 8*(3), 329–346.

Pascoe, C. J. (2011). Resource and risk: Youth sexuality and new media use. *Sexuality Research and Social Policy 8*(1), 5–17.

Peter, J. and Valkenburg, P. M. (2006). Adolescents' exposure to sexually explicit online material and recreational attitudes toward sex. *Journal of Communication 56*(4), 639–660.

Plummer, D. C. (2001). The quest for modern manhood. Masculine stereotypes, peer culture and the social significance of homophobia. *Journal of Adolescence 24*, 15–23.

Plummer, K. 2003. *Intimate citizenship: Private decisions and public dialogues*. Seattle: University of Washington Press.

Scarcelli, C. M. (2014). 'One way or another I need to learn this stuff!' Adolescents, sexual information, and the Internet's role between family, school, and peer groups. *Interdisciplinary Journal of Family Studies 19*(1), 40–59.

Scarcelli, C. M. (2015). 'It is disgusting, but…': Adolescent girls' relationship to internet pornography as gender performance. *Porn Studies 2*(2–3), 237–249.

Scarcelli, C. M. (2016). Adolescents, digital media and romantic relationship. *Interdisciplinary Journal of Family Studies 20*(2), 36–52.

Shaughnessy, K., Byers, E. S., Clowater, S. L. and Kalinowski, A. (2014). Outcomes of arousal-oriented online sexual activities: Perspectives of college, community, and sexual minority samples. *Archives of Sexual Behavior 43*, 1187–1197.

Silverstone, R. (1994). *Television and everyday life*. London: Routledge.

Simon, L. and Daneback, K. (2013). Adolescents' use of the in-ternet for sex education: A thematic and critical review of the literature. *International Journal of Sexual Health 25*(4), 305–319.

Stack, S., Wasserman, I. and Kern, R. (2004). Adult social bonds and use of internet pornography. *Social Science Quarterly 85*(1), 75–86.

Thiel-Stern, S. (2009). Femininity out of control on the Internet: A critical analysis of media representations of gender, youth, and MySpace.com in international news discourse. *Girlhood Studies 2*(1), 20–39.

Weeks, J. (1985). *Sexuality and its discontents*. London: Routledge.

Williams, R. (1961). *The long revolution*. London: Chatto and Windus.

4 Sex education in the digital age

Deb Levine

Overview

It is hard to believe, but it was only about one generation ago that the Internet went mainstream and changed the way people accessed explicit materials, learned about sex and sexuality and normalised their sexual experiences. Before that, we had to rely on word-of-mouth, X-rated magazines, embarrassed classroom teachers, cool parents and chatty friends. As far as young people's sexuality and the advent of the Internet, there have been stated benefits coupled with fears and challenges. Digital media has the potential to reach large numbers of young people with medically accurate sexual health information and education. And health professionals and educators around the world are still fearful about teaching young people about their sexuality and sexual health. Rationales abound, including, "[i]t will make them promiscuous" and "[t]hey'll only find pornography online". These justifications serve as reason that sex education has not yet gone viral. This chapter will set the scene for sex education and outline some of the major digital resources, including mobile phone apps, available at the time of writing, which help individuals get information whether they be young people who need their questions answered or teachers seeking to provide students with the information that they need.

Teen pregnancy and sexually transmitted infections (STIs) remain problems for adolescents. Rates of teen births in the US are much higher than the rates among other developed countries (The National Campaign to Prevent Teen Pregnancy, n-d). There are almost 19 million new STIs diagnosed annually, and 65 million Americans live with an incurable STI. Even though they represent only 25% of the total US population, youth under age 25 acquire nearly half of all new STIs (Wildsmith *et al.*, 2010).

Even with this unique place among developing countries, classroom sex education in the US has not changed much since the turn of the century. Content-wise, scare tactics are still commonplace tools to encourage young people to abstain from sex. The Netherlands is the only country that has embraced sexual pleasure as part of teenaged sex education.

The US 2002 National Survey of Family Growth (NSFG) found that formal instruction to teenagers about birth control methods declined from 1995 to 2002 (from 81% to 66% for males and from 87% to 70% for females). The most recent NSFG reported that these figures had not improved as of 2010: between 2006 and 2010 only 61% of male and 70% of female adolescents received formal instruction about birth control methods, and 82% of males and 89% of females received abstinence education (Center for Disease Control and Prevention, n-d). Notable public health and medical associations, including the American Medical Association, Society of Adolescent Health and Medicine, the American Public Health Association, and the Institute of Medicine all support a comprehensive approach to sex education (Boonstra, 2010).

Youth currently learn about sexual and reproductive health online, from health professionals, family, television and school. A 2011 white paper featured findings from extensive qualitative research into the impact of digital media and technology on the field of sexual and reproductive health (Boyar *et al.*, 2011).

Figure 4.1 highlights the relative importance of various venues for learning about sex and reproductive health, with "online" rising notably to the top. Over half of American youth grades 7–12 reported using the Internet to learn more information about a health issue affecting themselves or someone they know (Rideout *et al.*, 2010).

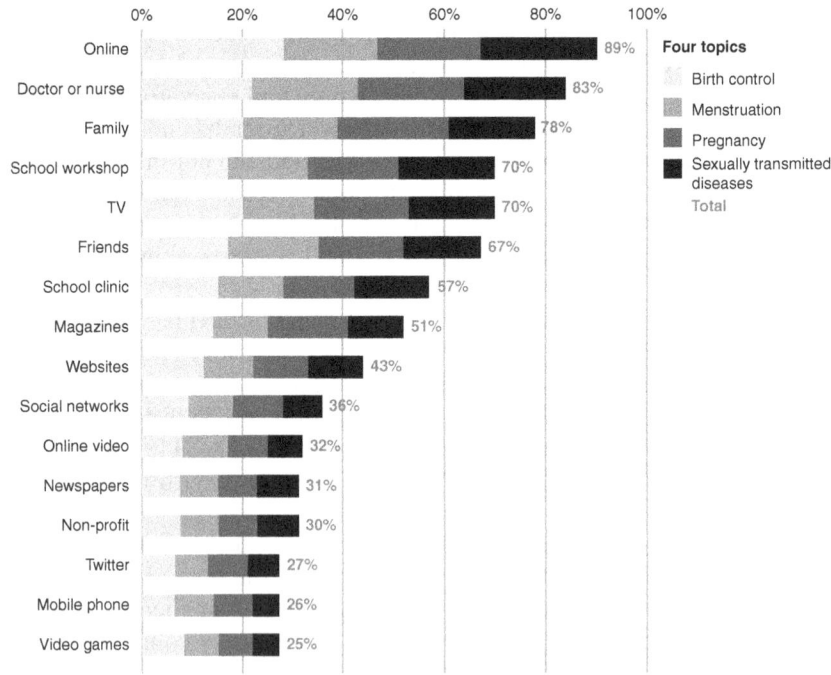

Figure 4.1 Sex education.

Youth typically view doctors and other health professionals as well-respected and trusted sources of information regarding sexual health, and at the same time often note that their teachers do not use appropriate tones when teaching sexual health information. Prior research by the author and others found that while high-school aged youth rarely visited a health professional, they found them to be good sources of sexual health information. Conversely, while they were exposed to sexual health information through schoolteachers, this was often in a tone that was overly joking or hyper-authoritative, neither of which were comfortable for students (Boyar *et al.*, 2011). Given the sensitive nature of many topics within sexual education curricula, teachers may be awkward or uncomfortable discussing sexual health with teenagers.

Many health educators have attempted to use out-of-the-classroom means, such as the Internet and mobile phones, to provide alternative comprehensive, sex-positive education for youth. Yet a recent study of 177 sexual health information websites reported that nearly half of websites addressing contraception and 35% of those addressing abortion provided inaccurate information (Buhi *et al.*, 2010). This points to the critical need for a digital strategy that will enable youth to access health information in a preferred manner, guided by scientific research on the efficacy of sexuality education, while also creating opportunities within real-time social media environments to access in-person youth-friendly medical services in a culturally appropriate manner.

A recent systematic review by Guse, Levine and colleagues of the use of digital media (i.e. the Internet, text messaging/mobile and social networking sites) as a tool for engaging youth in sexual health promotion and risk reduction found that these strategies were effective in delaying initiation of sex, and positively influencing psychosocial outcomes such as condom self-efficacy, and increasing knowledge of Human Immuno-Deficiency Virus (HIV), STIs or pregnancy (Guse *et al.*, 2012). Bull *et al.* (2012) conducted a cluster randomised controlled trial on Facebook called Just/Us that showed short term positive results for condom use and proportion of sex acts protected by condoms.

As a result of this and similar work, it is becoming more and more common for public health professionals who work with adolescents to use new media to educate, raise awareness, increase knowledge and encourage young people to change behaviours. However, there is lack of consistency in type and format of interventions, consistent evaluation and comparable outcomes, raising the need for a strategically researched model that is scalable and replicable to allow standardisation in public high schools.

Formative research with high school students online showed they preferred to receive their sex education online. In preparation for an HIV prevention intervention on a social networking site, online focus groups with 21 female and 15 male participants were conducted in synchronous and asynchronous discussion groups. Teens described social networking sites such as

MySpace and Facebook as online environments akin to both hanging out at the mall and keeping a personal diary. They share publicly and privately on social media, discussing their lives with friends and expressing their opinions freely. It appears that "[...] programs that use the immense reach of the Internet and social networking to market services that discretely and privately support youth and young adults will be better received" (Levine *et al.*, 2011, p. 40).

Online courses are the wave of the future. President Obama unveiled a bold, new initiative called ConnectED to connect 99% of America's students to the Internet through high-speed broadband and high-speed wireless by 2018 (The White House 2013) A number of companies are now creating online courses for high school students in a wide variety of subject matters (see www.pbslearningmedia.org for one such example), yet to date no one has developed or launched an online course for high schoolers in sexuality education.

Simultaneously, an explosion of online interactive courses is happening in US colleges and universities, largely through Massive Open Online Courses (MOOCs). MOOCs are aimed at large-scale interactive participation and open access via the web. In addition to traditional course materials such as videos, readings and problem sets, MOOCs provide interactive user forums that help build a community for the students, professors and teaching assistants (EDUCAUSE, n-d). They are usually free to students, with the educational institution partnering with a for-profit platform (i.e. Kahn Academy, Coursera, Udacity) to cover the costs. There is still, to date, no MOOC for college students that parallels Human Sexuality 101 in the classroom.

All signs point to a need for a program that will build on the national initiative for broadband and high speed wireless in schools and the successful expansion of MOOCs at the university level, taking the excitement of high-quality, interactive, open education to address a topic of critical public health importance – teen sex education.

Internet and mobile usage by teens

24% of teens aged 13–17 go online "almost constantly" and 92% of teens go online daily, facilitated by the widespread availability of smartphones. More than 70% of US teens have or have access to a smartphone, and most of the others (totally 90%) have a basic phone. Globally, 70% of the world's population (6.1 billion) people will own smartphones within five years time (Lenhart *et al.*, 2015).

In the US, African-American teens are the most likely of any group of teens to have a smartphone, with 85% having access to one, compared with 71% of both white and Hispanic teens. These phones and other mobile devices have become a primary driver of teen Internet use: Fully 91% of teens go online from mobile devices, and African-American and Hispanic youth report more frequent mobile Internet use than white teens (ibid). Social networking sites are extremely popular among teenagers. In the US, Facebook is the most frequently used platform, with Instagram and Snapchat in second and third place. Globally, Facebook is still in first place, with WhatsApp a close second and then QQ. Perhaps most importantly, most teens use more than one social networking site. Older teens (aged 15–17) are most likely to cite Facebook as their preferred platform. Teens of all ages globally use WhatsApp, and in the US, Kik (Lenhart *et al.*, 2015; Smith, 2016).

Teenage girls use social media sites and platforms – particularly visually oriented ones – for sharing more than their male counterparts do. For their part, boys are more likely than girls to own gaming consoles and play video games (ibid).

Teens average 44.5 hours per week in front of a screen, often multiple screens simultaneously (Boyar *et al.*, 2011). 31% of teenagers have searched online for information on a health topic that's hard to talk about (drugs, sex, etc.). In terms of health, technology is not an end for young people, but a means to accelerate information provision, widen social networks and sharpen the questions a young person might ask when they do access health services (Guse *et al.*, 2012).

Sex education outside the classroom

There are many websites that operate outside of the school system to provide comprehensive sex education, information and advice to youth and young adults. Ranging from Sex, Etc. to Scarleteen, to Planned Parenthood and Planned Parenthood International, they each have their own strengths and weaknesses. However, many teens do not know about these sites, so when they do have a sex question, they simply head to Google and search. Most times these informational sites are not first in the list of search results, because of a lack of knowledge by sex educators about search engine optimisation and how teens search online. Creators of these sites tag their pages with clinical terminology and medical language, whereas young people search conversationally. For example, when trying to find out more about ejaculation and wet dreams, a teenager might search for, "what happens when white goo comes out my peepee?" There is no mention of penises or ejaculate – simply a basic question in colloquial language without the clinically correct-ness to go with it. (FYI: The search results for this question range from advice for taking care of your dog to fan fiction.)

These days, there is a movement afoot to engage more philanthropists and corporate social giving in "learning outside the classroom", or sex education online. In order to do this effectively, we need to be able to put corporate marketing practices to work so that when a young person searches to find out the best ways to have sex or what to do if the condom broke, accurate relevant information comes to the top of the search engine results. Here are some of the most interesting websites and apps today that cover sex education outside the school classroom.

Websites

Many non-profit and non-governmental organisations have searchable websites with accurate information, and associated social media accounts to shout out their new content. Here are just a few sites that are long lasting and relatively complete.

Scarleteen: Their tagline is "sex ed for the real world". Scarleteen is a comprehensive, inclusive website with advice and answers about sexuality and relationships for youth and emerging adults. www.scarleteen.com/

Sex, Etc.: An online magazine with a mission to improve sexual health for youth in the US. Based out of the Rutgers University ANSWER centre, the e-zine is by youth, for youth and covers pretty much every sex, sexuality and sexual health topic under the sun in short articles and blog posts written by teens. http://sexetc.org/

KidsHealth.org: An incredibly comprehensive website for information about health, behaviour and development from before birth through the teen years. The teen sexual health section is medically accurate and covers just about everything under the sexual health umbrella. Includes coverage about STIs (sores, rashes and bumps), pregnancy and conception and prevention. http://kidshealth.org/en/teens/sexual-health/

One You by Britain's National Health Service: This is a healthy living website with a section on sexual health. Not particularly geared to teens, it does cover the full gamut of sexual expression and wellness as presented by government officials. www.nhs.uk/oneyou/sexual-health# lojUlmOF50d2pisl.97

Teens Pact: This organisation's site at Community Healthcare Network showcases youth made, short videos about sexual health and related topics. Awesome videos—very real. Highlights include videos about sexting and trust, feel-good sex and sex without stress. www.chnnyc. org/media-room/videos/more-than-just-sex

Karaz: Built by a software engineer with a yearning to help, this Arabic-language website has information and advice about sexual and relationship issues. Articles include Moderation during Ramadan and The Benefits of Reading Romance Novels, as well as frequently updated Questions and Answers (Q&A). www.karaz.net/

Social networking sex education: facebook, instagram, vine and more

Just/Us on Facebook: This was part of research study of an eight-week sexual health education program on Facebook. The study found that the intervention had positive short-term effects (such as increased condom use) on youth who participated. Content covered conversations starters such as geographic statistics about HIV, weekly tips including prom prevention and gender identity and labels. Current events and news were scattered within the feed. www.facebook.com/justusisis/

Instagram: Mostly used by youth on smartphones, searches for photos and short videos are by hashtags (#). A quick search for #sexed came up with selfies, alongside conference presentations and everything in between. There is room here for good solid sex info!

Vine: You can explore, watch and upload very short, looping videos. Searches are by hashtags, and the most popular videos inspire response videos. A search for #sexed on Vine came up with nothing. Sexual health had some very odd videos from Canada and London. Keep your eyes posted on Snapchat, Kik and other sites yet to be developed. Hashtags seem to be the commonality between sites right now so that it is easiest for users to find what they want and cultivate followers across multiple platforms. As of 17 January 2017, the app will turn into Vine Camera, allowing users to post 6.5 second looping videos on Twitter. The website is transitioning to an archive of Vines that were created and users can continue to browse old content but not upload any new content.

Mobile apps

Everyone is going mobile. Between phones and tablets, it is really time to integrate the best apps out there into your repertoire to educate youth about sex and connect them to clinical services. In the USA nearly three-quarters of teens have or have access to a smartphone (Lenhart *et al.*, 2015, p. 8); this number is only going to grow. Here are a few of the trendsetters in the sexual and reproductive health arena. All are free and downloadable in the iTunes and Google Play stores, unless otherwise noted.

Teens in NYC: An app created by the New York City Department of Health. It contains cool parts about access to services, and clinic experience videos created by real teens.

Condom Pro: This app was created by the National Campaign to Prevent Teen and Unplanned Pregnancies and distributed via their Bedsider program. The game is meant for "older" youth – 18–25, but could be played by anyone. There are two parts to each level – open the package without ripping or tearing the condom, then place the condom on an object – candlestick, carrot, etc. It gets harder each time you level up.

My Birth Control: This is a mobile website created by Planned Parenthood Federation of America. It works well for youth without smartphones as it can be accessed on regular phones with data plans. Youth answer a few lifestyle and health questions and get recommended forms of contraception and birth control. It is a virtual method chooser that can help women start a conversation with their provider about the best contraception matched to individual needs. www.mybirthcontrolapp.org/

The Kickback: This app was also created by Planned Parenthood Federation of America in mobile web format. This is an app that helps youth negotiate through common situations at parties, in high school, etc. with alternate endings and real consequences. https://kickbackapp.org/

Circle of 6: This app was created by a team of individuals and distributed by Tech4Good. Circle of 6 is a safety app designed to prevent sexual assaults and dating violence and abuse among teens and young adults by accessing the user's contact list before a bad situation escalates. This is one of the only "sex ed" apps that has hundreds of thousands of downloads in the app stores because it received extensive national press after winning a White House mobile challenge.

Juicebox: Students at the University of Tennessee, Knoxville created this app as a way for teens and college students to anonymously ask sex-related questions via text message. A sex expert or Planned Parenthood educator provides the answers. The app also provides a forum for students to post anonymous stories about their sexual experiences, creating a community and prevailing attitude of "we're all in this together".

Crisis Text Line: Text messaging is the universal app. Crisis Text Line, created by DoSomething.org, offers teens in a crisis a chance to text START to 741–741 and speak to a trained crisis counsellor about anything from relationships, to safer sex, to suicide prevention. This is also available in some countries globally. www.crisistextline.org

Planned Parenthood Federation of America's chat and text line: PPFA also offers answers to teens' questions about pregnancy, birth control, emergency contraception, sexually transmitted diseases (STDs) and abortion via chat or short message service (SMS) text message with answers provided by Planned Parenthood clinical staff (nurses, educators, psychologists). It is only available certain hours – check the website for up-to-date information. www.plannedparenthood.org/teens

Thrive App for Parents: This app was developed by the Society of Adolescent Health and Medicine for parents to guide them through their developing teen's emerging sexuality and wellness. Sanctioned by a large group of medical providers, it is one of the only apps to help adults navigate the world of parenting teens, and engage their adolescents without alienating them.

MyQuestion: This is a service in Nigeria created by the organisation Education as a Vaccine (EVA). MyQuestion allows young people to get answers to their questions about sex by text, phone or social media, from any location at any time of day or night. Seven advisors work at the service every day and young people can ask questions about anything, from sex and contraception, to periods and relationships. The service is popular – EVA says that 12,000–15,000 questions are sent by text alone each month – because it provides accurate, non-judgmental and confidential information anonymously. www.evanigeria.org/our-projects/my-question-and-answer/

Zana Africa Foundation: This organisation is doing incredible work in Nairobi, Kenya around girls' menstrual hygiene through comic books and soon, a mobile text Q&A service. It is a partner organisation to Zana Africa, a company that makes and distributes feminine hygiene products. www.zanaafrica.org/

In-classroom sex education

Working with students in an interactive way stimulates memory and critical thinking, so when they are in the heat of the moment, it is more likely they will remember what they learned. Technology can be used during in-classroom experiences as a teaching tool or a research tool. Both have benefits for students' enhanced learning and information retention.

Very little is being done in the classroom today vis-à-vis technology integration into sex education efforts. Advocacy efforts in the US have focused on monitoring sexuality education efforts, with little effort going to innovation. Most of what you will find are PDFs of approved, medically accurate lesson plans. They are often free of charge. Here are a few of the best sites for up-to-date lesson plans:

SIECUS Sex Ed Library: This is a comprehensive website of PDF lesson plans for teachers of all grades. Brought to you by the Sexuality Information and Education Council of the US, you can find lesson plans on topics such as sexual and reproductive health, puberty, abstinence, relationships, sexual orientation, body image, self-esteem, sexually transmitted diseases, HIV/AIDS, unintended pregnancy and more. www.sexedlibrary.org/

Teaching SexualHealth.CA: A site from Canada with lesson plans and instructional methods arranged by grade. Meant to be delivered by teachers in the classroom. http://teachers.teachingsexualhealth.ca/lesson-plans/

FLASH Comprehensive Sex Education Curriculum: This is a set of lesson plans for all grades, available via PDF for free, and via hard copy for a nominal fee from the Public Health Department at King County, Washington. High school FLASH users can purchase online access. www.kingcounty.gov/depts/health/locations/family-planning/education/FLASH.aspx

ReCapp Online Teen Scavenger Hunt: This Scavenger Hunt can be completed by students on their own, with a friend or with a parent. The goal is for high school-age students to gather information and identify resources related to teen pregnancy prevention using the Internet. http://recapp.etr.org/recapp/index.cfm?fuseaction=pages.LearningActivities Detail&PageID=174

The following lesson plans and curricula are for interactive learning in the classroom. Computers or access to the Internet are required. It's Your Game is the only evidence-based digital sex education curricula in the US.

BioDigital Human: It is a 3-D body, with lesson plans attached for various organ systems, including the reproductive system (must use a Chrome browser and be connected to the Internet). https://human.biodigital.com

Oakland Unified School District's Healthy Oakland Teens: This is a full curriculum for 6th and 9th graders in Oakland Unified School District, in compliance with State laws for comprehensive and inclusive sexuality education. One module is designed to connect youth to health centres, and the assignment is to find the nearest health centre either through search, via a paper brochure or by downloading a mobile app (called Oakland Teens) from the iTunes and Google Play stores.

PlayForward: Elm City Stories is an interactive world in which the player, using an Avatar (virtual character) they have created, "travels" through life, facing challenges and making decisions that bring different risks and benefits. Players have the ability to see how their choices affect their life and can move back in time to see how different actions might have led to different outcomes. www.schellgames.com/games/playforward/

It's Your Game: This is an excellent computerised middle school curriculum developed by University of Texas Center for Health Promotion and Prevention Research. This is the only interactive curriculum that is evidence-based. Evidence shows that a middle school-based HIV, STI and pregnancy prevention intervention can delay overall sexual behaviour. In particular, the intervention delayed overall sexual behaviour as well as oral and anal sex among female students who were sexually active in the 7th grade. www.hhs.gov/ash/oah/oah-initiatives/tpp_program/db/programs/ebp-iyg.html

Conclusion

There is no telling what is next in the world of mobile technology and social media. It will take a lot for the field of sexual health and educators themselves to become more agile and adept at using forms of technology as they are developed.

There is still a need for a programme that will build on the US national initiative for broadband and high speed wireless in schools and the successful expansion of MOOCs at the university level, taking the excitement of high-quality, interactive, open education to address a topic of critical public health importance, while entertaining the potential for commercialisation through partnerships with educational institutions and larger private companies. An inclusive, science-based curriculum designed for public high school students would be welcome in the US and replicable globally. The student curriculum could include a parent module where parents can preview the materials used in the classroom, sign permission slips and contact teachers with comments and concerns; and an information library for teachers containing scientifically sound videos, activities, fact sheets and images that reflect a variety of community norms and values. Student homework assignments could take place on social media – Wikipedia, Facebook, tumblr, Pinterest and Twitter – and should be designed to connect students to local, youth-friendly clinical services, such as school based and school-affiliated health centres, free and low-cost clinics and adolescent health specialists.

Given that teens' questions about sex and relationships have not totally changed in our lifetime, it should be do-able for youth-serving teams to stay on task with medically accurate information provided in a context and format that is comfortable for today's teens. A sexual-health based programme in line with pop culture, integrated into other health topics such as substance abuse prevention and fitness, would be welcome relief in the clutter of cyberspace and the app store. There is clearly much room for innovation in this space for the future.

References

Boonstra, H. (2010). Sex education: another big step forward—and a step back. *Guttmacher Policy Review 13(20)*, 27–28.

Boyar, R., Levine, D. and Zensius, N. (2011). *TECHsex USA: Youth Sexuality and Reproductive Health in the Digital Age.* Oakland: YTH.

Buhi, E.R., Daley, E.M., Oberne, A., Smith, S.A., Schneider, T. and Fuhrmann, H.J. (2010). Quality and accuracy of sexual health information web sites visited by young people. *Journal of Adolescent Health 47(2)*, 206–208.

Bull, S., Levine, D., Black, S., Schmiege, S. and Santelli, J. (2012). Social media-delivered sexual health intervention: a cluster randomized controlled trial. *American Journal of Preventive Medicine 43(5)*, 467–474.

Centers for Disease Control and Prevention (n-d). *Key Statistics from the National Survey of Family Growth.* Retrieved 18 July 2016 from the National Survey of Family Growth website: www.cdc.gov/nchs/nsfg/abc_list_s.htm#sexeducation.

EDUCAUSE (n-d). *7 Things You Should Know about MOOCs II* [Fact Sheet]. Retrieved 1 August 2013 from the EDUCAUSE website: http://net.educause.edu/ir/library/pdf/ELI7097.pdf.

Guse, K., Levine, D., Martins, S., Lira, A., Gaarde, J., Westmorland, W. and Gilliam, M. (2012). Interventions using new digital media to improve adolescent sexual health: a systematic review. *Journal of Adolescent Health 51(6)*, 535–543.

Lenhart, A., Perrin, A., Stepler, R., Rainie, L. and Parker, L. (2015). *Teens, Social Media & Technology Overview 2015, Smartphones Facilitate Shifts in Communication Landscape for Teens.* Washington, DC: Pew Research Center.

Levine, D., Madsen, A., Wright, E., Barar, R.E., Santelli, J. and Bull, S. (2011). Formative research on MySpace: online methods to engage hard-to-reach populations. *Journal of Health Communication 16(4)*, 448–454.

Rideout, V.J., Foehr, U.G. and Roberts, D.F. (2010). *Generation M2: Media in the Lives of 8 to 18-Year-Olds.* Menlo Park: Kaiser Family Foundation.

Smith, C. (2016). *By the Numbers: 20 Important Kik Messenger Stats. DMR Stats and Gadgets.* Retrieved 24 October 2016 from the Expanded Ramblings Website: http://expandedramblings.com/index.php/kik-messenger-stats/.

The National Campaign to Prevent Teen Pregnancy (n-d). *Teen Birth Rates: How Does the United States Compare?* [Fact Sheet]. Retrieved 15 July 2016 from the National Campaign Website: www.thenationalcampaign.org/resources/pdf/ TBR_InternationalComparison.pdf.

The White House (2013). *President Obama Unveils ConnectED Initiative to Bring American's Students into Digital Age* [Press release]. Retrieved 20 July 2016 from the White House website: www.whitehouse.gov/the-press-office/2013/06/06/ president-obama-unveils-connected-initiative-bring-america-s-students-di.

Wildsmith, E., Schelar, E., Peterson, K. and Manlove, J. (2010). Sexually transmitted diseases among young adults: prevalence, perceived risk, and risk-taking behaviors. *Child Trends Research Brief 10*, 1–8.

5 Love at our fingertips

Exploring the design implications of mobile dating technologies

Jessica L. James

Introduction

Tinder, a modern-day form of online dating that does not involve lengthy profiles, questionnaires or complicated algorithms. All you need is a smartphone, a functioning thumb and a series of enticing pictures and you have a dating profile fit for the ages. In today's digital landscape, speed and efficiency are increasingly becoming the driving forces behind our actions, and dating is no exception. Self-selection dating applications have become commonplace for many young singles looking for romance (Smith and Duggan, 2013).

With smartphone ownership figures at 72% of American adults (Poushter, 2016), the days of personal computer-based (PC) online dating where singles may chat for weeks before meeting in person (Mascaro *et al.,* 2012) have become a thing of the past. Thanks to location-based real-time dating (Handel and Shklovski, 2012), users can locate nearby people using the global positioning system (GPS) software available on all smartphone devices and meet within minutes of chatting online. With new niche forms of mobile dating applications appearing every day, understanding how these digital tools are changing the discourse of dating is fundamental to this research.

This chapter will focus on Tinder, a juggernaut in the mobile matchmaking market with 50 million users worldwide and 24 million matches per day (Smith & Anderson, 2016). Millennials, or anyone born between 1981–1997, represent 59% of all Tinder users (Smith & Anderson, 2016), a demographic who spends on average 14.5 hours a week using their smartphones, according to a 2014 a report from Experian Marketing Services. For many, its appeal is obvious: Tinder is free to download and allows users to select their ideal partner with the intention of meeting in person shortly after matching.

However, Tinder's novel design has gained widespread criticism for being a 'hook-up app' with some users downloading Tinder solely for purposes of finding casual sex. Indeed, after a 2014 report from the Centers for Disease Control and Prevention released figures citing a rise in Sexually Transmitted Diseases (STD), the AIDS Healthcare Foundation (AHF) blamed Tinder and similar dating applications for the spike in STD rates arguing that they:

> [...] are rapidly altering the sexual landscape by making casual sex as easily available as ordering a pizza. In many ways, location-based mobile dating apps are becoming a digital bathhouse for millennials wherein the next sexual encounter can literally be just a few feet away, as well as the next STD [...].
>
> (Whitney Engeran-Cordova, Senior Director,
> Public Health Division for AHF)

While no empirical evidence linking Tinder with increased STD rates exists, the digital capacities of Tinder bring into question the design and accessibility of self-selection dating applications and their use among Millennial populations. Studies examining the construction of online dating profiles have found a 'shopping' mentality for selecting matches, where users commonly evaluate other singles based on physical appearance and/or desired traits (Fullick, 2013; Gibbs *et al.,* 2006). Looks may be important for selecting a romantic partner, but the 'Hot-or-Not' (an online rating website that allows people to evaluate the attractiveness of user-submitted photos) like features of Tinder could increase the already gamified user experience. With emerging mobile applications rapidly intersecting with the routines of our daily lives, what we once called 'play' is quickly becoming the way we interact (Zichermann and Cunningham, 2011).

Representing a relatively new term in the field of Information and Communications Technology (ICT), gamification can be defined as a process by which non-game activities are designed to be more like a game (Morford *et al.,* 2014). As quoted by Zichermann and Cunningham, "[b]y turning the experience into a game, including some reward for achievement, we can produce unprecedented behavior change" (p. xv); "Games are able to get people to take actions that they don't always know they want to take, without the use of force, in a predictable way" (p. 15).

This study asks a series of questions related to mobile dating. First, how and why do people use Tinder, and what differences exists between men and women? Given the university setting where this research took place, Millennial users will be the primary audience. Second, how do people evaluate profiles? Specifically, do users, arguably by default, 'window shop' for matches because of Tinder's photo-centric interface? Finally, if the previous question does prove significant, how does Tinder's design impact its use and application for locating sexual partners?

Online dating then and now

In 1992, less than 1% of the population met their partner through printed personal advertisements or other intermediated sources (Laumann *et al.,* 1994). Even before online dating, using newspapers or magazines to find romance was largely stigmatised as many people who used personal advertisements were viewed as desperate or socially inept (Finkel *et al.,* 2012). But as the Internet started to gain popularity and cultural acceptance, the number of people turning to online dating also increased. Thanks largely to Web 2.0 technologies that allowed more opportunities for user-generated content (Hogan *et al.,* 2011), 1997 saw a large influx of online daters; a trend that has been on the rise ever since.

Today, more Americans are using online dating tools with 15% of adults saying they have used dating sites or mobile dating apps up from just 3% in 2008 (Smith, 2016). 66% of online daters have gone on a date with someone they met through a dating site or mobile application compared with 43% in 2005 (Smith, 2013). However, despite the number of online dating platforms available, only 5% result in marriage or a long-term committed relationship (Smith, 2016).

From a business perspective, media consumption usually involves entertainment or leisure. The hedonic consumption perspective highlights the enjoyment of consumer searching activities (Holbrook and Hirscham, 1982). Couch and Liamputtong (2008) explored conditions that led to online dating and found that seeking a soul mate, sex, fun, relaxation, boredom and "it's easier to meet people" were among key motivations. Whitty and Carr (2006) assessed the appeal of online dating, finding that nearly half (47%) of participants said the large number of potential matches was alluring. Additionally, 35% of respondents from that same study talked about liking the convenience of online dating, meaning they could access and search dating sites in their own home (Whitty and Carr, 2006).

Online dating profiles give users a face to the virtual world, serving as a means for browsing and evaluating other prospective singles. In this environment, users are presented in a virtual marketplace of potential dating partners, which Heino *et al.* (2010) describe "as a place where people go to 'shop' for romantic partners and to 'sell' themselves in hopes of creating a romantic relationship" (p. 429). Indeed, Witty and Carr (2006) found physical attractiveness to be an important characteristic when evaluating profiles for both men (96%) and women (83%). This 'shopping mentality' was also evident in a 2010 Long study, where one participant confirmed the market metaphor associated with online dating. As quoted in Long:

> [...] I can pick and choose; I can choose what size I want, it's like buying a car, what options am I looking for. I can test drive it, eh it's not really my fit, I'll put it back and go try another car.
>
> (p. 206)

Digital considerations on Tinder

In September 2012, Sean Rad and Justin Mateen piloted a mobile matchmaking application called Tinder at the University of Southern California. Today, Tinder is offered in 24 languages and has since been considered the fastest-growing dating application in the US (Baxter and Cashmore, 2013). As stated by Rad in a April 2013 Forbes article, "[w]e want to be the company you turn to when you want to meet somebody" (Colao, 2013).

Carrying the tagline, "[i]t's like real life but better", Tinder's innovative design allows Apple and Android smartphone users under the age of 50 to connect with nearby people using location-based software and basic Facebook information. Users can create a Tinder profile by uploading six pre-selected pictures from their Facebook account and providing an optional 500-character bio. Each Tinder user can customise the desired age, sex and proximity of potential matches in the "preferences" section of the application.

Tinder's photo-centric design enables users to filter through a series of profiles before rejecting (swipe left) or accepting (swipe right) other singles. After both users have displayed interest in each other by swiping right, a screen reading, "[i]t's a match" appears, authorising both users to chat in a private window. Users can have possibly hundreds of conversations simultaneously before deciding to meet with an individual face to face.

The design affords little effort on the part of the user and can be easily accessed throughout the day via a smartphone device. With just a swipe of the finger, Tinder users can find, or rather, select, matches based on individual tastes. Not surprisingly, the ease and convenience of Tinder has prompted a number of user intentions, including casual sex.

As a January 2014 article published on BetaBeat, a website dedicated to up-and-coming tech tools stated, "Tinder: High-speed digital dating (that) gets you more ass than the L Train" (Mulshine, 2014). Other critics contend that Tinder is more of a game than a tool for serious dating. For example, bar goers in England gather around groups of friends and approve or disapprove potential Tinder matches on behalf of one another (Dredge, 2014). A 2013 article from the Huffington Post quoted a Cornell University student who shared a similar stance: "[p]eople don't think of [Tinder] as online dating, they think of it as a game... I think of it as a beauty contest plus messaging" (Bosker, 2013).

In March 2015, developers announced the launch of Tinder Plus, a premium service for $9.99 a month that adds additional features, such as the ability to rewind a left swipe or search for matches in a different city (Crook, 2015). Tinder also added a new 'right-swipe limiter'. The limiter caps how many right swipes a user can make in a 12-hour period, but only by purchasing Tinder Plus can users receive more right swipes and increase the odds for more matches. With a plethora of singles available on Tinder, the app has seen "a small number of users who only swipe right just to see who likes them back" (Crook, 2015), a behaviour dubbed 'indiscriminate narcissism'.

Indeed, Crook (2015), attributes shallow behaviour on Tinder to its game-like design and the potential to secure one of our most basic psychological needs: sex.

> [...] It's not just a friend giving you a hat-tip on your photo or some random follower favoriting your tweet. It's someone who might actually like you, someone who may potentially want to have sex with you. The stakes are raised, and so is the reward.

Uses and gratifications of media consumption

Given the digital capacities on Tinder, applying a theoretical framework that incorporates the effects of media gratifications on user behaviour is appropriate for this study. Stemming from mass communication research, the uses and gratifications (U&G) theory seeks to understand how and why people use media to satisfy individual needs (Katz and Blumler, 1974). Compared with studies on passive media effects, U&G is an audience-centred approach, which posits that media users are active in their selection and have specific needs that drive media adoption (Rubin, 2009, p. 147).

Needs are the "combined product of psychological dispositions, sociological factors, and environmental conditions" (Katz *et al.*, 1973, pp. 516–517). Past studies on U&G determined that media gratifications are largely based on a user's pre-existing needs, rather than specific technological features of media (Greenberg, 1974; Lucas and Sherry, 2004). But as media becomes more interactive, it is important to remember differences between traditional media and newer forms of media (e.g. video games, tablets, smartphones), which usually offer Internet connectivity and more options for digital gratifications. Staying akin with the U&G approach, in this environment, media will compete with other information sources for user gratifications (Katz *et al.*, 1974, p. 22).

Earlier research often assessed the uses and gratifications of television, newspaper and radio (Berelson, 1949; Greenberg, 1974; Herzog, 1944; Rubin, 1983), finding that education, routine, information, relaxation, arousal, escape, learning, habit and sociability were among common gratifications received from traditional media. As consumption habits become more centred around two-way forms of communication, scholars have urged for updated studies on 'user gratifications 2.0' to better understand the latent effects of technology interaction.

A media model for digital gratifications

Sundar's MAIN model (2008, p. 73) addresses the digital affordances offered on smartphones and mobile applications. Sundar argues that the shift from old to new media creates new gratifications that develop with technology. This notion challenges conventional definitions of U&G re-search on the premise that needs or gratifications can also be satisfied by media characteristics. The model posits that such affordances provide cues to media users, which then trigger mental shortcuts about characteristics of the content they consume (Sundar and Limperos, 2013). As quoted in Sundar and Limperos (2013),

> [n]ewer media are characterised by newer functionalities, thereby alter-ing process gratifications (e.g. playing with technology) …. At the same time, they also determine content gratifications (e.g. information and entertainment) by influencing the nature of content accessed, discussed, and created when users interact with such media.
>
> (p. 511)

The MAIN Model identifies four potential areas of technological affor-dances: modality, agency, interactivity and navigability. Modality refers to the different methods of presentation of media content. The Internet pro-vides the option for users to provide content through multiple modalities (text, photo, audio video), which is why the term multimedia is often associ-ated with the Internet. Tinder displays this feature through its photo-centric design and interface.

Agency-based gratifications allow the user to be the 'agent' or source of the information. With the onset of Web 2.0 technologies, the rise in user-generated content has significantly altered the dynamic of online commu-nication. Research investigating this affordance found that digital media users enjoyed customising information in the sender role, which Sundar calls "agency-enhancement" (Sundar *et al.,* 2012, p. 402). Sundar summa-rises that agency-based gratifications are made possible because of new in-terface tools that relate to customisation (Sundar and Limperos, 2013), such as curating an online dating profile with text and photos.

Interactivity is the affordance that allows the user to make real-time changes to the content of the medium (Sundar and Limperos, 2013). Click-ing, dragging and moving are all examples of website interactivity. Sundar argues the very presence of interactivity on any digital application is likely to convey meaning to users. How the user receives and engages with the content is just as important as what's being communicated.

Navigability is a key aspect of the online experience as this affordance allows users to move through the medium. The medium's design is essential for understanding user navigation. An example is the sensation of freely navigating the Internet by searching different websites or filtering through dating profiles. Sundar (2008) calls this response the "browsing heuristic". Additionally, the navigation affordance also encompasses the 'play' grat-ification, emerging from the user enjoyment of moving through levels or spaces. Sundar suggests, "[t]he escapism and immersion that are induced by the affective state of play are best realised when the navigational structure of the interface affords a continuous sense of exploration and smooth transitions" (2013, p. 516).

Gamification of mobile applications

Games, as innocuous as they appear, are at the core of human psychology. How games are designed and what they accomplish is very much a conditioning mechanism for motivating specific behaviours (Zichermann and Cunningham, 2011). But what happens when game-like elements become infused with activities that are not traditionally "played?" iPhone app metrics company Flurry recently reported that after 30 days, a free iPhone app generally loses 95% of players, making gamified engagement, especially on mobile apps, critical for continued success (Zichermann and Cunningham, 2011).

Thanks to Tinder, online dating has also found a place in this gamified context. Never before has such an encounter been so accessible, and with that closeness comes a series of digital considerations tailored around the design and structure of mobile dating applications. The impetus behind Tinder's success may be explained by the human desire for sex. When combined with the central components of gamification, i.e. pleasure, reward and time (Zichermann and Cunningham, 2011), sex becomes the reward on Tinder. Successful game elements incorporate intrinsic motivators with an extrinsic reward or reinforcement for some type of external gain (Zichermann and Cunningham, 2011). For example, intrinsic motivators are things we cannot live without, such as sleep, food, shelter, sex, etc. By contrast, extrinsic forces are driven by material rewards, like money, praise and fame.

Methodology

For this study, a survey was administered at a US public university in fall 2014, producing a random sample of 578 respondents. However, of that number, only 38 individuals used Tinder and participated in the 30-question online survey. The questionnaire was developed by reframing questions from past and present U&G studies, in addition to online dating, to identify user behaviour on Tinder. Suggested questions from Sundar's MAIN Model were used to gauge user engagement with smartphone technology. However, these questions were more interpretative and were included to highlight general smartphone interactivity in relation to design.

While age was initially included in this research, the low number of participants in other ranges made comparing age differences difficult. Therefore, this study primarily focused on college-aged men and women as this was the largest demographic to participate in the research. Survey questions were measured using a single answer, five-point Likert scale (e.g. strongly agree,

agree, neutral, disagree, strongly disagree). A Chi-square test ($\alpha = .05$) was applied to this research since this analysis is often used to explain the relationship, or lack thereof, between variables, i.e. men and women. Therefore, this study produced a descriptive sample of Millennial-age Tinder users.

Results

From the online survey, three questions produced significant findings with $p > .05$. Question 11 asked if participants "downloaded Tinder to find casual sex". This question investigated why men and women decided to download Tinder. Question 11 produced higher averages for male participants compared to females with $r = .009$. Studies have found that people mainly use traditional online dating websites to find long-term relationships (Whitty and Carr, 2006), but there is also research confirming that the Internet allows for more sexual encounters (Bull *et al.*, 2004; Cooper *et al.*, 2003; Daneback, 2006; Hardey, 2004). The response demographic (i.e. men 18–24) could possibly skew this result as men in college are often more sexually promiscuous and less serious about finding romance compared with women (Grello *et al.*, 2006; Lyons *et al.*, 2013).

Question 13 asked if participants swipe right for all Tinder users to boost self-esteem with $r = .025$. This indicates that men largely use Tinder to improve confidence levels or potentially increase the odds of meeting more matches. With the addition of Tinder's 'right swipe' limiter, Question 13 produced a significant finding with $r = .025$. The general population of Tinder users strongly disagreed with this statement. However, it appears men are more likely than women to participate in this behaviour, possibly for increasing the chances of finding a compatible match or more sexual partners. Research on traditional online dating has found that men view more than three times as many profiles as women and are more likely to initiate conversation (Hitsch *et al.*, 2010). While the percentage of men swiping right for all Tinder users is unknown, the appearance of a limiter indicates that the behaviour is not desirable for Tinder's image.

Question 20 had a significance level of $r = .008$. This question asked if participants thought online dating was for desperate people. It appears that gender impacts how Tinder users view online dating with $r = .008$. Women do not think that online dating is for desperate people. However, men were more varied in their responses, but generally agreed with the above statement. As mentioned earlier, the Internet increases the odds of using online dating. Since smartphones are widely accessible and grant instant Internet access, people are generally more receptive of dating websites and/or applications. The disparity in responses between men and women could be explained by the above finding that alludes to women using Tinder for more serious/long-term purposes. Younger men might be reluctant to admit they used Tinder, which is a form of online dating, while women might employ the device in a more practical way.

Conclusion

This research offers insight into how and why people use mobile dating applications and the differences that exist between genders. It also examines possible gratifications of new media technologies in relation to design and user behaviours. While little research has explored if basic design principles impact the use and application of mobile applications, this study provides a novice analysis for the possible existence of such factors. Furthermore, as smartphones and mobile applications continue to play an increasing role in our daily lives, investigating the implications of new media contexts will add to the growing body of literature dedicated to human and computer interaction.

References

Baxter, H. and Cashmore, P. (23 November 2013). Tinder: The Shallowest Dating App Ever? Retrieved on 7 July 2016 from The Guardian website: www.theguardian.com/lifeandstyle/2013/nov/23/tinder-shallowest-dating-app-ever.

Berelson, B. (1949). "What 'missing the newspaper' means". In Lazarsfeld, P.F. and Stanton, F.N. (eds.), *Communication research 1948–1949* (pp. 111–129). New York: Harper.

Bosker, B. (9 April 2013). Why Tinder Has Us Addicted: The Dating App Gives You Mind-Reading Powers. Retrieved on 7 July 2016 from The Huffington Post website: www.huffingtonpost.com/2013/04/09/tinder-dating-app_n_3044472.html.

Bull, S., McFarlane, M., Lloyd, L. and Rietmeijer, C. (2004). The process of seeking sex partners online and implications for STD/HIV prevention. *AIDS Care 16*(8), 1012–1020.

Colao, J. (8 April 2013). Not Just For Hookups: Tinder Looks To Conquer Business Networking. Retrieved on 7 July 2016 from the Forbes website: www.forbes.com/sites/jjcolao/2013/04/08/tinder-for-business-dating-app-looks-to-conquer-other-matchmaking-verticals/.

Cooper, A., Mansson, S., Daneback, K., Tikkanen, R. and Ross, M. W. (2003). Predicting the future of Internet sex: Online sexual activities in Sweden. *Sexual and Relationship Therapy 18*(3), 277–291.

Couch, D. and Liamputtong, P. (2008). Online dating and mating: The use of the Internet to meet sexual partners. *Qualitative Health Research 18*(2), 268–279.

Crook, J. (12 March 2015). Hate It or Love It, Tinder's Right Swipe Limit Is Working. Retrieved on 7 July 2016 from the Tech Crunch website: http://techcrunch.com/2015/03/12/hate-it-or-love-it-tinders-right-swipe-limit-is-working/GAWJNn:13go.

Daneback, K. (2006). Love and Sexuality on the Internet. Unpublished doctoral thesis, Department of Social Work. Goteborg: Goteborg University. Retrieved on 7 July 2016 from the University of Gothenburg website: http://hdl.handle.net/2077/10169.

Dredge, S. (24 February 2014). Tinder: The 'Painfully Honest' Dating App with Wider Social Ambitions. Retrieved on 7 July 2016 from The Guardian website: www.theguardian.com/technology/2014/feb/24/tinder-dating-app-social-networks.

Finkel, E., Eastwick, P., Karney, B., Reis, H. and Sprecher, S. (2012). Online dating: A critical analysis From the perspective of psychological science. *Psychological Science in the Public Interest 13*(1), 3–66.

Fullick, M. (2013). "Gendering" the self in online dating discourse. *Canadian Journal of Communication 38*(4), 545–562.

Gibbs, J. L., Ellison, N. B. and Heino, R. D. (2006). Self-presentation in online personals: The role of anticipated future interaction, self-disclosure, and perceived success in Internet dating. *Communication Research 33*(2), 1–26.

Greenberg, B. S. (1974). "Gratifications of television viewing and their correlates for British children". In Blumler, J.G. and Katz, E. (eds.), *The uses of mass communications: Current perspectives on gratifications research* (pp. 71–92). Beverly Hills: Sage.

Grello, C. M., Welsh, D. P. and Harper, M. S. (2006). No strings attached: The nature of casual sex in college students. *Journal of Sex Research 43*, 255–267.

Handel, M. and Shklovski, I. (2012). Disclosure, Ambiguity and Risk Reduction in Real-Time Dating Sites. *Proceedings of the 17th ACM International Conference on Supporting Group Work*. Sanibel Island FL 175–178.

Hardey, M. (2004). Mediated relationships: Authenticity and the possibility of romance. *Information, Communication and Society 7*(2), 207–222.

Heino, R., Ellison, N. and Gibbs, J. (2010). Relationshopping: Investigating the market metaphor in online dating. *Journal of Social and Personal Relationships 27*(4), 427–447.

Herzog, H. (1944). "What do we really know about daytime serial listeners?". In Lazarsfeld, P.F. and Stanton, F.N. (eds.), *Radio research, 1942–1943* (pp. 3–33). New York: Duell, Sloan and Pearce.

Hitsch, G., Hortacsu, A. and Ariely, D. (2010). Matching and sorting in online dating. *American Economic Review 100*(1), 130–163.

Hogan, B., Dutton, W. and Li, N. (2011). A Global Shift in the Social Relationships of Networked Individuals: Meeting and Dating Online Comes of Age. Me, My Spouse and the Internet Project. *Oxford Internet Institute*. Retrieved on 7 July 2016 from the Oxford Internet Institute website: https://www.oii.ox.ac.uk/archive/downloads/publications/Me-MySpouse_GlobalReport.pdf

Holbrook, M. and Hirschman, E. (1982). The experiential aspects of consumptions: Fantasies, feelings and fun. *Journal of Consumer Research 9*, 132–140.

Katz, E., Blumler, J. and Gurevitch, M. (1974). "Utilization of mass communication by the individual". In Blumler, J. and Katz, E. (eds.), *The uses of mass communication: Current perspectives on gratifications research* (19–32). Beverly Hills: Sage.

Katz, E., Haas, H. and Gurevitch, M. (1973). On the use of the mass media for important things. *American Sociological Review 38*, 164–181.

Laumann, E. O., Gagnon, J. H., Michael, R. T. and Michaels, S. (1994). *The social organization of sexuality: Sexual practices in the United States*. Chicago: University of Chicago Press.

Long, B. L. (2010). Scripts for Online Dating: A Model and Theory of Online Romantic Relationship Initiation (Unpublished doctoral dissertation). Bowling Green State University, OH. Retrieved on 7 July 2016 from the Ohio Link website: http://rave.ohiolink.edu/etdc/view?acc_num=bgsu1268852623.

Lucas, K. and Sherry, J. L. (2004). Sex differences in video game play: A communication based explanation. *Communication Research 31*, 499–523.

Lyons, H. A., Manning, W. D., Giordano, P. C. and Longmore, M. A. (2013). Predictors of heterosexual casual sex among young adults. *Archives of Sexual Behavior 42*, 585–593.

Mascaro, C., Magee, R. and Goggins, S. (2012). Not Just a Wink and Smile: An Analysis of User-Defined Success in Online Dating. *Proceedings of the 2012 iConference Association for Computing Machinery.* New York 200–206.

Morford, Z., Witts, B., Killingsworth, K. and Alavosius, M. (2014). Gamification: The intersection between behavior analysis and game design technologies. *The Behavior Analyst 37*(1), 25–40.

Mulshine, M. (29 January 2014). Tinder Is The Night: High-Speed Digital Dating Gets You More Ass Than the L Train. Retrieved on 7 July 2016 from the Observer website: http://observer.com/2014/01/tinder-is-the-night-high-speed-digital-app-gets-you-more-ass-than-the-l-train/.

Poushter, J. (22 February 2016). Smartphone Ownership and Internet Usage Continues to Climb in Emerging Economies. Retrieved on 7 July 2016 from the Pew Research Center website: www.pewglobal.org/2016/02/22/smartphone-ownership-and-internet-usage-continues-to-climb-in-emerging-economies/.

Rubin, A. M. (2009). "The uses-and-gratifications perspective on media effects". In Bryant, J. and Oliver, M.B. (eds.), *Media effects: Advances in theory and research,* 3rd ed., (525–548), New York: Routledge.

Smith, A. and Anderson, A. (2016). 5 Facts about Online Dating. Retrieved on 7 July 2016 from the Pew Research Center website: www.pewresearch.org/fact-tank/2016/02/29/5-facts-about-online-dating/.

Smith, A. and Duggan, M. (20 October 2013). Online Dating & Relationships. Retrieved on 7 July 2016 from the Pew Research Center website: www.pewinternet.org/2013/10/21/online-dating-relationships/.

Sundar, S. S. (2008). "The MAIN model: A heuristic approach to understanding technology effects on credibility". In Metzger, M.J. and Flanagin, A.J. (eds.), *Digital media, youth, and credibility* (pp. 73–100). Cambridge: The MIT Press.

Sundar, S. S. and Limperos, A. (2013). Uses and grats 2.0: New gratifications for new media. *Journal of Broadcasting & Electronic Media 57*(4), 504–525.

Sundar, S. S., Oh, J., Bellur, S., Jia, H. and Kim, H. S. (2012). Interactivity as Self-Expression: A Field Experiment with Customization and Blogging. *Proceedings of the 2012 Annual Conference on Human Factors in Computing Systems,* 395–404. Retrieved on 7 July 2016 from the Digital Library website: http://dl.acm.org/citation.cfm?id=2207731.

Whitty, M. and Carr, A. (2006). *Cyberspace romance: The psychology of online relationships.* Basingstoke: Palgrave Macmillan.

Zichermann, G. and Cunningham, C. (2011). *Gamification by design.* Sebastopol: O'Reilly Media Inc.

6 Sexting

Michelle Drouin

Introduction

As cell phones have penetrated nearly every part of the globe (GSMA, 2015), communication, including romantic and sexual communication, has shifted to digital channels. Accordingly, researchers, especially in the social sciences, have become interested in the ways in which this computer-mediated communication has affected relationships. One branch of this research has focused on sexting, or the exchange of sexually-explicit material via technology (usually a cell phone). Sexting has gained considerable international attention during the last seven years from both the media and relationship researchers. Attention from media outlets typically centres on legal cases or school-wide sexting scandals involving adolescents (e.g. Martinez, 2015; Woolverton, 2015); however, researchers have mainly been interested in who is sexting, what their motivations are for sexting and the risk factors that are associated with this behaviour. Generally, the research has shown that sexting is more common among young adults than among adolescents and older adults, it is a predictor of physical sex among adolescents and it is associated with a number of risk factors, such as insecure attachments, risky sexual behaviour, physical abuse and depression (see Döring, 2014; Drouin, 2015; Klettke *et al.*, 2014). Far less research has focused on the potential benefits of sexting; however, there have been calls for more studies examining the benefits of sexting, particularly for adult couples (Wiederhold, 2015). In this chapter, I briefly discuss the research that has been summarised already in recent literature reviews and then focus on emerging research, including the most recent sexting prevalence statistics, coerced sexting as a risk factor for poly-victimisation and negative mental health symptoms, sexting deception and the differences in sexting with steady and committed relationship partners.

Sexting: summary of previous research

Over the past few years, fairly comprehensive papers have emerged that have summarised the findings from existing sexting research (e.g. Döring, 2014; Drouin, 2015; Gómez and Ayala, 2014; Klettke *et al.*, 2014). Typically, the research on sexting has focused on the prevalence of sexting in adolescent and adult populations, the demographic and personality correlates of sexting and the risk factors (e.g. sexual, drug and alcohol use and mental health) associated with sexting.

Prevalence statistics

In terms of prevalence, statistics vary widely based on the population studied and the way in which sexting has been measured. For example, Mitchell *et al.* (2012) conducted a telephone survey in the US of youth aged 10–17 and found that only 1% of those in this age group had sent a sexually explicit photo (i.e. displaying breasts, genitals or bottom) and only 6% reported receiving a photo of this nature. In contrast, in that same year, Dake *et al.* (2012) used a paper and pencil assessment with US youth aged 12–18 and found that 17% had engaged in sexting. In both studies, and across the wider body of research, the incidence of sexting increased as teens edged towards young adulthood. Meanwhile, the prevalence statistics for adult sexting (usually utilising young adult populations) have also varied widely from 12% to 88%, depending on the type of sext, gender of sexter and direction of transmission. As an example, Gordon-Messer *et al.* (2013) found that 30% of their college sample had sent a nude or nearly nude photo, whereas Henderson and Morgan (2011) found that 60% of their college sample had sent a nude or nearly nude photo and 69% had sent a sexually suggestive text. Despite the fact that researchers have suggested that there be more consistency in the definition and measurement of sexting across studies for greater comparability (e.g. Drouin, 2015; Drouin & Langdraff 2012; Klettke *et al.*, 2014; Lounsbury *et al.*, 2011), there is still much inconsistency and no validated, reliable measure of sexting practices exists. Moving forward, it will be integral for researchers worldwide to adopt a consistent definition and measurement of sexting, so that there can be greater comparability across studies.

Sexting: personality traits

With regard to the personality traits of those who sext, a rather large body of work has focused on the attachment characteristics of those who send sexually-explicit messages (e.g. Drouin and Landgraff, 2012; McDaniel and Drouin, 2015; Weisskirch and Delevi, 2011; Weisskirch *et al.*, 2016). Overall, these studies have found those with insecure attachment styles, either anxious (those who fear that they might lose their partner) or avoidant (those that want to keep their independence from partners), are more likely to engage in sexting. An exception to this is recent work by Weisskirch *et al.* (2016), who found that those with higher levels of anxiety (both dating anxiety and attachment anxiety) were more likely to sext, but those with lower levels of attachment avoidance were also more likely to sext. These disparate findings with regard to attachment avoidance may reflect a shift in culture that has made sexting more desirable among those who want to remain close to romantic partners. Additionally, sexting has been associated with a variety of personality characteristics, such as neuroticism (Benotsch *et al.*, 2013; Delevi and Weisskirch, 2013), histrionic symptoms (Ferguson, 2011), negative urgency (Dir *et al.*, 2013), low self-esteem (Delevi and Weisskirch, 2013) and extraversion (Benotsch *et al.*, 2013) (See Gómez and Ayala (2014) for a review). Considered together, these studies suggest that the psychological characteristics associated with sexting are mostly negative. However, in the last few years, there has been a shift in the characterisation of sexting from a pathological act, perhaps worthy of a DSM classification (Wiederhold, 2011) to an act of fun and flirtation that may possibly be beneficial to couples (Burkett, 2015; Drouin *et al.*, 2013; Lee and Crofts, 2015; Parker *et al.*, 2013; Wiederhold, 2015). Although individuals still acknowledge that there is risk associated with sexting (see Gómez and Ayala, 2014, for review), this cultural shift in the perception of sexting may make it more appealing and commonplace among those in secure relationships with healthy psychological traits. Moreover, considering the call from Wiederhold (2015) to continue to examine the potential benefits of sexting within adult relationships, researchers may begin to approach the study of sexting in terms of its benefits rather than its risks.

Sexting: demographic characteristics

In terms of demographic characteristics that relate to sexting, results have been rather consistent that older teens and young adults are more likely to sext than younger youth (Klettke *et al.*, 2014), but sexting prevalence statistics are also low for those who are older and married (McDaniel and Drouin, 2015). Of the 355 heterosexual married individuals in McDaniel and Drouin's (2015) study, only 12% had ever sent a nude or nearly nude photo to their partner and 29% had engaged in sexy talk with their partner. Findings are also rather consistent with regard to sexual orientation: Higher sexting prevalence rates are common among LGBTQ individuals (Klettke *et al.*, 2014). Meanwhile, findings with regard to gender and race have been mixed: Some studies report gender and race differences in one direction (e.g. women and Caucasians are more likely to sext) and others report differences in a different direction (e.g. men and minorities are more likely to sext) (see Klettke *et al.*, 2014 for a review). These mixed findings suggest that engagement in sexting may not be influenced directly by one's gender or race; instead, it likely reflects a complex interplay between socio-demographic variables, which may include the views on the acceptability of sexting within one's peer group. That said, women have more negative expectancies with regard to sexting than men do (Dir *et al.*, 2013) and they also report more negative sexting experiences, including feeling pressure to sext (Englander, 2012), engaging in unwanted sexting (Drouin and Tobin, 2014; Drouin *et al.*, 2014) and enduring reputational damage as a result of the sexts they send (Lippman and Campbell, 2014; Ringrose *et al.*, 2012; Walker *et al.*, 2013).

Sexting: associated risk factors

The existing research has also focused on risk factors associated with sexting. In their comprehensive review, Klettke *et al.* (2014) found eleven studies that focused on risk factors and Drouin (2015) delineated these risks into sexual, substance abuse and psychological/interpersonal categories. Overall, the research is rather consistent that sexting is a form of sexual activity. In fact, in one of the only known longitudinal studies on the topic Temple and Choi (2014) found that sexting among adolescents was predictive of sexual behaviour a year later. However, interestingly, in their study, sexting was not predictive of engaging in *risky* sexual behaviours. This is in contrast to much of the research on sexting among both teens and adults (e.g. Benotsch *et al.*, 2013; Crimmins and Siegfried-Spellar, 2014; Dake *et al.*, 2012; Dir *et al.*, 2014; Ferguson, 2011; Gordon-Messer *et al.*, 2013), which has shown that sexting is associated with potentially risky behaviours, such as unprotected sex, sexual hook-ups, sex with multiple partners and web-chatting with strangers. Some of these same studies have shown that sexting is related to substance use, including problematic alcohol use or binge drinking and marijuana use (Benotsch *et al.*, 2013; Dake *et al.*, 2012; Dir *et al.*, 2014) and mental health issues, such as attempted suicide and hopeless feelings (Dake *et al.*, 2012). However, even within these studies, there is some inconsistency, as Gordon-Messer *et al.* (2013) found no association between having multiple partners, unprotected sex and sexting, and no differences between sexters and non-sexters in depression or anxiety. Considering these inconsistencies, and especially as cultural values shift and sexting becomes more normative, it will be important to re-examine these issues with diverse populations.

Sexting: current and future directions

Today, sexting research has moved beyond just examining the prevalence and correlates of sexting; although arguably, as cultural attitudes towards sexting continue to shift, this will remain an active and necessary area of research. Instead, researchers have begun to investigate other aspects of this phenomenon, including links between sexting and intimate partner violence, sexting deception and differences in sexting based on relationship type (e.g. casual and steady partners).

Unwanted sexting, sexting coercion and intimate partner violence

In a series of studies, Drouin and Tobin (2014), Drouin *et al.* (2015) and Ross *et al.* (2016) have been examining unwanted but consensual sexting, sexting coercion and links with intimate partner violence and sexting coercion as a component of poly-victimisation. In contrast to previous sexting work that focuses on risk behaviours, these studies distinguish between wanted and unwanted sexting, based on the premise that some individuals may be engaging in sexting voluntarily but as a result of some coercion (e.g. repeated asking) from partners.

Overall, we have found that engaging in unwanted sexting is quite common within committed romantic relationships. For example, in Drouin and Tobin (2014), 52% of our young adult participants had sexted with a committed partner when they did not want to. Their motivations for doing so were typically for flirtation, foreplay, or to meet a partner's needs, but there were also some who engaged in the behaviour to avoid an argument. Moreover, for women, attachment anxiety was linked to engagement in unwanted sexting, and this was mediated by desire to avoid an argument with one's partner.

In a follow up study (Drouin *et al.*, 2015), we extended our inquiry to examine the extent to which men and women had felt coerced into sexting and whether this related to the experience of intimate partner violence. One fifth (22%) of the 480 young adults in this study had engaged in unwanted sexting and a similar percentage (21%) stated that they had experienced sexting coercion. For comparison, only 6% of the teens and young adults in the Associated Press-Music Television (AP-MTV) (2009) study indicated that they had been pressured by someone to send a naked photo or video themselves. In our study (Drouin *et al.*, 2015), women were significantly more likely than men to have engaged in sexting when they did not want to; however there were no significant differences between men and women in their experience of sexting coercion. This implies that women may be more susceptible to the influence of sexting coercion. Most importantly, we found that sexting coercion and sexual coercion were both related to the experience of intimate partner violence and to symptoms of anxiety, depression and traumatic stress. This significant association occurred among both men and women. On the basis of these findings, we proposed that sexting coercion may be a new vehicle for the expression of intimate partner violence within couples.

Finally, in Ross *et al.* (2016), we found that among young adults ($N = 885$), sexting coercion was a cumulative risk factor for attachment dysfunction, negative mental health symptoms and sexual problems. Sexting coercion was independently related to each of these symptoms. However, additionally, men who had experienced intimate partner aggression along with sexting and sexual coercion were significantly more likely to have symptoms of avoidant attachment and sexual problems than those who experienced only intimate partner aggression. Meanwhile, women who had experienced intimate partner aggression along with sexting and sexual coercion were significantly more likely to have symptoms of anxious attachment and depression. Thus, when there was some sexual coercion (either sexting or sexual) in the relationship, there were more psychological symptoms than when one experienced only traditional forms of intimate partner violence. However, sexting and sexual coercion did not always co-occur; therefore, we suggested that sexting coercion be considered independently as a new, digital form of intimate partner violence.

Sexting deception and fantasy

Another new avenue of research regarding sexting relates to the conceptualisation of sexting as a deceptive or fantasy-based behaviour. Drouin
et al. (2014) examined sexting deception among 155 young adults and found
that 45% of active sexters had lied to a committed partner about what they
were wearing, doing, or both during a sexting interchange. This was more
common among women than men and it was also more common among
those with higher levels of attachment avoidance. Although most participants (67%) had lied during sexting to serve others (e.g. to make a partner
happy or fulfil their fantasy), some (33%) also lied for self-serving reasons
(e.g. to get in the mood or because they were bored). In a follow up study
with older adults (average age = 32.2), Drouin *et al.* (2016) found that 79%
had sexted with romantic partners and 43% had sexted with those they knew
only online. In terms of deception, 50%–63% had lied about what they were
wearing, doing, or their sexual intentions, and these adults were more likely
to lie to those they know only online than to romantic partners. More importantly, only slightly more than half intended to engage in the specific
sexual acts they mentioned in sexting with romantic partners (60%) and even
fewer (20%) expected to engage in the sexual acts they mentioned in sexting
with those known only online. When asked about their motivations for lying
during sexting, the majority of participants cited fantasy as a primary motivation for lying with both types of partners (71% of those who lied in both
relationship types cited this motivation), but a significantly greater number
of participants lied during sexting to make it better for romantic partners
(71%) than to make it better for those known only online (43%). This suggests that deception during sexting, especially within offline romantic relationships, may not be a symptom of malice or discontent, but rather it could
serve as a means for a partner to meet a relationship goal. Further, we suggest that for many, sexting may just be a virtual dance of fun and flirtation,
meant to please the partner and spur engagement in fantasy play.

Sexting in different relationship contexts

In an early study on the topic, Drouin *et al.* (2013) found that a greater
percentage of their young adult participants had sexted via text-only (no
pictures) with committed relationship partners than with casual sexual or
cheating partners. However, they were almost just as likely to have sent
sexually-explicit pictures or videos to cheating partners (45%) as they were
to send them to committed partners (49%), and they were less likely to have
sent sexually-explicit pictures to casual sex partners (37%). Based on these
results, we suggested that relationship context is a meaningful construct to
consider when examining the prevalence of sexting. Other researchers, too,
have made distinctions in sexting behaviour based on the target of the message. For example, AP-MTV (2009) found that most of the teens and young

adults in their study who had sent a naked picture or video had shared it with a romantic partner or romantic interest, 29% had sent those sexts to people they knew only online and 24% sent sexts to someone with whom they wanted to initiate a romantic or sexual relationship.

More recently, Davis *et al.* (2016), found that sexting adult minority men were more likely to sext with casual than with steady partners. Additionally, there were different risk factors associated with sexting in these different relationship contexts. More specifically, those who sent sexts to steady partners (of any type, including sexually suggestive or explicit words, pictures or videos) were more likely to have had unprotected sex (both vaginal and oral) and those who sent sexts to casual partners were more likely to report more sexual partners. Also, those who received sexts from casual partners were more likely to engage in unprotected oral sex and have sex while under the influence of substances. Meanwhile, in another recent study, Drouin *et al.* (2016), found that the positive and negative consequences of sexting (in this case, sending sexually explicit pictures or videos) varied by relationship type. Those in committed relationships were significantly more likely to experience positive emotional and sexual relationship consequences and those in casual relationships were more likely to experience negative emotional and sexual consequences. Moreover, those who sent sexually-explicit messages to casual partners were more likely to experience discomfort and trauma both when they sent them and afterwards, have regret and worry about sending the pictures, and they were also more likely to have had their pictures forwarded to others. Combined, the results of these studies re-emphasise the importance of examining sexting within different relationship contexts and also provide possible avenues for the development of interventions with teens (e.g. emphasising the risk factors and negative consequences associated with sexting with casual partners).

Conclusion

The first empirical studies of sexting emerged only seven years ago, but since that time, the number of studies on this topic has grown tremendously. In fact, we now have numerous comprehensive works that have summarised the existing research from various angles (e.g. Döring, 2014; Drouin, 2015; Gómez and Ayala, 2014; Klettke *et al.*, 2014.) Among both teens and young adults, sexting has been portrayed mainly as a risk behaviour, associated with a variety of negative personality and relationship characteristics. However, there has been a dramatic shift in its conceptualisation among a handful of researchers, with some suggesting that sexting might actually be good for adult romantic relationships. In fact, Parker *et al.* (2013) even suggested that sexting might be used as an intervention technique with couples, and Wiederhold (2015) called for researchers to examine the potential benefits of sexting within adult relationships.

Although this research avenue remains open for exploration, it may be that the theme of risk that dominates the sexting research is not just a theme of convenience or happenstance. Instead, it is likely that researchers focus on the negative consequences of sexting and its associated risk factors not because of some cultural bias against sexting but rather as a reflection of the data trends. Interestingly, even in Parker *et al.'s* (2013) study, the strongest correlate of sexting was hedonism, which had a stronger association with sexting than intimacy, affirmation, coping and other relationship dynamics. In addition to this, we have years of research that link sexting with insecure attachment patterns (Drouin and Landgraff, 2012; McDaniel and Drouin, 2015; Weisskirch and Delevi, 2011) and the most recent work on the topic (Weisskirch *et al.*, 2016) suggests that both attachment anxiety and fear of negative evaluation from a partner (an element of relational anxiety) both predict engagement in sexting among young adults. Thus, there are at least two undesirable routes to sexting behaviour (i.e. sensation seeking and insecure attachment patterns), so even if one of these routes is eliminated through a cultural shift in public opinion (e.g. sexting becomes so commonplace that it is no longer associated with sensation seeking), the other route may still exist. Moreover, and perhaps more importantly, when we open the door to the exploration of sexting as a potential relationship benefit, we may inadvertently be reinforcing this behaviour among youth and teens, providing dangerous models for digital interactions with romantic partners.

In sum, although future research should explore the possibility that sexting might be associated with relationship benefits, it would be prudent to also continue to track prevalence statistics and examine risk factors associated with the behaviour. Empirical studies in this area are becoming more common; however, many questions still exist with regard to the potential benefits and detriments of sexting.

References

Associated Press (AP) and MTV. (23 September 2009). AP-MTV digital abuse study, executive summary. Retrieved on 26 November 2014 from the A Thin Line website: www.athinline.org/MTV-AP_Digital_Abuse_Study_Executive_Summary. pdf.

Benotsch, E.G., Snipes, D.J., Martin, A.M. and Bull, S.S. (2013). Sexting, substance use, and sexual risk behavior in young adults. *Journal of Adolescent Health 52*, 307–313.

Burkett, M. (2015). Sex(t) talk: A qualitative analysis of young adults' negotiations of the pleasures and perils of sexting. *Sexuality & Culture: An Interdisciplinary Quarterly 19*, 835–863.

Crimmins, D.M. and Siegfried-Spellar, K.C. (2014). Peer attachment, sexual experiences, and risky online behaviors as predictors of sexting behaviors among undergraduate students. *Computers in Human Behavior 32*, 268–275.

Dake, J.A., Price, J.H., Maziarz, L. and Ward, B. (2012). Prevalence and correlates of sexting behavior in adolescents. *American Journal of Sexuality Education 7*, 1–15.

Davis, M.J., Powell, A., Gordon, D. and Kershaw, T. (2016). I want your sext: Sexting and sexual risk in emerging adult minority men. *AIDS Education & Prevention 28*, 138–152.

Delevi, R. and Weisskirch, R.S. (2013). Personality factors as predictors of sexting. *Computers in Human Behavior 29*, 2589–2594.

Dir, A.L., Coskunpinar, A., Steiner, J.L. and Cyders, M.A. (2013). Understanding differences in sexting behaviors across gender, relationship status, and sexual identity, and the role of expectancies in sexting. *Cyberpsychology, Behavior, and Social Networking 16*, 1–7.

Döring, N. (2014). Consensual sexting among adolescents: Risk prevention through abstinence education or safer sexting? *Cyberpsychology: Journal of Psychosocial Research on Cyberspace 8*(1), article 9.

Drouin, M. (2015). "Sexual communication in the digital age". In Rosen, L.D., Cheever, N.A. and Carrier, L.M. (eds.), *The Wiley handbook of psychology, technology and society* (pp. 176–191). Chichester: Wiley-Blackwell.

Drouin, M., Coupe, M. and Temple, J. (2017). *Is sexting good for your relationship? It depends.* Manuscript submitted for publication.

Drouin, M., Hernandez, E. and Wehle, S. (2017). *Sexting—Is it all just lies, fantasy, and role play?* Manuscript in preparation.

Drouin, M. and Landgraff, C. (2012). Texting, sexting, attachment, and intimacy in college students' romantic relationships. *Computers in Human Behavior 28*, 444–449.

Drouin, M., Ross, J. and Tobin, E. (2015). Sexting: A new, digital vehicle for intimate partner aggression? *Computers in Human Behavior 50*, 197–204.

Drouin, M. and Tobin, E. (2014). Unwanted but consensual sexting among young adults: Relations with attachment and sexual motivations. *Computers in Human Behavior 31*, 412–418.

Drouin, M., Tobin, E. and Wygant, K. (2014). Love the way you lie: Sexting deception in romantic relationships. *Computers in Human Behavior 35*, 542–547.

Drouin, M., Vogel, K.N., Surbey, A. and Stills, J.R. (2013). Let's talk about sexting, baby: Computer-mediated sexual behaviors among young adults. *Computers in Human Behavior 29*, A25–A30.

Englander, E. (2012). Low risk associated with most teenage sexting: A study of 617 18-year-olds. *MARC Research Reports*, 1–12. Retrieved on 30 June 2016 from the Bridgewater State University website: http://vc.bridgew.edu/cgi/viewcontent.cgi?article=1003&context=marc_reports.

Ferguson, C.J. (2011). Sexting behaviors among young Hispanic women: Incidence and association with other high-risk sexual behaviors. *Psychiatric Quarterly 82*, 239–243.

Gómez, L.C. and Ayala, E.S. (2014). Psychological aspects, attitudes and behaviour related to the practice of sexting: A systematic review of the existent literature. *Procedia—Social & Behavioral Sciences 132*, 114–120.

Gordon-Messer, D., Bauermeister, J., Grodzinski, A. and Zimmerman, M. (2013). Sexting among young adults. *Journal of Adolescent Health 52*, 301–306.

GSM Association (2015). The global economy 2015. Retrieved on 30 June 2016 from the GSM Association website: http://gsmamobileeconomy.com/GSMA_Global_Mobile_Economy_Report_2015.pdf.

Henderson, L. and Morgan, E. (2011). Sexting and sexual relationships among teens and young adults. *McNair Scholars Research Journal 7*, 31–39.

Klettke, B., Hallford, D.J. and Mellor, D.J. (2014). Sexting prevalence and correlates: A systematic literature review. *Clinical Psychology Review 34*(1), 44–53.

Lee, M. and Crofts, T. (2015). Gender, pressure, coercion and pleasure: Untangling motivations for sexting between young people. *British Journal of Criminology 55*, 454–473.

Lippman, J.R. and Campbell, S.W. (2014). Damned if you do, damned if you don't… if you're a girl: Relational and normative contexts of adolescent sexting in the United States. *Journal of Children and Media 8*, 371–386.

Lounsbury, K., Mitchell, K.J. and Finkelhor, D. (2011). The true prevalence of sexting. Retrieved on 30 June 2016 from the University of New Hampshire website: www.unh.edu/ccrc/pdf/Sexting%20Fact%20Sheet%204_29_11.pdf.

Martinez, M. (9 November 2015). Sexting scandal: Colorado high school faces felony investigation. *CNN*. Retrieved on 30 June 2016 from the CNN website: www.cnn.com/2015/11/07/us/colorado-sexting-scandal-canon-city/index.html.

McDaniel, B.T. and Drouin, M. (2015). Sexting among married couples: Who is doing it, and are they more satisfied? *Cyberpsychology, Behavior, and Social Networking 18*, 628–634.

Mitchell, K.J., Finkelhor, D., Jones, L.M. and Wolak, J. (2012). Prevalence and characteristics of youth sexting: A national study. *Pediatrics 129*, 13–20.

Parker, T.S., Blackburn, K.M., Perry, M.S. and Hawks, J.M. (2013). Sexting as an intervention: Relationship satisfaction and motivation considerations. *American Journal of Family Therapy 41*, 1–12.

Ringrose, J., Gill, R., Livingstone, S. and Harvey, L. (2012). A qualitative study of children, young people and "sexting": A report prepared for the NSPCC. London: National Society for the Prevention of Cruelty to Children. Retrieved on 30 June 2016 from the website of the London School of Economics website: http://eprints.lse.ac.uk/44216.

Ross, J., Drouin, M. and Couple, M. (2016). Sexting coercion as a component of intimate partner polyvictimization. *Journal of Interpersonal Violence, 1–23*, online publication ahead of print (20 July 2016).

Temple, J.R. and Choi, H. (2014). Longitudinal association between teen sexting and sexual behavior. *Pediatrics 134*, 1287–1292.

Walker, S., Sanci, L. and Temple-Smith, M. (2013). Sexting: Young women's and men's views on its nature and origins. *Journal of Adolescent Health 52*, 697–701.

Weisskirch, R.S. and Delevi, R. (2011). "Sexting" and adult romantic attachment. *Computers in Human Behavior 27*, 1697–1701.

Weisskirch, R.S., Drouin, M. and Delevi, R. (2016). Relational anxiety and sexting. *Journal of Sex Research 31,* 1–9, published online before print.

Wiederhold, B.K. (2011). Should adult sexting be considered for the DSM? *Cyberpsychology, Behavior, & Social Networking 14*, 481.

Wiederhold, B.K. (2015). Does sexting improve adult sexual relationships? *Cyberpsychology, Behavior, & Social Networking 18*, 627.

Woolverton, P. (2 September 2015). NC law: Teens who take nude selfie photos face adult sex charges. *Fayetteville Observer*. Retrieved on 30 June 2016 from the Fay Observer website: www.fayobserver.com/news/local/nc-law-teens-who-take-nude-selfie-photos-face-adult/article_ce750e51-d9ae-54ac-8141-8bc29571697a.html.

7 "Nude selfies til I die" – making of 'sexy' in selfies

Katrin Tiidenberg

Introduction

"Nude selfies til I die" was the extent of Kim Kardashian's Webbly awards acceptance speech in 2016, when she won an award for her unparalleled success online. And while she is in no terms the measure of female sexual subjectivity or the selfie[1] culture today, the 'speech' can be seen as an indication that sexy selfies are out of the closet. We cannot exactly claim that taking and sharing nudes is a marginal practice, when many of the images leaked in the celebrity photo hack (the Fappening) and the Snapchat hack (the Snappening) of 2014 were sexy selfies. Or when one recent study claims a whopping 82% of 18–82-year-old Americans to have sexted during the past year (Stasko and Geller, 2015). Yet, both mass media and much of academic discourse seem to regard sexy selfies as shameful, dismissible or a source of paternalistic worry.

Working with a community of sexy selfie enthusiasts on Tumblr for five years, I have noticed when presenting my work, that it is common to assume that sexy selfies could only possibly increase individual people's limited sense of life satisfaction, but that they do nothing for or are even harmful in terms of the broader struggle against patriarchy. This relies on a widespread premise that sexy selfies cannot be anything but a postfeminist glorification of internalised objectification. Jumping ahead here – that is not true. Sexy selfies are not, *a priori*, sociologically insignificant, nor do they necessarily detract from a feminist agenda.

In this chapter I will thus articulate how women can find both their politics and a comfort in their own skin through sexy selfie practices. The two are not mutually exclusive, but become possible in confluence. This is as much an analysis of empirical material as it is my explicit statement in an on-going debate. Critical feminist work (Evans and Riley, 2015) has pointed out that there are two conflicting positions readily available for women – (1) postfeminist self-objectification and (2) joyless rejection of neoliberal sexiness. I show that reflexive selfie-practices can carve out subject positions that fit in between the two. To do this, I rely on ethnographic analysis conducted with a community of sexy selfie practitioners on Tumblr, and supplement it with contextual analysis (visual, textual and hyper textual data are analysed as intertextually relational) of data such as photographs, captions, comments, hashtags and interviews from 2011–2015 relating to two female bloggers – Katie and Rachel.

What is sexy, how is it done and why does it matter?

'Sexy', which is used by many groups but here pertains to 'sexy for Cis women', seems exceedingly hard to pin down for analysis. If approached as one's 'sexual subjectivity', it can be defined as "a person's experience of herself as a sexual being, who feels entitled to sexual pleasure and sexual safety, who [can] make...active sexual choices, and who has an identity as a sexual being" (Tolman, 2012, pp. 749–750). Research on women's experiences of sexiness tends to focus more on girls than adults, but is useful in pointing out the strain women experience in discursively distinguishing sexiness from its negative alternative of sluttiness. This is accomplished by imbuing the concept of sexiness with a sense of confidence, thus making it about being comfortable in one's own skin (Lamb *et al.*, 2015, p. 7). The tension between sexiness as being vulnerable to judgment versus sexiness as an independent practice of 'owning it' is evident both in everyday discourse and existing literature. Consumer products are marketed with the rhetoric of a sexually assertive woman, who knows what she wants and is not afraid to take it. Yet, modesty is still lauded as a virtue and used to police girls and women in both interpersonal (i.e. slut-shaming) and institutional settings (i.e. skirt length controversies at schools). In similar vein, scholarship on the effects of sexualised culture points to social institutions (e.g. mass media) constructing a narrow ideal of white, young, thin, heterosexual femininity (cf. Mager and Helgeson, 2011), wherein sexual subjecthood, particularly of white, middle-class girls is passive and in need of protection, (Renold and Ringrose, 2011). Contrary to this, other work (Dobson, 2015) describes a neoliberal, postfeminist rhetoric that posits an ideal of a choice-making, pleasure seeking, powerful subject with working class, and black girls often hyper-sexualised.

Recently, Adrienne Evans and Sarah Riley elaborated on their own and other authors' Foucault inspired framework of 'technologies of sexiness', "to account for women's engagement with material and non-material practices in the pursuit of (hetero)sexy subjectivity" (2015, p. 39). They examine how intersections of consumerism, post feminism and neoliberalism offer an ideal subject position of the empowered pleasure pursuer, but take a step further, to show how technologies of sexiness can also produce subject positions that subvert existing normative expectations, even while having to repeat dominant discourses to be legible as subversions. This is significant, as critical feminist scholarship has a history of coming to an impasse regarding women's agency in negotiating their sexual subjecthood (for discussions on empowerment vs sexualisation cf. articles in *Sex Roles*, Volume

66 (11/12), 2012). In Evans' and Riley's framework, agency becomes defined as "a self-reflexive method of adopting and potentially subverting one discourse over another" (2015, p. 56), which allows us to contemplate women's experiences of control without erasure of the structural conditions they find themselves in.

The dominant norms of what an embodied 'sexy' looks like have obviously changed over time, neither are they uniform across societies and groups.[2] Today's ideal of a (white, young) thin[3] body can be traced to the 19th century, when wealthy people began to systematically deny themselves food for the sake of an aesthetic ideal, which then gradually became a status symbol and spread through all layers of society (Bordo, 2003). The end of the 19th century also launched the use of images of nude women in advertising (1871, Pearl Tobacco). But while the sexualisation of women's bodies in media and advertising continued throughout the next century, it was only in the 1980s, when it became particularly raunchy as a "less regulated, more commercialized sexual culture" could be seen to emerge (McNair, 2002, p. 12). Research of media images over the past 50 years has shown that bodies in media have become progressively sexualised and ever more thin (Hatton and Trautner, 2011; Graff *et al.*, 2013). Thus today, at least in wealthy consumer economies, our worth as a person is linked to the appearance of our bodies, but practically no one's body seems to live up to the ageist, sexist and ableist (Gill, 2012) standards.

Selfies and the making of sexy

Selfies are receiving continuing popular and scholarly attention.[4] Interpreted as assemblages of subjectivities within a massively mediated and networked society (Hess, 2015), and as simultaneously photographic objects and socio-cultural practices, indicative of what different cultures value or dismiss (Senft and Baym, 2015), selfies function as communicative acts, social currency and a self-making tools.

Not everyone agrees with this understanding of selfies as self-expression and self-reflection. Alarmist accounts of narcissism are abundant in popular writing and some psychological scholarship (cf. Weiser, 2015). Diagnoses of (self) objectification and commodification are common in some feminist and media scholarship (cf. Barnard, 2016). The debate on agency introduced in the previous section thus follows extant work on selfies. It is not surprising; after all, as Anne Burns says: "there are parallels between the discipline of women's bodies and the regulation of women's photographic practice – indeed, often these principles are achieved simultaneously" (2015, p. 43). Often the controversy of women's agency is operationalised with the concept of visibility. While selfies are occasionally linked with particular groups gaining visibility,[5] women's gendered, embodied and sexual visibility have a long tradition of being treated as a Foucauldian trap (1977, p. 200), which – within the confines of existing discourses and structures of inequality – leads to objectification (c.f. Donaghue *et al.*, 2011; Gill, 2008; Levy, 2005). While I agree that the popularity of particular aesthetics, sensibilities or practices in specific contexts needs to be questioned for their structural and discursive power implications, it should be done without collapsing analyses of the phenomena into statements about practitioners' lack of freedom (Attwood, 2010, p. 5). Recent empirical work exemplifies this well – contrary to Western perspectives on gendered selfie shaming (cf. Burns, 2015), selfies' association with feminine vanity does not devalue them among Singaporean Influencers. Instead, there, selfies are unabashedly admired for their aesthetic ideals and commercial value (Abidin, 2016, p. 1742).

Work on sexy selfies specifically has shown that (young) people carefully curate the (re)presentations of their sexual subjecthood on social media. Warfield's (2014) participants said they would post cute selfies on Facebook, but not sexy ones, which they might post on Instagram. Both Albury (2015) and Miguel (2016) found a double standard for men's and women's sexy selfies. Albury (2015, p. 4) showed that men are protected by the cultural readiness to dismiss their nude selfies as funny or stupid, whereas young women always bear an extra burden of representation. Some of Miguel's (2016) male participants interpreted women's sexy selfies as cheap self-sexualisation, while they did not see their own similar images as such. My previous work with a community of sexy selfie enthusiasts on Tumblr has led me to argue that in addition to the sexting-based interpretation of sexy selfies as communicative acts of foreplay or sex, taking and sharing sexy selfies can function as a practice of (re)claiming control over the aesthetic of what is and is not 'sexy' (Tiidenberg, 2014). Elsewhere (Tiidenberg *et al.*, 2015), I have suggested that sexy selfie practices may engage with visual and consumer culture's normative, ageist and sexist assumptions, and allow women new ways of experiencing both their bodies and their embodied, gendered, sexual selves.

Speaking to the capacity selfies have for being a practice in the pursuit of sexual subjectivity, I have argued (Allaste and Tiidenberg, 2015; Tiidenberg, 2014; Tiidenberg *et al.*, 2015) that taking and sharing selfies – quite like Foucault's (1988) letter writing or note taking – can become an endeavour that teaches self-care, critical self-awareness and aestheticises the self. When this self-care is critical, I would go as far as saying that selfie practices have potential for transgressive self-invention, as they become practices of freedom (Foucault, 1996; Rose, 1998). In a body-positive atmosphere, selfies expand community members' understanding of what is photographable (Bourdieu, 1996, p. 6) by giving practitioners new ways of seeing (Bordo, 2003). In addition to questioning the narrow standards of appearances that our sexualised visual culture (McNair, 2002) mandates us to exhibit and observe, these selfie practices reject many of the consumerist aspects of this culture by sharing nudity for no monetary gain or using one's own body (instead of that of a supermodel or a fitness subscription) as an inspiration.

Rachel and Katie's selfies making their sexy

Katie and Rachel both started posting sexy, naked selfies on Tumblr around 2011, and I have had the privilege of witnessing their journeys. I have interviewed both of them four times over the five-year period, starting with a more general interview on their Tumblr experiences, following up with specific thematic interviews (i.e. on selfies, friendship, body-image or non-monogamy). During our first interview Katie identified as kinky, bisexual and in a consensual non-monogamous marriage; while Rachel identified as a closeted bisexual in a monogamous marriage. Both of their partners were aware of and reasonably supportive of their self-exploration on Tumblr. Today Katie is in her early thirties and her identifications have remained largely the same, while Rachel is in her mid-forties and her Tumblr experience has led to her now identifying and living as polyamorous. I have decided to focus on their stories, because they have been prolific posters of selfies with highly popular and impactful blogs (tens of thousands of followers). They have also both independently articulated the links they believe exist between their bodies, selves, selfies and politics in our interviews and on their blogs. Those experiences are common among my informants. Katie's and Rachel's experiences offer a lot of nuance and thus allow me to demonstrate the unfolding of those processes of becoming.[6]

In Rachel's first interview, she mentioned three reasons for why she takes and posts sexy selfies. First, she found it sexually exciting; second, seeing herself on the laptop screen allowed her to, for the first time in her life, realise that she could look 'hot'. And finally – as a then nearly 40-year-old woman, afraid of becoming invisible – the feedback helped her realise that her sexual shelf-life was not over.

> Body dysmorphic disorder is a very real kind of thing and it is only through taking the laptop cam pix that I could see myself from outside, more clearly [...].
>
> (Rachel, interview 2011)

In Katie's first interview, she just mentioned that her selfies help her scratch her exhibitionist itch, but a year later, in an interview specifically on selfie practices, she described her years' worth of taking and posting sexy selfies as allowing her to:

> [...] empower myself to really own this new way I was seeing my body, like a force, a thing of beauty, like mine. It was amazing to have these thoughts after years of body image issues. And on the bad days, where my old monsters rear their ugly heads, my blog and self-shooting are now ways I can kick its ass.
>
> (Katie, interview 2012)

The key moment in Katie's and Rachel's (and my other female participants') selfie-awareness, and a moment that is crucial in sexy selfie practices becoming a technology of sexiness (Evans and Riley, 2015), which subverts existing discourses in an agentic way, is when their blogs become popular. Amassing a large enough following that goes beyond interaction partners or silent, but regular 'heart button' pushers, towards a more anonymous crowd of viewers, tends to drastically change the feedback women get for their sexy selfies. In the following interview excerpt Rachel is just starting to articulate it for herself:

> There is a sleazy crowd, who think you're a performing seal, and they don't respect that you're doing it for [...] they think that [...] they misunderstand the whole transactional nature of Tumblr [...].
>
> (Rachel, interview 2011)

The metaphor of a performing seal became one that Rachel often used, when explaining to her followers, why she would not fulfil their desires or demands. It apparently resonated really well with other women in the community, because Katie has referenced it to describe her own process of boundary setting in a group chat with some female informants:

> [T]he comment about demands from users (the ever-present "show us your pussy!") resonated. I operate from the same idea, my blog is always for me, end of story. I use it for whatever I need from it at the time. I think it was Rachel, who said she once felt like a performing seal taking requests. There are some self-shooters who like that, but I'm not one of them.
>
> (Katie, interview 2012)

Thus, it is the struggle to set and maintain the boundaries between self-expression, self-exploration and relevance that elevates sexy selfie practices to self-reflexivity, and transforms them into a technology of sexiness. Rachel was able to eloquently articulate the importance of those boundaries in our most recent interview.

> The first thing that happens, when you start putting images out there and gaining a following is that you start getting requests from people, who think you are there for their pleasure. So I understood early on that I had to take step back and take control over my self-imaging and remember that I am doing it for me. That this is a pleasurable thing I am doing for me – and I had to articulate this really clearly to my followers – so I could maintain a clear sense of self through it. I could initially feel it slipping away as these messages started coming through from people.
>
> (Rachel, interview 2015, describing her experience back in 2011 and 2012)

Now this process of activating boundaries is not easy and should not be dismissed. It may seem or even be framed as a moment's decision in interviews, but is more of an emotionally expensive period of trial and error. A subject position that a woman has never before deemed possible, felt a need for, or known how to articulate is slowly built in that process. Hints towards this are evident in some of Rachel's exchanges on her blog, where she explicitly says that filling photo requests that do not resonate with her own idea of what is sexy or interesting make her feel really bad and taken advantage of.

Thus, sexy selfie practices become self-aware. Taking and posting images moves from an impulsive search for a pleasurable subject position, to a reflexive choice of actualising one's subject position through this practice and having a firm sense of personal politics about it. For Rachel, the next stage of selfie practices meant exploring different personas with different lovers, eventually leading to her embracing her non-monogamous preferences. Katie told me, in an interview in 2013 that posting selfies made her pay more attention to how her cycle, emotions and circumstance affect her sexuality. Thus experiences, selfie practices have a felt, positive impact on (a) the lived body; (b) the sense of sexiness; and (c) the actual sex life. But most importantly to the argument at hand, those are clearly experienced by practitioners as mindful positions within the patriarchal discourses of female sexuality. Thus, for Rachel, her final stage of selfie posting, before she stopped completely, was almost entirely at the service of body-positivity.

> I really felt that there had to be a purpose to posting selfies, there was much more of a politicisation to it, I was doing it for body positivity. So it went from kind of pure sexual exhibitionism to testing out different personas to a more explicitly politicised thing, to now nothing, it's just political jokes on there now.
>
> (Rachel, interview 2015)

Katie points out that posting sexy selfies and blogging about non-monogamy have given her an agentic voice that she explicitly calls feminist, and directly links to being able to stand up for what she believes to perhaps change perceptions and show there is pride and power to owning your sexuality. Recently, Katie trusted someone she knew with her blog and her trust was abused. Instead of retreating, she reflects on it as follows:

> I know I have the right to autonomy over my body. I know I will be glad I revelled in my physical form, when I am old and grey. I know that taking and posting selfies does not make me any less of a feminist or any less worthy of respect.
>
> (Katie, excerpt from blog, 2015)

This is not meek, postfeminist, consumerist enjoyment of orgasms and pink vibrators. This is politically self-aware sexual subjectivity illustrated further by both Katie and Rachel moving towards increasingly interspersing their 'conventionally sexy' content with explicitly feminist content relating to issues such as rape culture, sex work, LGBT rights, body fascism, body positivity, pubic hair, sex-education, non-monogamy and consent. While this is produced in original text posts, quotes and reading recommendations, they also occasionally post 'statement selfies'. Katie, for example, has posted an image of her in an aggressive, wide legged stance, wearing no pants but a t-shirt that reads "well, the patriarchy isn't going to fuck itself" (can be seen in Tiidenberg *et al.*, 2015), while Rachel has created a series of images captioned with an essay length verbal smack down of an anonymous commenter, who had suggested she keep her "slightly overweight mommy body" off the Internet (a detailed analysis of this series in Tiidenberg, 2014). Would this rhetoric have been possible without the experiences these women had with posting sexy selfies, drawing boundaries around them and defending their right to do so? These highly personal and individualized experiences might also be woven into a wider reaching, structural opposition to cultural gender imbalances.

Conclusion

I am not claiming that every picture of women's bodies is automatically empowering or will start a revolution. But the women whose selfie practices I have followed over the years post pictures, where they like what they see. The more pictures they take, the more they find to like. Their blogs end up becoming catalogues of evidence that they like their own bodies. Relying on the succinct summation Caroline Caldwell's (2015) art-project-become-internet-meme: "in a society that profits from your self-doubt, liking yourself is a rebellious act". Or, in more scholarly terms, if an important aspect of sexual subjectivity is the ability to feel comfortable in one's skin, then establishing that baseline is both a sociologically relevant phenomenon, and a building block for any kind of self-actualisation. Sexy selfie practices thus have the power to become a tool that produces a body that looks and feels good. A tool that is controlled by ordinary women, unlike the pens, printing presses and cameras that wrote the history, systematically erasing or caricaturising some groups and experiences.

Beyond that, when women post sexy selfies in a culture that expects their public self-depictions to be sexualised, but only in a manner that is "acceptable for the male, heterosexual viewer" (Burns, 2015, p. 168), it is often followed by critique and humiliation, or demands for more. What my fieldwork has shown, though, is that this clash between women's sexual(ised) practices and the toxic chauvinist responses of a neoliberal, heteronormative culture may be a fertile space. My informants' experiences have shown, that women can, at this point of tension, self-reflexively assess their practices and work on setting the boundaries that subvert (Evans and Riley, 2015) the toxic discourse for others that position posting sexy selfies as a feminist technology of sexiness.

Notes

1 Selfie = (photo taken of oneself with an extended hand or in a mirroring surface and shared on social media).
2 Researchers have pointed out the whiteness of the slenderness ideal, noting that for example black women's ideal body image is more curvaceous (cf. Overstreet et al., (2010) for a comparison of black and white women's body ideals). However, recent research also suggest that the thin ideal is far reaching, and can lead to a paradoxical body image, where the thin ideal is contrasted with a curvier counter image (cf. Viladrich et al., 2009 on paradoxical body image among Latinas). A meta-analysis of studies (published since 1990) of ethnicity and body dissatisfaction among women in the US showed that women from white, Asian American, Hispanic, and black American ethnic groups had similar body dissatisfaction levels (Grabe et al., 2008).
3 Some scholars have questioned whether the reign of slenderness might be over. A closer look shows that both the 'curvy' (Harrison, 2003) and the 'strong' ideals that are often proffered as examples of change, still presume a thin frame, just enhanced with ample breasts or sharp muscle definition. Both are unattainable for most women (Tiggerman and Zaccardo, 2015). Content analysis of #fitspiration posts on Instagram (Tiggerman and Zaccardo, 2016) and in web searches (Boepple et al., 2016) showed that even in expressly strength focussed body ideals thin continues to be the prevailing body type.
4 cf. special issues in International Journal of Communication, (eds.) Senft and Baym, 2015, or Social Media and Society, (eds.) Warfield et al., 2016.
5 Various recent hashtag happenings like #blackout, #feministselfie, #whatbilookslike are a case in point. In 2015 Tumblr user Y.R.N. created #BlackOutDay (http://whatwhiteswillneverknow.com/post/112575747932/colorthefuture-tv-on-expect-the-greatest) in an effort to promote solidarity and acceptance of black beauty. In 2013 Jezebel (http://jezebel.com/selfies-arent-empowering-theyre-a-cry-for-help-1468965365) published a story indicating that all selfies were a cry for help. Jamie Nesbitt Golden (@thewayoftheid) and Kate Averett (@convergecollide) started the #feministselfie hashtag took onTwitter in response. In 2014 Huffington Post (www.huffingtonpost.com/2014/08/16/whatbilookslike_n_5682347.html) started a #whatbilookslike hashtag campaign on Twitter to offer more authentic visibility to bisexuals.
6 Becoming is used here in line with the authors who rely on Deleuze to emphasise the fluid aspects of people's identities by focusing not on being, but on becoming.

References

Abidin, C. (2016). "Aren't these just young, rich women doing vain things online ?": Influencer selfies as subversive frivolity. *Social Media + Society, April-June 2(2)*, 1–17.
Albury, K. (2015). Selfies, sexts, and sneaky hats: Young people's understandings of gendered practices of self-representation. *International Journal of Communication 9*, 1734–1745.
Allaste, A.A. and Tiidenberg, K. (2015). "Sexy Selfies of the Transitioning Self". In Woodman, D. and Bennett, A. (eds.), *Youth Cultures, Belonging and Transitions* (pp. 113–127). Basingstoke: Palgrave Macmillan.
Attwood, F. (2010). *Porn.com: Making Sense of Online Pornography*. New York: Peter Lang Publishing, Inc.
Barnard, S.R. (2016). Spectacles of Self(ie) empowerment? Networked individualism and the logic of the (post)feminist selfie. *Communication and Information Technologies Annual 11*, 63–88.

Boepple, L., Ata, R.N., Rum, R. and Thompson, J.K. (2016). Strong is the new skinny: A content analysis of fitspiration websites. *Body Image 17*, 132–135.

Bordo, S. (2003). *Unbearable Weight: Feminism, Western Culture, and the Body.* Berkeley: University of California Press.

Bourdieu, P. (1996). *Photography: A Middle-Brow Art.* Stanford: Stanford University Press.

Burns, A. (2015). *SELFIE CONTROL: Online Discussion of Women's Photographic Practices as a Gendered Form of Social Discipline.* Doctoral Thesis Submitted, Loughborough University.

Caldwell, C. (2015). In a Society That Profits from Your Self Doubt, liking Yourself is a Rebellious Act. Retrieved on 20 September 2016 from the Twitter website: https://twitter.com/dirt_worship/status/600028189113581569.

Dobson, A.S. (2015). *Postfeminist Digital Cultures: Femininity, Social Media, and Self-Representation.* New York: Palgrave Macmillan.

Donaghue, N., Kurz, T. and Whitehead, K. (2011). Spinning the pole: A discursive analysis of the websites of recreational pole-dancing studios. *Feminism & Psychology 21*, 441–455.

Evans, A. and Riley, S. (2015). *Technologies of Sexiness: Sex, Identity, and Consumer Culture.* New York: Oxford University Press.

Foucault, M. (1977). *Discipline and Punish: The Birth of the Prison.* London: Penguin Books.

Foucault, M. (1988). "Technologies of the Self". In Martin, L.H., Gutman, H. and Hutton, P.H. (eds.), *Technologies of the Self: A Seminar with Michel Foucault* (pp. 16–49). Amherst: University of Massachusetts Press.

Foucault, M. (1996). What is Critique? In Schmidt J. (ed.), *What is Enlightenment: Eighteenth-century Answers and Twentieth-century Questions.* Berkeley, CA: University of California Press, 382–398.

Gill, R. (2008). Empowerment/sexism: Figuring female sexual agency in contemporary advertising. *Feminism & Psychology 18(1),* 35–60.

Gill, R. (2012). Media, empowerment and the 'sexualization of culture' debates. *Sex Roles 66(11–12),* 736–745.

Grabe, S., Ward, L.M. and Hyde, J.S. (2008). The role of the media in body image concerns among women: a meta-analysis of experimental and correlational studies. *Psychol Bull 2134*, 460–476.

Graff, K.A., Murnen, S.K. and Krause, A.K. (2013). Low-cut shirts and high-heeled shoes: Increased sexualization across time in magazine depictions of girls. *Sex Roles 69(11),* 571–582.

Harrison, K. (2003). Televisino viewers' ideal body proportions: The case of the curvaceously thin woman. *Sex Roles 48*, 255–264.

Hatton, E. and Trautner, M.N. (2011). Opportunity objectification? The sexualization of men and women on the cover of rolling stone. *Sexuality & Culture 15(3),* 256–278.

Hess, A. (2015). The selfie assemblage. *International Journal of Communication 9*, 1629–1646.

Lamb, S., Farmer, K.S., Kosterina, E., Sariñana, S.L., Plocha, A. and Randazzo, R. (2015). What's sexy? Adolescent girls discuss confidence, danger, and media influence. *Gender and Education 28(4),* 527–545.

Levy, A. (2005). *Female Chauvinist Pigs: Women and the Rise of Raunch Culture.* New York: Free Press.

Mager, J. and Helgeson, J. (2011). Fifty years of advertising images: Some changing perspectives on role portrayals along with enduring consistencies. *Sex Roles 64(3/4),* 238–252.

McNair, B. (2002). *Striptease Culture: Sex, Media and the Democratisation of Desire.* London: Routledge.

Miguel, C. (2016). Visual intimacy on social media : From selfies to the co-construction of intimacies through shared pictures. *International Journal of Communication, April–June 2(2),* 1–10.

Overstreet, N.M., Quinn, D.M. and Agocha, B. (2010). Beyond thinness: Exploring the influence of a curvaceous body ideal on body dissatisfaction in Black and White women. *Sex Roles 63,* 91–103.

Renold, E. and Ringrose, J. (2011). Schizoid subjectivities? Re-theorizing teen girls' sexual cultures in an era of 'sexualization'. *Journal of Sociology 47(4),* 389–409.

Rose, N. (1998). *Inventing Our Selves: Psychology, Power, and Personhood.* Cambridge: Cambridge University Press.

Senft, T.M. and Baym, N.K. (eds.). (2015). What Does the Selfie Say? Special Section, *International Journal of Communication 9,* 1588–1606.

Stasko, E.C. and Geller, P.A. (2015). *Reframing Sexting as a Positive Relationship Behavior.* American Psychological Association Convention. Toronto, Canada

Tiggeman, M. and Zaccardo, M. (2015). "Exercise to be fit, not skinny": The effect of fitspiration imagery on women's body image. *Body Image 15,* 61–67.

Tiggemann, M. and Zaccardo, M. (2016). "Strong is the new skinny": A content analysis of #fitspiration images on Instagram. *Journal of Health Psychology 3,* 1–9.

Tiidenberg, K. (2014). Bringing sexy back: Reclaiming the body aesthetic via self-shooting. Cyberpsychology. *Journal of Psychosocial Research on Cyberspace 8(1),* article 1.

Tiidenberg, K. and Gómez-Cruz, E. (2015). Selfies, image and the re-making of the body. *Body & Society 21(4),* 77–102.

Tolman, D.L. (2012). Female adolescents, sexual empowerment and desire: A missing discourse of gender inequity. *Sex Roles 66(11–12),* 746–757.

Viladrich, A., Yeh, M.C., Bruning, N. and Weiss, R. (2009). "Do real women have curves?" Paradoxical body images among Latinas in New York City. *Journal of Immigrant Minority Health 11,* 20–28.

Warfield, K. (2014). Making Selfies/Making Self: Digital Subjectivities in the Selfie. Retrieved on 1 March 2015 from the Kwantlen Open Resource Access website: http://kora.kpu.ca/facultypub/8/.

Warfield, K., Cambre, M.C. and Abidin, C. (eds). (2016). Me-diated Inter-faces. *Social Media and Society 2(2).*

Webbly Awards (2016). 2016 Webby Award Winner KIM KARDASHIAN WEST, SPECIAL ACHIEVEMENT, Break the Internet Award. Retrieved on 23 June 2015 from the Webby Awards website: http://webbyawards.com/winners/2016/special-achievement/special-achievement/break-the-internet-award/kim-kardashian-west/.

Weiser, B.E. (2015). #Me: Narcissism and its facets as predictors of selfie-posting frequency. *Personality and Individual Differences 86,* 477–481.

8 Nothing to hide

Selfies, sex and the visibility
dilemma in trans male online
cultures

Tobias Raun and Cáel M. Keegan

Introduction

The images of two naked men (one of which is Figure 8.1),[1] their genitals covered only by pairs of women's hands, went viral in 2015. The photographs circulated side by side, but they were actually taken at different points in time: Maroon 5 singer Adam Levine posed in 2011 in *Cosmo* to raise awareness for prostate and testicular cancer, while transgender activist and video blogger Aydian Dowling posed in 2015, in order to create visibility for the trans masculine spectrum. Both are similar in pose, posture and body type with a white, slim and well-built body covered by tattoos looking directly into the camera. The female partners of Levine and Dowling, respectively, appear only as hands in the photographs, covering the men's genitals with fingers marked distinctively by shining red nail polish. In all cases, the hands not only obstruct and redirect our sight, but also draw our attention towards certain areas of the body – almost but not quite revealed.

This kind of image clearly intends to arouse the spectator's curiosity, and with it, desire. According to Ballard, who shot Dowling's image, the idea to recreate the photo of Levine was a matter of showing similarities between trans and non-trans men: "We by no means mean to say that this is what all transgender males look like, but this is what one of us looks like and it's no different from our cisgender counterparts" (Sieczkowski, 2015). What is telling about this statement is on the one hand the anticipation of critique from trans/queer communities about the body image communicated – not attainable or wanted by all trans men – and on the other hand the appeal to a mainstream, non-transgender public to acknowledge trans men as a legitimate part of the category "men". While it plays with notions of trans male bodies as lacking, the image of Dowling also evokes a set of questions: What constitutes the ultimate erotic object for a heterosexual female desiring gaze? And, probing deeper: How is maleness itself visually constructed by such desire?

This chapter takes the juxtaposed images of Dowling/Levine as its point of departure in order to address the dilemmas that trans men face in seeking to create images of themselves as male and as sexually desirable. While

Figure 8.1 Dowling in Ballard's recreation photo.

trans men must struggle to pass as "male enough" in order to be considered men by non-trans people, their success in this performance is often criticised for upholding oppressive gender norms attached to ideal masculinity. Acknowledging this paradoxical situation, we suggest that the image of Dowling offers a rare and wide exposure of a trans male body as worthy of sexualised consumption. We argue that in order to understand the gendered and sexual complexities of this image, it is necessary to contextualise it within Dowling's comprehensive selfie-practice on YouTube and Instagram. Although this image is not a selfie *per se*, it is almost impossible to separate from Dowling's exploration of his trans male self as an embodied image, as both a subject and object of representation. Hence, Dowling's selfies – as well as the image comparison with Levine – can be seen as a persistent attempt to work with and through what Jameson Green labels "the visibility dilemma for transsexual men" (Green, 2006). As trans men (through medical transition) become more recognisable as men, they simultaneously become more invisible as trans. If trans men are open about being or visible as transgender, this potentially puts them in awkward if not harmful situations in which they risk being perceived as not men. Hence, 'trans' and 'man' seem to eradicate each other.

Balancing on a knife's edge: visibility/invisibility

The portrait of Dowling confronts the fundamental problematic around visuality and the trans (male) body that Prosser (1998) points out when he mentions that transsexuality, as a condition of embodiment across time, resists portrayal in photography. Anticipating Green's observation of the "visibility dilemma", Prosser notes that photographs of transsexuality are "situated on a tension between revealing and concealing transsexuality" (Prosser, 1998, p. 209), caught in a conundrum between exposing the body as transsexual and smoothly occupying a re-sexed category. Dowling's portrait attempts to resolve this problematic: The obvious similarities in pose and body type between Levine and Dowling seek to manifest trans men unquestionably as "men". However, the body of Dowling also signifies differently than the body of Levine. While the image of Levine (like any image of a man hiding his genitals) evokes a number of questions and desires concerning the look and size of what is hidden, the image of Dowling ties into always-already preconceived notions of trans men as lacking genital surplus. Trans men are typically thought of and depicted as "deficient, castrated, as having 'not enough' genitals", assumed "to lack a genital status reserved for cisgender men alone, and can therefore never be 'real men.'" Even if genital surgery has been pursued, trans men's genitals are typically "demoni[s]ed as monstrous, 'insensate,' or 'mutilated'" (Keegan, 2016, p. 3; see also Cotton, 2012, p. 3). In other words, the hands might not be hiding something, but "nothing".

The comparison between Dowling and Levine in Ballard's photo had the predicted effect of fascinating and arousing viewers. A cut-together image of the two photos soon began circulating on Facebook, Tumblr and Instagram and was published on a number of high-profile LGBTQ websites. Responses ranged from sexual appreciation, to confusion, to curiosity about Dowling's body, to disbelief that Dowling could actually be transgender – a response anticipated by both Ballard and Dowling in their design of the image. Ballard noted this reaction in an interview: "'We've had comments saying 'he doesn't look trans' which brings up a great point on what does trans even look like?' he added. 'Perhaps we're struggling so hard for our rights here because people have a false sense of who we are. So besides the entertainment factor of a sexy naked man, there is an element of positive visibility too'" (Sieczkowski, 2015). However, not all viewers agreed that the image was a 'positive' form of representation: Some responses in queer and transgender online spaces criticised the image as reinforcing hegemonic masculinity and dominant beauty norms for trans people. For example, trans male writer Tony Zosherafatain says of the comparison image, "[w]hite, able-bodied, heterosexual trans men with toned physiques are the only ones deemed worthy of media attention. (...) Our own community re-inforces this, by concentrating on proving that our bodies are 'attractive' rather than challenging normative ideas about gender, masculinity, and beauty" (Zosherafatain, 2015). Indeed, the image and Ballard's comments about it could be accused of depicting medical transition as delivering a secure, binary gender through a triumphal journey from "self-hatred to a celebration of liberal individuality" (Keegan, 2013).

In their own virtual communities, trans men have developed a range of strategies for navigating this visibility paradox, the most noticeable of which is self-documentation through both video blogging (vlogging) and the selfie. Negative responses to these practices from within queer and transgender culture, which are often invested in a deconstructive relation to the gender binary, nonetheless simultaneously strip trans men of any resistant agency in the creation of their own images. Reactions that accuse the Dowling/ Levine portrait comparison of simply replicating oppressive gender norms tend to overlook the manner in which the image is a meta-cognitive exten-sion of Dowling's selfie practice. In an interview with *The Advocate*, Dowling himself characterised his selfie-taking as a kind of modelling in preparation for the more formal portrait, saying, "I'm not a professional model of any kind, *unless selfies count* [emphasis added], so I wasn't really sure what to expect leading up to the shot" (Ennis, 2015). A consideration of selfies and the self-modelling that this practice offers to trans men necessarily compli-cates the debate over how trans men seek to represent themselves as male, sexy and desirable.

Entrepreneurial trans self-modelling

Aydian Dowling emerged into public visibility through video blogging, which he began in 2009. Like many other trans people he has openly shared his thoughts and feelings about being trans, documenting and discussing his transition (Raun, 2016). These vlogs serve various purposes, including functioning as "self-help how-to manuals", shedding light on "what is hap-pening bodily, psychologically and socially when transitioning", while also eliciting pride in trans male identity (Raun, 2012, pp. 171, 178). In addition to vlogging, Dowling is a persistent Instagram user, uploading both pho-tographs and videos. Dowling also owns Point5cc.com, an online clothing company that e.g. sells t-shirts and hoodies with self-affirming and encour-aging statements such as "I am enough", and, "Transcend your binaries. Embrace your journey", as well as "BroTherhood" (with an enlarged T and a drawing of a needle), referring to (medically transitioning) trans men as a collective group. The company was established in 2011 in order to raise money for Dowling's chest surgery, and is now part business and part activ-ism, working to "highlight transgender commonalities and create a sense of pride" (http://point5cc.com/about-us/).

Dowling's social media presence is part of a persistent attempt to attain the status of a "micro-celebrity". Platforms like YouTube and Instagram have indeed popularised celebrity processes, encouraging people to create a "publici[s]able personality" (Marwick, 2013, p. 117), hence promising democratic access to (self-)representation while also promoting self-commodification. Within Dowling's image, the current social mediascape intersects with a neoliberal technology of subjectivity, giving rise to an entrepreneurial or "enterprising self" that advocates the use of technology for identity creation and presentation, rooted in the contemporary idea that the self is – or should be – constantly improving (Marwick, 2013, pp. 169, 192). Dowling's social media presence can thus be seen as part of a persistent self-branding, through which he deploys and maintains the image of himself "as if it were a branded good" (Senft, 2013, p. 346).

The trans male selfie

Dowling started posting images of himself on Instagram in 2014, but his popularity and visibility accelerated in 2015 when he ran for and was included in the final competitive round for the title of "Ultimate Men's Health Guy", a contest to appear on the cover of *Men's Health*. While he did not win, he became the first trans man to ever appear in the magazine: He was included on the special collector's edition cover, although only in half-figure and not alone (*Men's Health*, November 2015). In his posts to Instagram the images are 'classical' selfies, typically taken from within an arm's length and showing the visual presence of Dowling's hand/arms holding the camera, which function as deictic pointers highlighting the images' own making.

As noted by Theresa Senft and Nancy Baym, a selfie is both a photographic *object* and *practice* – a *gesture* that one can send to different individuals, communities and audiences (Senft and Baym, 2015, p. 1589). Hence, the selfie is a special "mode of presentation" that is exchanged as a form of visual communication and "a contemporary strategy of flirting and erotic play" (Lasén and García, 2015, p. 717). Dowling's selfies typically situate him in a domestic setting or at the gym. For example, this selfie (Figure 8.2) epitomises Dowling's selfie production while self-reflexively underscoring the "labor" that goes into creating and marketing himself as an attractive trans male object. Dowling faces not the spectator, but rather his own image. The photograph thus inscribes itself as a meta-self-reflection, a kind of "see me showing you me", emphasising a "self-enacting itself" and pointing to "the performance of a communication action;" the act of taking on and assuming an image (Frosh, 2015, p. 1610).

Dowling's selfie makes visible its own construction as an act and a product of mediation (a reflexive image), just as it points to Dowling himself as an object and agent of representation (a reflexive self) (Frosh, 2015, p. 1621). As the spectator is allowed full access to his naked, sculptured upper-body,

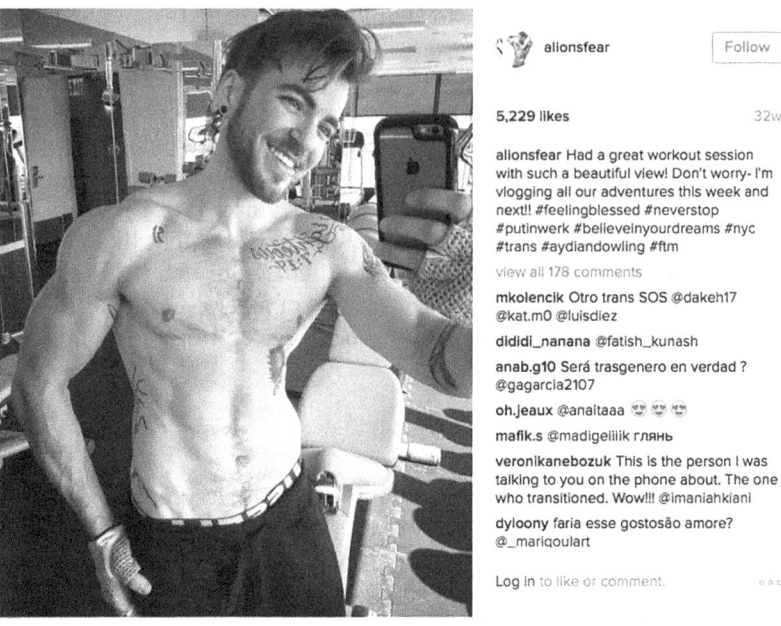

Figure 8.2 Dowling poses for his own camera in a classical selfie.

Dowling is voluntarily objecting himself to – and encouraging – the spectator's sexualised consumption. But he is also an active agent in the objectification process, self-consciously controlling what and how to represent himself, allowing a kind of 'backstage' view into the process behind becoming/assuming the status of an attractive object. Here, as well as in most of his other selfies, Dowling appears semi-naked, profiling his upper body with a clear muscle definition of chest, abdomen and arms. The built body is not the body one is born with; it is the body made possible by the application of thought and planning, just like the medically modified trans body itself (Raun, 2016, p. 69). There is, as Susan Bordo argued back in 1993, social power ascribed to the ability to control the size and shape of the body. The slender and worked-on body operates as a symbol for the emotional, moral or spiritual state of the individual: "It means that one 'cares' about oneself and how one appears to others, suggesting willpower, energy, control over infantile impulse, the ability to 'shape your life'" (Bordo, 1993, p. 195). A muscular body is one of a number of ways to produce masculinity – a way to produce male 'realness' through the bodily feeling and/or visual appearance of strength (Boucher, 2011, p. 223). A slim and muscular upper-body circulates as *the* desirable male body that most men today (trans or not) strive for or concern themselves with living up to, not least when taking selfies (e.g. Lasén and García, 2015, p. 724; Tiidenberg, 2014). In this sense, the images of Dowling discussed here point to a paradoxical form of popularly represented masculinity that can actually be difficult to incarnate or obtain for trans men, as well as for men in general.

While taking selfies is to a certain extent experienced as a stigmatised and potentially de-masculinising act by white, straight, non-trans men (Lasén and García, 2015, pp. 723–724; Williams and Marquez, 2015, p. 1780), more *subordinate masculinities* (black and latino men, and white trans men like Dowling) tend to see selfies as way to "express their style of masculinity as a positive sense of self-importance", acting as a barrier to ongoing discrimination and potentially making them feel empowered and attractive (Williams and Marquez, 2015, p. 1782; see also Connell, 2005 [1993]; Connell and Messerschmidt, 2005). However, the genre of the selfie is often pigeonholed as evidence of low self-esteem and/or self-absorption – the ultimate expression of a contemporary narcissistic culture – and less often as an expression of empowerment (Senft and Baym, 2015, pp. 1588–1592). To return to the concept of a "visibility paradox", on the one hand Dowling's images (his selfies as well as the Dowling/Levine photo) are inscribed in a neoliberal self-commodification and "attention economy" (Senft, 2013, p. 350) where success is based on web traffic – on one's "spreadability" (Jenkins *et al.,* 2013, p. 5). On the other hand, these images clearly instantiate a personal sense of empowerment while also carrying an important political weight that compensates for stigmatisation and counteracts the absence of trans male representation in mainstream culture. Hence, the visual representation of Dowling's body is a strong 'voice' in and of itself.

Renegotiating gender and desire

Attention to the agential aspects of selfie practice in trans male subcultures can aid in establishing a more cohesive discussion of how trans men negotiate the sexualised image economy from within "multiple, apparently indiscriminate, erasures" (Hale, 2009, p. 46). Returning to Ballard's portrait of Dowling, we might read how the photo replicates the selfie's meta-aware qualities by inscribing him in a circuit of gender and desire that is self-consciously designed to make the trans male body cognisable as an ideal sexual object. The image, like Levine's, is an intentional negotiation with the history of erotic male portraiture, which Abigail Solomon-Godeau argues is generally divided either into muscular, virile heroes or graceful, lissom youths (Solomon-Godeau, 1997, p. 62). Although these representations occasionally include the flaccid male penis, the symbolic labour of evoking the phallus was – and is – usually performed otherwise, leaving phallic power just as, or all the more, potent (Still, 2003, pp. 7, 2–3). These conventions inadvertently permit Dowling's entry into the symbolic register of the photograph as not needing to 'prove' maleness through the display of a penis. His body is positioned intentionally to draw favourable comparisons between his exceptionally masculine physique and Levine's. He looks into the camera confidently, his eyes communicating a sexual availability and an awareness that he has permitted himself to be put on display, inscribing himself in a "complex gaze game" with self and others (Lasén and García, 2015, p. 718). Dowling's knowing stare claims his position as sexually desirable and dares the audience to deny his maleness.

Revisiting the Dowling/Levine comparison, we might imagine a range of reactions to and interpretations of these two images: A paranoid[2] reading would assert that, in positioning Dowling as comparable to Levine, Ballard's photo merely reflects and therefore reproduces the logic of dominant, white, able-bodied, non-trans masculinity and its ideological force. In this reading, Dowling's masculinity is the 'wrong kind of trans' in that it does not overtly deny non-trans masculinity as an erotic ideal. From this perspective, the touching of Levine's image by Dowling's has the effect of infecting Dowling's image with an over-determining heteropatriarchal message, which crystallises across the photo and transfers virally out from it to contaminate the audience. This critique echoes the familiar accusations historically asserted by both medical professionals and radical feminists (Lothstein, 1983; Raymond, 1979) that transsexuals are fundamentally deluded by and fetishize the gender binary, rather than realising that gender is socially constructed and abandoning it. This reading of the images, while familiar, offers no position from which Dowling might assert anything but a totally colonised participation in his own and others' oppression: His image becomes a pure extension of patriarchal domination. Under such an interpretation, trans men who seek self-representation as ideally, desirable can only ever reiterate a toxic logic of dominant masculinity.

In contrast, a reparative reading would consider Dowling's image here in additional contexts that acknowledge his agential relationship to the glaring lack of documented trans male histories and images. Ballard's portrait of Dowling must be considered a formalised extension of Dowling's own selfie production, a subcultural praxis through which trans men engage in an "empowering exhibitionism", exploring their "embodied identity as sexual being(s)" (Tiidenberg, 2014) to the (here, female) gaze. In both portraits, the strategic placing of the women's hands has the effect of both blocking the sight of the men's genitals, but also of *producing the phallus* as an absence, endowing the photos with an equally shared sexual charge. These hands, which cup what is not seen, also generate the images' heterosexual register. What makes each man desirable is the cupping – perhaps even eager touching – of his genitalia by these hands, which signals a desiring audience of women for his masculinity. Reading the images together, the hands create the effect that *what is behind them does not matter*: So long as the hands appear desiring, then what they desire must be male. What makes a man ideally, (heterosexually) desirable? That women want him. The hands, then, become each man's prosthetic genitals and a sign of his maleness and his phallic energy. Ballard's reinterpretation of Levine's portrait draws our attention to a circuit of substitutions in the original image (hand/penis/man/male/phallus) that are loose enough to accommodate a trans male body, but that only become obvious when Dowling's body becomes proximal to Levine's.

The photo of Dowling therefore works on a number of reparative levels – by providing Dowling with an aesthetic economy in which he can appear as something more than a "still a woman" (Hale, 2009, p. 45) and/or castrated, but also by 'touching' the other photo in a manner that deconstructs Levine's ownership of hegemonic masculinity. The photo comparison consequently "arous(es) the dreadful" (Cromwell, 1999, p. 115) suspicion that whatever hides behind either set of obscuring hands will ultimately fail to meet expectations. While both his and Levine's bodies appear phallic, neither can ultimately possess the phallus. In response to this admission of lack – disguised in Levine's photo, yet drawn out in and by Dowling's – the muscular upper-body is "installed as a displaced phallus and invested with sexual potency and desire" (Raun, 2016, p. 69). Thus, the photo of Dowling suggests a critical flexion, rather than a simple emulation of, dominant ideals of masculine beauty. It is this visual rhetoric that allows Ballard to assert an equivalence between Dowling's masculinity and Levine's as equally the product of fantasy, and therefore equally paradoxical as simultaneously 'real' and 'not real'.

Exit: the dilemma of having nothing to hide

Ballard's portrait of Dowling thus demands we recognise how a cloaked visibility dilemma haunts all representations of ideal masculinity, not only those of trans men. The photo reveals how the presence of a transgender body in or even next to a non-trans image might have the effect not of 'appearing', but rather of *disappearing the non-trans ideal itself*. Rather than merely claiming 'positive visibility' for trans male bodies, as Ballard claims the photo is intended to do, his portrait of Dowling carries an accompanying deconstructive effect when placed next to Levine's. The comparison between Dowling's and Levine's bodies illustrates how the non-trans ideal is a non-existent, imaginary form that must always fail in reality. As hegemonic or normative versions of masculinity might always already be "phantasmatic sites, impossible sites", and hence "alternately compelling and disappointing" (Butler, 1993, p. 188). Figure 8.1 marks and makes readable the manner in which all ideal male bodies 'pass' through a constructed visual economy that preserves their phallic potential – a pattern of self-representation mastered by many trans men who engage in selfie culture. Dowling does not 'pass' as non-transgender (this would spoil the point of the image), but rather, both he and Levine successfully 'pass' as ideally desirable male objects. Like Dowling's selfies, Ballard's portrait of Dowling illustrates how all-ideal masculinity, not merely trans masculinity, creates desire through a visibility paradox in which what is indicated (the phallus) must always be missing. This 'gap' in all images of ideal masculinity, where an unspoken lack becomes the very source of erotic longing, offers trans men an ironic representational interstice from where to become recognised as fully sexually embodied. From this un-acknowledged space in the image, trans men emerge into desirability by 'hiding nothing', baring themselves to the camera even as they sustain the alluring absence at the heart of visual desire.

Note

1 The second figure can not be displayed for copyright reasons.
2 Sedgwick distinguishes between paranoid and reparative reading strategies. According to Sedgwick, queer studies have a particular distinctive history of and intimate relationship with the paranoid imperative (Sedgwick, 2003, p. 126). Although Sedgwick acknowledges the importance of paranoid exigencies and makes the claim that they are often necessary for non-paranoid knowing and utterance, she also points out that they foreclose other ways of knowing, less oriented toward suspicion. As she argues, to produce other kinds of knowledge than paranoid readings does not in itself entail "a denial of the reality or gravity of enmity or oppression" (Sedgwick, 2003, p. 128).

References

Bordo, S. (1993). *Unbearable Weight: Feminism, Western Culture, and the Body.* Oakland: University of California Press.

Boucher, M. (2011). "'Do You Have What It Takes to Be a Real Man?': Female-to-Male Transgender Embodiment and the Politics of the 'Real' in A Boy Named Sue and Body Alchemy." In Shaw, M. E. and Watson, E. (eds.). *Performing American Masculinities: The21st-Century Man in Popular Culture* (pp. 192–232). Bloomington: Indiana University Press.

Butler, J. (1993). *Bodies that Matter. On the Discursive Limits of "Sex."* New York: Routledge.

Connell, R. W. (2005). *Masculinities.* Berkeley: University of California Press.

Connell, R. W. and Messerschmidt, J. W. (2005). Hegemonic Masculinity. Rethinking the Concept. *Gender & Society 19(6),* 829–859.

Cotten, T. T. (2012). "The Jury's Still Out: Rethinking the Verdict on Female-to-Male Genital Surgery." In Cotton, T.T. (ed.). *Hung Jury: Testimonies of Genital Surgery by Transsexual Men* (pp. 1–11). Oakland: Transgress Press.

Cromwell, J. (1999). *Transmen and FTMs: Identities, Bodies, Genders, and Sexualities.* Chicago: University of Illinois Press.

Ennis, D. (March 2015). "The Naked Truth About Trans Man's Re-Creation of Adam Levine Photo." *The Advocate.* Retrieved on 8 May 2016 from the Advocate website: www.advocate.com/politics/media/2015/03/02/naked-truth-about-trans-mans-re-creation-adam-levine-photo.

Frosh, P. (2015). The Gestural Image: The Selfie, Photography Theory, and Kinesthetic Sociability. *International Journal of Communication 9*, 1607–1628.

Green, J. (2006). "Look! No, Don't! The Visibility Dilemma for Transsexual Men." In Stryker, S. and Whittle, S. (eds.). *The Transgender Studies Reader* (pp. 499–508). New York: Routledge Press.

Hale, C. J. (2009). "Tracing a Ghostly Memory in My Throat: Reflections on FTM Feminist Voice and Agency." In Schrage, L. J. (ed.). *You've Changed: Sex Reassignment and Personal Identity* (pp. 43–65). New York: Oxford University Press.

Jenkins, H., Ford, S. and Green, J. (2013). *Spreadable Media: Creating Value and Meaning in a Networked Culture*. New York: New York University Press.

Keegan, C. M. (2013). Moving Bodies: Sympathetic Migrations in Transgender Narrativity. *Genders 57,* 1–29.

Keegan, C. M. (2016). "Junk Politics: The Visual Economy of Trans Male Genitalia." In Cotton, T.T. (ed.). *Below the Belt: Genital Talk by Men of Trans Experience* (pp. 7–18). Oakland: Transgress Press.

Lasén, A. and García, A. (2015). '… but I haven't got a body to show': Self-pornification and Male Mixed Feelings in Digitally Mediated Seduction Practices. *Sexualities 18(5–6),* 714–730.

Lothstein, L. (1983). *Female-to-Male Transsexualism: Historical, Clinical, and Theoretical Issues*. Boston: Routledge Press and Kegan Paul.

Marwick, A. E. (2013). *Status Updates. Celebrity, Publicity & Branding in the Social Media Age*. New Haven and London: Yale University Press.

Men's Health (November 2015). Special Collector's Edition, The Reader Issue. Emmaus: Rodale Inc.

Prosser, J. (1998). *Second Skins: The Body Narratives of Transsexuality*. New York: Columbia University Press.

Raun, T. (2012) "DIY Therapy: Exploring Affective Self-Representations in Trans Video Blogs on YouTube." In Karatzogianni A. and Kuntsman A. (eds.). *Digital Cultures and the Politics of Emotion: Feelings, Affect and Technological Change* (pp. 165–180). Basingstoke and New York: Palgrave Macmillan.

Raun, T. (2016). *Out Online: Trans Self-Representation and Community Building on YouTube*. London and New York: Routledge.

Raymond, J. (1979). *The Transsexual Empire: The Making of the She-Male*. Boston: Beacon Press.

Sedgwick, E. K. (2003). "Paranoid Reading and Reparative Reading, or You're So Paranoid, You Probably Think This Essay Is about You." In Sedgwick, E.K. (ed.). *Touching Feeling: Affect, Pedagogy, Performativity* (pp. 123–152). Durham: Duke University Press.

Senft, T. (2013). "Microcelebrity and the Branded Self." In Hartley J., Burgess, J. and Bruns, A. (eds.). *A Companion to New Media Dynamics* (pp. 346–354). Blackwell Publishing.

Senft, T. and Baym, N. (2015). What Does the Selfie Say? Investigating a Global Phenomenon Introduction. *International Journal of Communication 9*, 1588–1606.

Sieczkowski, C. (20 February 2015). "Transgender Model Has A Powerful Reason For Recreating Racy Adam Levine Nude Portrait." *The Huffington Post*. Retrieved on 8 May 2016 from the website of the Huffington Post: www.huffingtonpost.com/2015/02/20/transgender-model-adam-levine-nude_n_6717064.html.

Solomon-Godeau, A. (1997). *Male Trouble: A Crisis in Representation*. London: Thames and Hudson.

Still, J. (2003). (Re)presenting Masculinities: Introduction to 'Men's Bodies'. *Paragraph. A Journal of Modern Critical Theory 26(1/2)*, 1–14.

Tiidenberg, K. (2014). Bringing Sexy Back: Reclaiming the Body Aesthetic Via Self-shooting. *Cyberpsychology: Journal of Psychosocial Research on Cyberspace 8(1)*, 3.

Williams, A.A., and Marquez, B.A. (2015). The Lonely Selfie King: Selfies and the Conspicuous Presumption of Gender and Race. *International Journal of Communication 9*, 1775–1787.

Zosherafatain, A. (28 February 2015) "Community Voices: Panel Continues the Conversation on Race and Racism in the Trans Community." *Dapper Q*. Retrieved on 8 May 2016 from the Dapper Q website: www.dapperq.com/2015/02/community-voices-panel-continues-the-conversation-about-race-and-racism-in-the-trans-community/.

9   Supporting one another

Nonbinary community building on Tumblr

Abigail Oakley

Introduction

Although the word "community" is difficult to define, it is one of the more important factors in our lives as we strive for connections with others. Communities often provide a safe place where we can go to be with others that share our interests and identity markers. In this chapter, I present a case study analysis of one nonbinary Tumblr blogger. This blogger, whom I will call 'Daniel', is an early-twenty-something nonbinary transman who manages a personal Tumblr blog. Though Daniel's blog theme is simplistic, with a white background and sans-serif font, he interacts regularly with his followers by blogging responses to questions they submit. Answering 'asks' like this is one common way that Tumblr bloggers interact with their followers, so it is in the act of publicly answering these asks that I examine community building practices. I build upon existing literature about online communities and counterpublics, noting the differences between the two and how the theorisation of counterpublics may positively influence our understanding of online communities. I then discuss the community-building practices shown by both Daniel and his followers, with a focus on interpersonal relationships, shared resources and support. Through a strategy of openness about his personal life, Daniel builds *ethos* and connects with other community members who express both commonality and desire for connection in the questions and comments they submit.

Tumblr asks

In this case study, I focus on Tumblr's 'ask' feature as an indication of community communication. The ask feature is similar to an inbox where readers may submit character-limited questions or comments to bloggers. The ask feature may be turned on or off at any time a blogger wishes. Bloggers also have the opportunity to allow or disallow anonymous asks. Generally, nonbinary bloggers keep anonymous asks on to allow readers to ask questions about gender and sexuality without it being linked to their Tumblr username or their real life friends and family – something that often leads to self-censorship (de Laat, 2008; Tiidenberg, 2013). It is also optional to publish asks to one's blog. Bloggers often refer to the people who submit anonymous asks as 'anons'.

Methods

In my initial data collection, I collected blogs of users over the age of 18 who self-identified as nonbinary either in relation to their gender or their sexuality utilising ten community-defined hashtags to locate the blogs. I excluded from the search results posts that contained #lovewins or #love wins because there were many heterosexuals using those tags in celebration of the *Obergefell v Hodges* (2015) court ruling as well as blogs run by minors, blogs run by groups of people, duplicates and porn blogs (though I did not exclude blogs with occasional sexually explicit content). The initial data set was collected in June and July of 2015. The first 20 blogs under each search term – #gay, #girlswholikegirls, #bi, #ace, #queer, #lgbtq, #nonbinary, #gender fluid, #genderqueer and #trans – that did not meet the exclusionary criteria were collected. During the first round of analysis I found that an additional 14 blogs met the exclusionary criteria making the data set 186 blogs. It is from this initial data set that I selected the blog for the case study in this chapter. In order to examine community-building practices, I needed to be able to see an indication of the blogger wanting to connect to others on Tumblr. Within my initial data set, the most apparent mode of communication was answers to submitted asks. Out of the initial 186 blogs, 18 (9.7%) of them linked either a Frequently Asked Question (FAQ) or answers to asks on their blogs.

Following Robert K. Yin's (2014) parameters for conducting case study research, I designed this project as an embedded single case study of an extreme case. I chose a blog from the initial sample that represents an extreme case regarding the volume of answered asks; Daniel has not only linked his answered asks but does so prolifically. This case study examines 90 answered asks for elements of community communication (as outlined in Table 9.1). In April of 2016, I collected FAQs and up to ten pages of answered asks (multiple posts per page, exact number per page depending on the blog theme). Only ten of these 18 blogs were still active under their original usernames from the initial sample at that time. Of these ten blogs, I excluded blogs where the blogger talked openly about any mental illness they had such as anxiety or depression to maintain protection of that special group. Daniel's blog was chosen from the remaining seven blogs. This single case study does limit the generalisability of this study, but it also allows me to closely examine community-building practices of nonbinary Tumblr bloggers who actively engage with their audiences. This in turn may provide insight for examining community-building practices in other online communities.

For the brief quotations included in this chapter, I have used ethical fabrication as suggested by Annette Markham (2012) and done by Katrin Tiidenberg (2014) in her study of not safe for work (NSFW) Tumblr blogs. This was done to help protect the identity of the individual included in this case study. Specifically, I have altered any quotations that may be entered into a search engine to find the blog in this case study. In these instances, I altered the specific wording of the quotations to remain true to the sentiment of the blogger, but eliminate the possibility that these quotations would lead anyone back to his blog. Although in rhetorical analysis wording is often important, since these quotations remain true to the sentiment, for which this data was coded, this does not adversely impact the analysis here.

Communities and counterpublics

The word *community* is a loaded term with a wide body of scholarship across several fields that interrogate its definition, how it works and what it means to the individuals in the community. The complexity of community has not escaped Internet scholars, and the idea of community has easily coupled with research of new media e.g. Rheingold's (1993) *The Virtual Community*. There is also reluctance on the part of scholars to give a single definition of *community*. Instead, most scholars provide lists of *aspects* of community, sometimes referenced as qualities (Baym, 2015), themes (Parks, 2011), elements (Willson, 2006) or dynamics (Renninger, 2015). Things also become more complicated when we consider online publics, or, as danah boyd (2011) names them, networked publics. Considering publics, as boyd (2011) and Bryce J. Renninger (2015) do, is valuable in examining communities in online spaces primarily because of the significant impact of platform affordances on platform usage. Renninger (2015) builds upon boyd's (2011) four affordances of networked publics – (1) *persistence*, how information lingers in online spaces; (2) *replicability*, how information is easily reproduced; (3) *scalability*, the potential for large audiences; and (4) *searchability*, the ability to easily find information through search (p. 46) – to construct Tumblr as a place that not only allows for but encourages counterpublic communication. He makes this clear through his additional six dynamics that "can be used to understand why Tumblr has become such a prominent venue for counterpublic communication" (Renninger, 2015, p. 11). However, in his examination of Tumblr as a networked counterpublic and the asexual community's use of it, Renninger (2015) does not make a distinction between the terms 'community' and 'counterpublic'.

Publics/counterpublics and communities do have some differences. The key point of difference between publics/counterpublics and communities is that communities must be aware of their status as a community (Parks, 2011), but publics/counterpublics need not be aware of their status as a public or counterpublic (Warner, 2002). Thus while communities are often publics/counterpublics, publics/counterpublics are *not* always communities. Although Andre Cavalcante (2016) describes counterpublics in the same way that one might describe a community – "[i]n offering platforms for interpersonal association, publics can create new worlds, social relations, and forms of citizenship and belonging that exist outside of the state and family" (pp. 117–118) – boyd (2011) and Renninger (2015) focus on public/counterpublic space and Michael Warner (2002) on the discourse. By Cavalcante's (2016) account, counterpublics and communities are not so different. However, counterpublics are formed in specific response to and subordination of dominant publics whereas communities have no such stipulation; it is then in the 'counter' where we see another difference. Communities may be formed by those with or without social, economic and power privileges, whereas counterpublics are more specifically composed of those without one or more of those privileges.

In teasing out these subtle differences between publics/counterpublics and community, they are shown as two separate but related phenomena that cannot and should not be collapsed, conflated or used interchangeably. Far from being kept separate, though, the theorisation of networked publics can be fruitfully integrated into considerations of online communities. The four affordances that boyd (2011) lays out describe the *space* that makes it possible for publics, counterpublics and communities to form; boyd (2011) and subsequently Renninger (2015) effectively describe the *networked* portion of networked publics. Their definitions of networked publics/counterpublics are absolutely necessary in considering how, like physical space, the architecture of online space affects the publics, counterpublics and communities therein. It is therefore necessary to blend the consideration of online space into how we think about online communities. Space or location is traditionally considered an important factor of real-world communities (Parks, 2011; Willson, 2006), but that significance is not always included as an influencer of online communities; of the scholars mentioned here, Baym (2015) is the only one who acknowledges the impact of space in online community.

Aspects of online communities

Since Baym (2015), Parks (2011), Renninger (2015) and Willson (2006) all theorise online communities in different ways, I have compiled these to create a list of defining aspects of online communities. Though, like these scholars, I do not seek a single definition, I also see community as defined through its aspects, therefore this list provides an abstract definition of what constitutes an online community. Mapping the lists of aspects each author gave allowed me to see overlap and discrepancies between them and create a composite list of aspects that form the basis of online community. In making this list, I have borrowed terminology primarily from Baym (2015) and Willson (2006), though the description of each has been modified. Table 9.1 outlines the six

Table 9.1 Aspects of online communities

Aspects of online communities	
Support and Shared resources	Emotional, esteem (confidence/self-esteem) and informational support (Baym, 2015); bonding and reciprocity between members (Willson, 2006); one-to-many connections (e.g. giving advice); Social capital (Baym, 2015), the ability to be politically motivated (Baym, 2015; Parks, 2011), any kind of material support such as monetary or other gift-giving (Baym, 2015)
Commonality	Community members share something in common relating to their interests or identity (Willson, 2006). There is a connection between members (Parks, 2011).
Shared norms	The community has agreed upon (explicit or implicit) norms (Baym, 2015), rituals (Parks, 2011) and patterned interactions (Parks, 2011).
Shared identity	There are sometimes distinct roles in the community that members take on (Baym, 2015). The community is aware of its status of community (Parks, 2011). Identity markers may or may not be the basis for constitution of the community.
Interpersonal relationships	One-on-one relationships that help to sustain the community (Baym, 2015), contacting and reaching out to others within the community, not just the community as a whole (Parks, 2011); one-on-one connections with others (Parks, 2011). This does not necessitate offline relationships (Renninger, 2015).
Space	A shared space that is the hub of a community (Baym, 2015; Renninger, 2015).

aspects of community that guide my interpretation in this study: Support and Shared Resources (Baym, 2015), Commonality (Willson, 2006), Shared Norms, Shared Identity (Baym, 2015), Interpersonal Relationships (Baym, 2015) and Space (Baym, 2015).

These aspects indicate what constitutes a community. It follows, then, that community-building practices work toward strengthening or forming these aspects. I have found that the most common aspects observed as *community-building* practices are support and shared resources, commonality and interpersonal relationships. Shared identity and shared norms mark a community, but they are something to be worked toward rather than something that plainly shows in community-building discourse. While Daniel and his anonymous askers exhibit shared norms of Tumblr (including communicating through asks and using common Tumblr jargon), there are few indications of shared norms from the nonbinary community in these posts.

Tumblr and queer online communities

The Internet has had incredible impact on the ability of people both from around the world and locally to organise themselves, and the ability to find and confide in others online has significantly impacted queer culture by allowing queer individuals to connect with others like them. The Internet has affected queer rural youth to help develop their identities and their 'queer realness' (Gray, 2009), lesbian mothers struggling against heteronormativity (Hunter, 2015), transgender activists after being abandoned by the medical community (Shapiro, 2004) and the asexual community who have gained both support and positive exposure due to their online home base, Asexual Visibility and Education Network (AVEN) (Renninger, 2015). Critically, the Internet allows "activists to provide their own framing and to challenge medical and social understanding of gender nonconformity" (Shapiro, 2004, p. 170). The aspects of community outlined in Table 9.1 show, generally, the aspects that define an online community. While not all communities are identity-based, many of the communities on Tumblr are. The communal aspects of those within the LGBTQIA community are heavily identity-based, though those are not the only commonalities within the community; after all, "[e]veryone may have sexuality, but not everyone defines their identity around their sexuality" (Cameron and Kulick, 2003, p. 8).

In this case study, there were a total of 90 asks (88 anonymous) for Daniel. Only eleven of those asks included discussion of gender or sexual orientation, whereas another 26 were general inquiries about Daniel and his interests including videogames and television shows. These exchanges, made public, illustrate how community building is directly affected by platform affordances; Tumblr's most prominent form of direct communication between blogger and audience is the ask feature as commenting is only available on certain posts and Tumblr has no in-house chat feature (though there is also a way to send private messages if the blogger has enabled it). By allowing anonymous asks, bloggers encourage the audience to ask questions they may not otherwise. Questions about gender, sexual orientation and sexuality become easier to ask and move forward a dialogue about nonbinary genders, sexual orientations and sexualities that is productive both in disturbing hegemonic gender and sexuality discourse as well as signalling commonality to other nonbinary persons.

Tumblr's tagging system, which makes posts on Tumblr searchable, is also an indication of how affordances/space shapes community discourse. In my initial data collection, every blog was found because the blogger used a tag that indicated a nonbinary gender or sexuality. Those tags then function both as a form of identity construction *and* community discourse by making posts searchable under common terms and, often, expressing a blogger's gender or sexuality. More specifically for the transgender community, tagging on Tumblr can function as an ontological practice that helps to locate "transgender [...] within a wider [...] identity development framework" which in turn "provides internal stability, opens up avenues of support, and makes possible access to necessary medical care if desired" (Dame, 2016, p. 24). The network of trans tags such as #ftm and #trans has affected "the so-called 'transgender community'", bringing them "together by their shared practices and identities" (Dame, 2016, p. 25). In this way, tagging helps to bring nonbinary individuals, or those interested in learning about nonbinary individuals to blogs that are usually, at a minimum, nonbinary friendly.

While there are many similarities across differently identifying LGBT-QIA bloggers, there are also distinct differences between different parts of the community. For example, individuals who identify as queer, asexual and pansexual are more likely than those who identify as bisexual, gay and lesbian to label their gender and preferred pronouns somewhere on their blogs (Oakley, 2016). I have also noticed, more informally, that individuals identifying as trans, queer, genderfluid, genderqueer, nonbinary and agender tend to be more forthcoming about their knowledge of nonbinary genders, what life is like as a nonbinary person, and with those who are transitioning. Although for Daniel his transition is not the focus of his blog, he does answer specific questions about whether he is taking testosterone (he is not), and if/how he binds his upper body (binding is uncomfortable, so he prefers to pass as female more often than not). While his transition is not the focus of his blog, as with some other transgender blogs, it is a part of his life he is willing to talk openly about on Tumblr. On his blog, there is a link where readers may donate money to help fund his top surgery to create a more masculine-looking torso.

In the exchange between answers and asks on Daniel's blog, his answers are not the only sites of community building. Askers take steps toward a personal relationship with Daniel by at times requesting contact outside of Tumblr and/or Tumblr's ask system, but also by asking general get-to-know-you questions, responding to Daniel's requests for asks, expressing sexual desire for Daniel and providing and asking about personal information. But one thing that happens more often in asks than in Daniel's answers is that users express some kind of solidarity with the blogger. One asker simply states "I'm here, fellow transman", while others include more casual references to their experiences as nonbinary persons. For example, one anon asks how Daniel can 'stand' to learn biology as a trans person, because it is something they cannot imagine doing. Daniel responds:

[T]hat's a good question. it's very complicated [...]. human biology is very scientific and [...] can overlook the fact that transgender and nonbinary ppl exist. [...] for me i think understanding biology has actually helped me to see how blurred the line bt male and female really is in nature.

(Daniel's Blog, 2016)

In this particular example, the asker signals commonality by implying that, as a nonbinary person, it is difficult for them to learn about biology. One reason for this may be that the inclusion commonality may make it more likely that Daniel will respond and/or post an ask on his blog because of that sense of commonality or connection.

Askers not only expressed commonality but also showed support for Daniel. Askers offered monetary support (offering to purchase sex toys for Daniel and contributing to his top surgery fund), but there is also emotional support in the form of praise and the expressions of desire which fall under esteem support that Baym (2015) mentions. More specifically, the anonymous asks complementing Daniel on his appearance (16 in total) may have a similar effect to McKenna and Bargh's (1998) study on Usenet groups for homosexuals that when self-disclosure is performed – in this case Daniel's public status as transmasculine – and confirmed – by positive *anon* interaction – there is a positive change to that person's self-esteem. Since the overwhelming majority of Daniel's posted asks are anonymous, Daniel himself does very little reciprocal praise, but instead expresses gratitude in varying degrees of seriousness that usually matches the degree of seriousness in the ask. For example one exchange reads:

> **Anonymous asked: *"you! got! a! nice! face!"***
> *"thanks! anon!:)!"*
>
> (Daniel's Blog, 2016)

However, some are slightly more serious:

> **Anonymous asked: *"You're one seriously handsome guy"***
> *"omg thank u so much that's really sweet:)))))".*
>
> (Daniel's Blog, 2015)

But both illustrate esteem support on the part of the asker with emotional gratification for the asker in the form of Daniel's gratitude for the compliment.

Digital ethos and community

Daniel's blog was chosen for this case study due to his, by comparison, prolific amount of answered asks linked on his blog. Daniel's asks include a good bit of discussion regarding nonbinary genders. In one interaction, an anon asked: "does nonbinary mean that you don't identify as any gender? I'm just not sure and I want to educate myself" (Daniel's Blog, 2015). In his response, Daniel enacts informational support, noting that his response is for "anyone who doesn't know" about nonbinary genders:

[...] Nonbinary is an umbrella term for anyone who doesn't really identify as just a man or just a woman. So it sometimes means you identify with more than just one gender but that's not the only definition.
You can be genderfluid, agender, neutrosis, bigender, etc there's a whole
bunch of things.

(Daniel's Blog, 2015)

Continuing in that vein, Daniel goes on to share his personal experience:
"For me, I'm nonbinary bc I feel more masculine than feminine even though
I was designated female at birth but I also don't feel quite like a man. So I'm
somewhere between" (Daniel's Blog, 2015). This interaction again shows indication of shared resources: one community member is struggling with the
definition of nonbinary and Daniel is able to help with his knowledge and
lived experience of being nonbinary. However, one might also wonder how
this *anon* knew to ask Daniel and that he would have a reasonably sound
answer. While the simple answer is that Daniel indicates on his main blog
page that he is nonbinary transmasculine, the actual answer is more complicated than that. Arguably, through a combination of using nonbinary tags,
identifying as nonbinary in his bio on his main page and having a history of
being responsive to asks have all contributed to Daniel's *ethos* as a source of
information about nonbinary genders and, more specifically, the transmasculine experience. While I am unable to speculate, from this data, exactly
how Daniel's blog became a hub of community action, it is still possible to
examine influencing factors.

Aristotle argues that if speakers show they have good sense, good moral
character and goodwill, they have good *ethos* and are more persuasive to
their audiences. Aristotle notes a speaker's *ethos* makes them "worthy of
credence" and is directly tied to the speaker's virtue and how that speaker
enacts that virtue (Fleckenstein, 2007). While this Aristotelian definition
provides important context for *ethos*, I am instead focusing on modern con-
ceptions of *ethos,* which consider not necessarily the *virtue* of the author,
but rather their credibility and trustworthiness. Kristie Fleckenstein (2007)
in her article on *ethos* and digital poetry argues that "what *ethos* exposes
is that participation need not require a user's textual contributions", and
that boundaries between speaker and participant become blurred. Sonia
Livingstone (2005) notes that even traditional media audiences are "often
participatory seekers after meaning, not always accepting but sometimes
negotiating or even resisting textual meanings" (p. 30). Likewise, other feminist teachers and scholars work to position audiences (in the form of readers or students) as *knowers* rather than positioning the speaker as the sole
knower (see bell hooks' (1994) foundational text: *Teaching to Transgress*).
Taking this into consideration, I argue that *ethos* is constructed differently
online where *ethos* is participatory and often authors are actively engaging
with their audiences – such as in answers to asks on a Tumblr blog. Online,
we engage both synchronously and asynchronously as well as through text,

image, video and gif. Consequently, with a change in the way people interact with one another, *ethos*, then, evolves, becoming a hybrid of what we have known it to be in the past and something that has adapted to new modes of communication.

Not only does *ethos* work differently in online spaces, its function as it relates to gender and sexuality is also different than in other online situations. When movements such as feminism are rooted in activism, it is difficult for the slow and (at times) cumbersome process of academic publishing to catch up with the fast-paced evolution of societal views on things like gender and sexuality. This is especially true when considering individuals who identify outside of the male/female and heterosexual hegemonic binaries (Shapiro, 2004). In these cases, individuals turn to communities rather than academic texts in order to find a place of acceptance, of people who are 'like me'. However, in the face of these differences, it can be difficult to construct a believable *ethos*, though a significant influencing factor is how one imagines their audience. In a socially mediated world, it can be difficult to know if intended and actual audience will match up and it is entirely likely that actual audience will differ a great deal from an author's intended audience (Brake, 2012; Marwick and boyd, 2010; Tufekci, 2007). With the inability to know one's audience, constructing a reliable *ethos* can be quite difficult.

One of the strongest contributing factors to Tumblr blogger *ethos* is openness. More specifically, nonbinary bloggers implement identity-constructing moves such as self-labelling of nonbinary gender and sexuality as part of establishing their credibility or trustworthiness. These identity-constructing moves include nonbinary bloggers self-labelling their gender and sexual orientation on the main page of their blogs, but also in FAQs, answered asks and About Me pages. To be clear, it does not follow that this *ethos*-building tactic happens on every blog created by nonbinary persons. Rather, it is a tactic of those who seek to either educate their audience about nonbinary genders and sexualities or those who seek to build a community by sharing knowledge resources and support in an effort to connect with similar persons. In that particular sense, openness is both an indicator of community building *and* an ethos building strategy. Nonbinary bloggers show openness not only through the public labelling of their gender and sexual orientation on their blogs in their bios, blog posts and post tags (Oakley, 2016), but also through responses to asks on their blog. In the answer to the ask at the beginning of this section, Daniel exhibits elements of shared resources, commonality and shared identity, but he also shows his willingness to be open about his own personal experiences. Further, what his willingness to talk openly about a range of topics – from gender to video games – does, is create an environment of openness on his blog, indicating Daniel's receptiveness and willingness to answer, post and track almost any type of ask.

Conclusion

Here I have shown the ways in which platform affordances shape the discourse of communities on that platform. Through answered asks on Tumblr, one of the most prominent forms of communication on the platform, Daniel both performs and receives community-building practices. *Anons* signal commonality and support Daniel both monetarily and through bolstering his self-esteem. In turn, Daniel provides emotional support through gratitude as well as sharing his informational resources, and, in order to be seen as a trustworthy source of information about nonbinary genders and sexualities, Daniel structures his *ethos* through strategies of openness about his life, his interests and his experiences as a nonbinary person. Openness as a strategy for both *ethos* and community building may help us to better understand the function of both in an online environment.

References

Baym, N. K. (2015). *Personal connections in the digital age* (2nd ed.). Malden: Polity Press.

boyd, danah. (2011). Social network sites as networked publics: Affordances, dynamics, and implications. In Papacharissi, Z. (ed.), *Networked self: Identity, community, and culture on social network sites* (pp. 39–58). New York: Routledge.

Brake, D. R. (2012). Who do they think they're talking to? Framings of the audience by social media users. *International Journal of Communication 6*, 1056–1076.

Cameron, D., & Kulick, D. (2003). *Language and sexuality.* Cambridge: Cambridge University Press.

Cavalcante, A. (2016). "I did it all online:" Transgender identity and the management of everyday life. *Critical Studies in Media Communication 33*(1), 109–122.

Dame, A. (2016). Making a name for yourself: Tagging as transgender ontological practice on Tumblr. *Critical Studies in Media Communication 33*(1), 23–37.

De Laat, P. B. (2008). Online diaries: Reflections on trust, privacy, and exhibitionism. *Ethics and Information Technology 10*(1), 57–69.

Daniel's Blog (2016). Tumblr *(case study – anonymous source).*

Fleckenstein, K. S. (2007). Who's writing? Aristotelian ethics and the author position in digital poetics. *Kairos 11*(3). Retrieved on 5 July 2016 from the Karios website: http://kairos.technorhetoric.net/11.3/binder.html?topoi/fleckenstein/index.html.

Gray, M. L. (2009). *Out in the country: Youth, media, and queer visibility in rural America.* New York: New York University Press.

hooks, b. (1994). *Teaching to transgress: Education as the practice of freedom.* New York: Routledge.

Hunter, A. (2015). Lesbian mommy blogging in Canada: Documenting subtle homophobia in Canadian society and building community online. *Journal of Lesbian Studies 19*(2), 212–229.

Livingstone, S. (2005). "On the relation between audiences and publics". In Livingstone, S. (ed.) *Audiences and publics: when cultural engagement matters for the public sphere.* Changing Media – Changing Europe Series (2) (pp. 17–41). Bristol: Intellect Books

Markham, A. (2012). Fabrication as ethical practice: Qualitative inquiry in ambiguous Internet contexts. *Information, Communication & Society 15*, 334–353.

Marwick, A. E., & boyd, d. (2010). I tweet honestly, I tweet passionately: Twitter users, context collapse, and the imagined audience. *New Media & Society 13*(1), 114–133.

McKenna, K. Y., & Bargh, J. A. (1998). Coming out in the age of the internet: Identity "demarginalization" through virtual group participation. *Journal of Personality and Social Psychology 75*(3), 681–694.

Oakley, A. (2016). Disturbing hegemonic discourse: Nonbinary gender and sexual orientation labeling on Tumblr. *Social Media + Society 2*(3), 1–12.

Obergefell *et al.* v. Hodges, Director, Ohio Department of Health *et al.*, 14–556 S.C.O.T.U.S. (2015).

Parks, M. R. (2011). Social network sites as virtual communities. In Papacharissi, Z. (ed.), *A networked self: Identity, community and culture on social network sites* (pp. 105–123). New York: Routledge.

Renninger, B. J. (2015). "Where I can be myself… where I can speak my mind": Networked counterpublics in a polymedia environment. *New Media & Society 17*(9), 1513–1529.

Rheingold, H. (1993). *The virtual community: Homesteading on the electronic frontier*. Addison-Wesley Publishing Company. Retrieved on 5 July 2016 from the Rheingold website: www.rheingold.com/vc/book/.

Shapiro, E. (2004). 'Trans'cending barriers: Transgender organizing on the internet. *Journal of Gay & Lesbian Social Services 16*(3–4), 165–179.

Tiidenberg, K. (2013). How does online experience inform our sense of self? NSFW bloggers' identity narratives. In Allaste, A. A. (ed.), *Change and continuities of lifestyles in transforming societies* (pp. 177–203). New York: Peter Lang.

Tiidenberg, K. (2014). Bringing sexy back: Reclaiming the body aesthetic via self-shooting. *Cyberpsychology: Journal of Psychosocial Research on Cyberspace 8*(1) (published online).

Tufekci, Z. (2007). Can you see me now? Audience and disclosure regulation in online social network sites. *Bulletin of Science, Technology & Society 28*(1), 20–36.

Warner, M. (2002). Publics and counterpublics. *Public Culture 14*(1), 49–90.

Willson, M. A. (2006). *Technically together: Rethinking community within technosociety*. New York: Peter Lang.

Yin, R. K. (2014). *Case study research: Design and methods* (5th ed.). Thousand Oaks: SAGE.

10 'Cake is better than sex' – AVEN and asexuality

Agata Pacho

Given asexuality being a relatively un-researched concept, it seems worthy to begin with a definition provided by the Asexual Visibility and Education Network (AVEN), the largest association of asexual people in the world. Launched in 2001, AVEN hosts an archive of educational resources on the phenomena of asexuality available to academic researchers and the press. AVEN's enterprise may be defined as an effort intended to serve as a catalyst for widening the definition and discussion about sexuality. AVEN's members are actively engaged in distributing pamphlets, leading workshops and organising meetings. AVEN defines asexuality as a sexual orientation, in which there is no sexual attraction. Asexual people distinguish themselves from celibates who choose not to have sex, and, therefore, must control their sexual drive. They also emphasise their ability to form intimate relationships, as their orientation does not affect their emotional needs (AVEN, 2008).

Establishing asexual identity and community are imperative projects when research suggests that asexuality continues to be pathologised and medicalised (see for e.g. Cerankowski and Milks, 2010). Asexual people tend to be described as not yet fully developed and/or sexually experienced and asexuality often provokes questions about past trauma and sexual abuse. What has been also revealed as a problem asexual individuals face is the alienation that comes from lacking sexual desire in a world that presumes that everyone has, or should have, sexual desire (Cerankowski and Milks, 2010, p. 650). Alongside efforts made by asexual individuals to raise awareness of their sexual orientation, researchers coming from various disciplines such as psychology, gender studies, sociology and queer theory have strived to validate and legitimise asexual community and experience (e.g. Scherrer, 2008), depathologise asexuality by separating it from 'disorder' (Bogaert, 2004, 2006, 2015) and point out the potential of asexuality for broadening notions of sexual diversity (Cerankowski and Milks, 2014). This research joins the efforts to acknowledge experiences of asexual people while using the challenges they are facing to offer a critique of representation. In particular, I will focus on the challenge of representing a sexual orientation that has been defined in terms of absence, i.e. of sexual drive, desire and practices. I will offer an analysis that suggests how asexual communities overcome the issue of invisibility. I will propose that by adopting practices of eating cake and celebrating an annual cake day, asexuality is performed in a way that challenges common stereotypes to which asexuals have been subjected.

Asexuality: challenges of representation

While research exploring asexual identity, orientation and the politics of an asexual movement has endeavoured to reimagine and reframe what has commonly been viewed as dysfunctional and repressed sexuality, it has been also noted that raising awareness of asexuality appears to meet significant challenges. The absence of sexual practices, which lies at the core of asexual identity, contributes significantly to the asexual orientation remaining invisible. This could result from asexual people not needing to seek acceptance for their sexual practices in a way that, for instance, gay people may, and, therefore, they may lack willingness to declare being asexual (Pacho, 2013 p. 30). Importantly, the lack of visibility and awareness of asexuality is a substantial barrier to its inclusion in other sexuality-based political action groups (Scherrer, 2008, p. 636).

Further, Ela Przybylo (2011) argues, a representation of asexuality that is binary-bound and emphasises absences of practices is problematic as it provokes new discourses of sexuality potentially coercing us into becoming defendants of sexuality. While to be asexual is commonly understood as to be 'a-fun', boring or prudish, our attachments to sexuality may be strengthened. In this fashion, asexuality functions to reaffirm the space of sexuality and re-establish its margins (Przybylo, 2011, p. 452). For this reason, Przybylo suggests the need for a shift from "declarations of absence, to an enacting of difference, both linguistically and actually" (2011, pp. 456–457). Przybylo suggests that a genuine resistance would mean that asexuality repeats itself differently, plurally and complexly. If articulated and enacted differently, asexuality has the potential to transform society in which sexuality and sex play central roles suggesting alternative repetitions and destabilising those existing and presumed normalised (2011, pp. 456–457).

Asexuality and the problem with essentialism

Representing asexuality may also face challenges resulting from the diversity within the community. As argued by Kristin S. Scherrer, while lack of sexual attraction and desire has been a highly common feature of participants' descriptions of their asexuality, it is by no means a universally shared definition of asexuality (Scherrer, 2008, p. 626). Similarly, CJ DeLuzio Chasin points out that despite a clear and widely accepted definition of asexuality as a lack of sexual attraction there is a significant diversity among those who participate in the broad asexual community. The name of the community remains discussed as some of its members then prefer to adopt the term 'ace', a phonetic abbreviation of asexual, which they perceive as more inclusive (Chasin, 2013, p. 406). Among variations of asexuality there are: greysexuality (individuals may occasionally feel sexual attraction), demisexuality (being incapable of feeling sexual attraction without having a close bond with the person), apothisexuality (being repulsed at the thought of sex), akoisexuality (where individuals feel sexual attraction, but do not wish for those feelings to be reciprocated by the object of their affection), fraysexuality (feelings of sexual attraction fade over time as individuals bond with the person) and placiosexuality where individuals do not wish to have sexual acts performed on them, but are willing/want to perform them on others (Apps, n.d).

Notwithstanding, the need for a coherent representation of asexuality that can serve as basis for the community's politics remains. The further complexity embedded in the debates on asexuality lies in the complex relationship between asexual identities and essentialist notions of sexuality (see for example Pacho, 2013; Scherrer, 2008). As asexuality still lacks legitimisation and acceptance from LGBTQ communities, the general public and medical institutions (Prause and Graham, 2007), essentialist notions of sexual orientation may aid the process of establishing asexuality as legitimised. On the other hand, Scherrer (2008) argues, while asexuals continue to draw from understanding of essential sexuality in describing and forming their sexual identity, they simultaneously challenge essentialist notions of sexuality as naturally being part of human experience (Scherrer, 2008, pp. 629–630).

In *Gender trouble: feminism and the subversion of identity,* Judith Butler (2006) argues that even though the coherence is desired and idealised, any identification needs to be understood as an enacted fantasy. By suggesting that identity is performative, Butler argues that it is constituted by the very 'expressions' that are said to be its result. In other words, words, acts and desire produce the effect of an internal substance, but never revealing their work. Yet, Butler's performative body has no ontological status apart from the various acts which constitute reality (Butler, 2006, p. 185). The notion that identity categories are not essences but rather contingent outcomes of performative work has also been widely deployed in the field of science and technology studies (STS). Shared among STS scholars the empirical focus of ontological investigations on the practices of world-making emphasises the generative power of the practices involved in the constitution of reality. Such an approach challenges the assumption that the world pre-exists representational practices and favours instead the implication that practices perform the world (Woolgar and Lezaun, 2013, p. 4). In agreement with those propositions, the subsequent analysis will consider the practices employed by asexual people, in particular eating and sharing cake, and celebrating an annual cake day, in order to consider what asexuality becomes through those practices and what that means for the communities.

Two appetites: food and sex

Before moving on to the analysis of data gathered on AVEN's website, it is imperative to reflect on the evolving relationship between food and sex embedded in Western culture. For instance, Bell (in Wiederman, 1996) argues that for centuries it was common among certain religious women to engage in an exercise of self-starvation as a way of developing self-discipline and avoiding sexual temptation. In various cultures and at different points in history, slender female bodies were idealised in an apparent attempt to restrain women's sexual desire (Weiderman, 1996).

Further, John Coveney (2000) elaborates on the similarities between attitudes towards food and sex pointing out that the pleasures derived from food are also the sources of anxieties around eating, which continue to give rise to concerns about the very moral fabric of society. At the heart of the problem Coveney sees the fact that food pleasure challenges self-control. In this way, food pleasure matches sex. Coveney adopts a Foucauldian approach pointing to how the problem has required different forms of individual concern and conduct during different historical periods. Coveney argues that just as ancient Greeks assumed that both appetites required the exercise of moderation in order to demonstrate that one was truly civilised, the early Christian fathers thought that the appetite for food was even more harmful and distracting than the appetite for sex in the quest for spirituality (Coveney, 2000, p. xii). Today, scientific and technical knowledge of nutrition forms the basis for the moral judgements we make about ours and other's appetite and eating habits. It is the food's nutritional quality that makes it, as well as those eating it, 'good' or 'bad' (Coveney, 2000, p. xiii). Applying Foucault's concept of ethics, understood as determining how the individual is supposed to constitute himself as a moral subject of his own actions accordingly to socially and historically patterned ethics, Coveney proposes that current concerns about nutrition are not only a science but also an ethos which presents a problem for modern individuals in regard to their food choices (2000, p. xvi). The modern subject of food choice is constructed at the level of the body via 'regimes of truth' of medical science and nutrition, which justify the importance of health, longevity and so on. Simultaneously, it is constructed at the level of the soul via ethics as individuals are expected to know themselves as morally acceptable eaters (Coveney, 2000, p. 45).

Existing discourses around pleasures derived from food provoke a number of questions that may be asked in relation to the practices of eating cake and celebrating an annual cake day by asexuals. For instance, what is the significance of going against the ethics of a 'good' eater? What are the consequences for the discourses of the relation between food appetite and sex drive when the two are being decoupled? How are the present association between food and self-control, often tied to religious beliefs, being used by asexual communities in forming new ways of representation?

Methods: researching the virtual

The research is based on the analysis of data collected from the Internet sites set up and managed by members of asexual communities. The decision to base the research on online data was influenced by the findings suggesting that the Internet has been functioning as an imaginary home for asexual individuals. While Turkle (1995) argues that the Internet has made virtual space available for highly stigmatised, marginalised groups to find community and support for their identity, AVEN has been called a 'sanctuary' by its members for whom it gives an opportunity to express asexual identity (Pacho, 2013). Such spaces are interesting for researchers who can examine the implications of the ongoing online interactions for the emergence of asexual community and the processes of formulating community politics. Moreover, Karli June Cerankowski (2014) draws attention to how online activity has enabled the development of multiple discourses of asexuality. With reference to Cerankowski, as asexuals invent their own wikis and zines, video blogging and Live journaling, the diversity of voices expands and troubles the discourse put forth on the AVEN website reminding us that AVEN's literature is not the only voice on the topic of asexuality. Cerankowski stresses that the wider community based on the use of new media does not merely decentralise a political movement, but it "reveals its diversities, its possibilities, and its wilful and productive obscurities" (2014, p. 140).

'Emotionless, cold and generally apathetic' – stereotypes of asexuality

Reading AVEN's forums, one is likely to encounter discussions about the stereotypes asexual people are subjected to. The exchanges suggest that asexual people suffer from a number of stereotypes associated with the lack of sexual desires. As assumptions about innate sexual desires and impulses of human beings are deeply rooted in shared cultural and religious beliefs (Seidman, 2003, p. xi), asexuals become the sexual minority that is considered to be ' deficient' and lacking in terms of human nature. Asked in the forum post about stereotypes they are aware of Scotthespy replies:

> Cold. Emotionless. Driven by logic. Unable to understand society and its relationships, even the non lust/romance driven ones.
>
> (Scottthespy, AVEN, 7 March 2015)

Scotthespy's answer highlights how the lack of sex drive can be translated into a deficiency of emotions, and the ability to engage with or/and understand others. In other words, asexual people may be subjected to being judged as less equipped to be a full member of society. Similarly, AlexPeyton writes:

I'm usually stereotyped as a misanthrope, emotionless, cold and generally apathetic because of it.

(AlexPeyton, AVEN, 10 March 2015)

Again, the emphasis rests on the suspected lack of emotions, especially warm feelings towards others.

Being aware of how asexuality can be perceived may have an impact on how asexual people feel about themselves:

Personally I know I might come across as cold sometimes but that's a defence mechanism since I tend to be in touch with how others feel to a ridiculous extent. I'm definitely capable of love, I love most people in general.

(~Tyrant~, AVEN, 9 March 2015)

~Tyrant~ emphasises his ability to love and care for others in an attempt to dismiss stereotypes he is subjected to. Being aware of the possibility of being seen as cold is the reason ~Tyrant~ insists on having a greater capacity for empathy.

The way asexuality is associated with not being able to fully engage with others may be a barrier to understanding one's identity and sexual orientation:

[W]hen I was a lot younger I had gotten the impression [...] that asexuality meant wanting to be alone and not being a part of any kind of relationships – [...] for the longest time I had thought that I couldn't consider myself asexual due to my romantic attractions.

(SamiBat, AVEN, 9 March 2015)

SamiBat shares her experience of coming to understand her sexual orientation pointing out how that process was complicated by the stereotypes of asexuality. It was the associations around asexuality that made it difficult for SamiBat to recognise herself as asexual.

'Too immature to handle sex' – other stereotypes

Another AVEN member, Alchemistress draws attention to a different set of stereotypes from which asexual communities suffer:

No one's mentioned childish O-O which I've heard a lot online.

(Alchemistress, AVEN, 7 March 2015)

She then explains:

Such as asexuals are too oblivious/immature to handle grown up things like sex. It's really a really condescending and annoying stereotype in my opinion. Then again I'm pretty sure most stereotypes are.

(Alchemistress, AVEN, 7 March 2015)

Stereotypes described by Alchemistress describe asexual people being not fully developed or sexually experienced. They directly evoke medicalised discourses that have historically pathologised the lack of sexual drive as a disorder (Bogaert, 2004).

jennybunny adds to the discussion:

> I've definitely experienced being labelled with the childish/cute/innocent/naive stereotype (which, if true, I don't think has anything to do with my asexuality to be honest). I've also had people say 'but you're so nice' as though they expect an asexual to be completely cold and anti-social.
>
> (jennybunny, AVEN, 10 March 2015)

Reading this particular forum thread points to the language employed to describe asexuality and which stresses the absence of experience and/or knowledge of self and sexuality, of maturity. It may be argued that the lack of sex drive that lies at the core of definition of asexuality is being translated into other forms of lacking.

In the article titled 'Here's What It Means To Be Asexual In 2015', James Michael Nichols quotes Kara Kratcha, an individual who identifies as genderqueer and 'grey ace':

> "The stereotypes about asexuality are that aces are boring or childish—which I really hate", Kratcha shares. "Where you can't be an adult unless you're having sexual relationships—you're stunted in some way socially or developmentally... I think it's a hard thing to represent".
>
> (Here's What it Means to be Asexual in 2015, 2015)

Kratcha voices challenges of representation resulting from ongoing subjectification of asexuals to stereotypes that stress their suspected immaturity that, as I argued above, could be interpreted in terms of lacking. Now, I would like to reflect on the practices adopted by asexual communities which allow new ways of representing asexuality that challenge the stereotypes discussed here.

'Cake is better' on the superiority of cake over sex

Since 2013, the community of asexuals holds an annual cake day on 20 May. On this day the focus is on raising awareness of asexuality. Members of the community are encouraged to invite all their family and friends to join and show their support for each other by sharing cakes, pies, cupcakes and more. Some suggested that annual cake day may create an opportunity for asexual individuals to come out to their close ones. As AVENwiki explains:

> The AVEN forum has a long tradition of welcoming new members with cake [...] in the Welcome Lounge and AVENchat. [...] [I]t has become an informal symbol of asexuality and is often referenced to in [...] asexual media. Cake is also given for congratulations, comfort, or when a poster does something particularly asexy.
>
> (AVENwiki)

A Facebook community called 'Cake Day-Asexuality Awareness' regularly shares pictures, often humorous, that aim to engage public with the topic of asexuality. Sadly we are unable to reproduce those images here due to copyright restrictions. In one there is a slice of cake on a purple background, one of the colours of the asexual flag. The text says "Sex? Too mainstream. Cake is better". Similarly, another image states that "Cake is better than sex". In both cases, we notice positioning eating cake as opposite to and better than sexual practices. Both pictures use devalourising language, often used against asexual people, to describe sex as too 'mainstream'. By doing this, they challenge the notion of sex as a necessary part of one's life. While asexual people often stress that asexuality, just as other sexual orientations, is not a matter of choice, they simultaneously employ a discourse of choosing cake over sex in order to contest the idea that sex is essential. This reflects complexity embedded in the debates where the asexuality both, mobilises and rejects the essentialist notions of sexuality (Scherrer, 2008). Another image posits: "I want a relationship cake that lasts". Here, it is implied that, for asexual people, cake replaces a relationship. Again, it challenges the idea of a relationship being an essential part of life and, therefore, of those who are not willing to engage in relationships as deficient. The absence of sexual practices and desires is filled with practices of sharing and eating cake.

Yet another example describes being asexual in the form of a comic. It tackles a number of stereotypes that asexual people face, some of which were discussed above. For instance, it suggests that asexuality may be viewed as a rejection or unwillingness to engage in a relationship. Or that it may be mistaken for abstaining from sex for religious reasons. Above the statement "What I actually do" there is a picture of a woman enjoying a chocolate cake. In this instance, asexuality is yet again translated into being appreciative of cake. Interestingly, while food indulgences have been considered as close to pleasures derived from sex (Coveney, 2000), the discourse introduced by asexual communities decouples the long-standing association.

Problematising asexuality as indulgence

Introducing practices of sharing and eating cake where the absence of sexual practices led to the asexual orientation remaining invisible has created possibilities for new ways of representing asexual orientation. Yet, if we employ the approach to identity categories as not essences but rather contingent outcomes of performative work, it becomes possible to consider the practices of sharing and eating cake as performative practices with generative power for constituting asexuality. Through adopted practices of cake consumption, asexuality is being performed not as lacking, e.g. sex drive or desire, but as indulgent. The representational practices not only change association of asexuality with inability to experience pleasure and being constrained, but they perform new realities of being asexual.

Importantly, asexual communities adopt the idea of indulging in cake when medical and popular discourses around eating patterns remain morally charged and promotion of fitness and slimness is a significant site of stigmatisation (Turner, 1994). This raises questions about the potential negative consequences for asexual communities which may become targeted by the discourses of individuals' responsibility for controlling their appetite in the pursuit of current concerns about nutrition and health.

In addition, the question of asexual people enjoying cakes as a new stereotype has been discussed on the AVEN's forums. Kirbyfan66 voiced her opinion on the association of asexuality and cake:

> My Ctrl + F might not be working, but has nobody discussed the whole cake stereotype yet? That seems to be the one that most ace people enjoy the most, at least from my experiences. Myself included-I think it's a slightly odd yet very amusing stereotype.
>
> (Kirbyfan66, AVEN, 17 March 2015)

Kirbyfan66's observation points to the possible disagreement with the representational practices adopted by the asexual communities. Further, as those practices create new realities of being asexual, this may lead to further complications for the process of self-identification when an individual identifies as lacking sex drive but concurrently rejects the idea of food indulgence.

Conclusion

This chapter outlines a small scale research focused on the challenges of representing asexual orientation that has been defined in terms of absence, i.e. of sexual drive, desire and practices. It began with the reflections on the lack of visibility of asexuality, which has been identified as a substantial barrier to its inclusion in other sexuality-based political action groups. While, on one hand, the invisibility of asexuality may be attributed to the absence of sexual practices, on the other hand, it is also a result of particular stereotypes to which asexuals are being subjected. Among others misrepresentations, AVEN members pointed to being seen as unable to engage emotionally with others or to be empathetic. What is more, others stressed the harmfulness of describing asexual people as being not fully developed or sexually experienced. Those stereotypes directly evoke medicalised discourses that have historically pathologised the lack of sexual drive as a disorder. They also translate the lack of sex drive that lies at the core of definition of asexuality into other forms of lacking.

Later, I advanced the debate on the representation of asexuality by analysing practices of sharing and eating cake, adopted by asexual communities. I proposed that such practices can potentially challenge existing stereotypes and open new ways of representing asexual orientation through filling the absence of sexual practices and desires with practices of indulging in cake. Approaching identity categories as not essences but rather contingent outcomes of performative work, I argued that new representational practices do not only change association of asexuality with an inability to experience pleasure and being constrained, but they perform new realities of being asexual. I have also shown how this may lead to further complications for the process of self-identification when an individual identifies as lacking sex drive but concurrently rejects the idea of food indulgence. Another problem embedded in establishing new representational practices is related to the current 'regimes of truth' of nutrition. I have suggested that adopting of the practice of indulging in cake may lead to potential negative consequences for asexual communities that may become targeted by the discourses of individuals' responsibility for controlling their appetite in the pursue of current concerns about nutrition and health.

References

Apps, A. (n.d). Your Guide to the Asexual Spectrum. Retrieved 25 May 2016 on the Amino Apps website: http://aminoapps.com/page/virtual-space/2092947/your-guide-to-the-asexual-spectrum.

AVEN. (2008). *Welcome.* Retrieved 25 May 2016 on the AVEN website: www.asexuality.org/home/.

Bogaert, A.F. (2004). Asexuality: Prevalence and Associated Factors in a National Probability Sample. *The Journal of Sex Research 41*, 279–287.

Bogaert, A.F. (2006). Toward a Conceptual Understanding of Asexuality. *Review of General Psychology 10*, 241–250.

Bogaert, A.F. (2015). Asexuality: What It Is and Why It Matters. *The Journal of Sex Research 52*, 362–379.

Butler, J. (2006). *Gender trouble: feminism and the subversion of identity.* New York: Routledge.

Cake Day-Asexuality Awareness. Retrieved 25 May 2016 on Facebook: www.facebook.com/Cake-Day-Asexuality-Awareness-171003989723981/?fref=ts.

Cerankowski, K.J. (2014). "Spectacular Asexuals: Media Visibility and Cultural Fetish". In Cerankowski, K.J. and Milks, M. (eds.): *Asexualities. Feminist and Queer Perspectives* (pp. 139–161). New York: Routledge.

Cerankowski, K.J. and Milks, M. (2010). New orientations: Asexuality and its implications for theory and practice. *Feminist Studies 36(3),* 650–664.

Cerankowski, K.J. and Milks, M. (eds.). (2014). *Asexualities: feminist and queer perspectives, Routledge research in gender and society.* New York, London: Routledge, Taylor & Francis Group.

Chasin, CJ DeLuzio. (2013). Reconsidering Asexuality and Its Radical Potential. *Feminist Studies 39*, 405–426.

Coveney, J. (2000.) *Food, morals, and meaning: the pleasure and anxiety of eating.* London, New York: Routledge.

Simply Human (2016). *Discrimination and Asexuality.* Published 5 May 2016 on the Simply Human: Blog. Retrieved 25 May 2016 on TUMBLR: http://odrallag73.tumblr.com/post/140368604919/discrimination-and-asexuality.

Here's What It Means To Be Asexual In 2015 (n.d.). Retrieved 25 May 2016 on the Huffington Post website: www.huffingtonpost.com/entry/heres-what-it-means-to-be-asexual-in-2015_us_55ca42bfe4b0f73b20bad3a6.

Pacho, A. (2013). Establishing Asexual Identity: The Essential, the Imaginary, and the Collective. *Graduate Journal of Social Science 10*, 13–35.

Prause, N. and Graham, C.A. (2007). Asexuality: Classification and Characterization. *Archives of Sexual Behaviour 36*, 341–356.

Przybylo, E. (2011). Crisis and Safety: The Asexual in Sexusociety. *Sexualities 14*, 444–461.

Scherrer, K.S. (2008). Coming to an Asexual Identity: Negotiating Identity, Negotiating Desire. *Sexualities 11*, 621–641.

Seidman, S. (2003). *The Social Construction of Sexuality*. London, New York: W. W. Norton & Company.

Turkle, S. (2005). *The second self: computers and the human spirit*. Cambridge: MIT Press

Turkle, S. (2011). *Life on the Screen*. London, New York, Toronto, Sydney: Simon and Schuster.

Turner, B. (1994). "Preface". In Falk, P. (ed.): *The Consuming Body*. London: SAGE.

Wiederman, M.W. (1996). Women, Sex, and Food: A Review of Research on Eating Disorders and Sexuality. *The Journal of Sex Research 33*, 301–311.

Woolgar, S. and Lezaun, J. (2013). The Wrong Bin Bag: A Turn to Ontology in Science and Technology Studies? *Social Studies of Science 43*, 321–340.

11 Gay men and the internet

Unlimited possibility, lived reality

David Gudelunas

Gay men and the Internet can possibly be best described as a series of paradoxes. Just as the World Wide Web helped bring together geographically isolated communities, the Internet also helped spur further bifurcations of this 'community' into countless subcultures; as the Internet helped mainstream gay culture and provided a platform for the advancement of gay civil rights, it also became a space where unfiltered hate and discrimination flowed freely; while the Internet helped bring gay men out of closets and shadows across the globe, the same technological platform also allowed for these men to hide behind aliases, torsos and profiles that relied on subterfuge; when the Internet promised to unite the global gay diaspora, the same Internet also gave us cautionary clauses like 'no fats, no fems, no Asians, no Blacks'. Like so much pontification on the Internet generally, the history of gay men online can best be described as a mix of unlimited possibility and lived reality.

The Internet has always, in its relatively short history, been a contested terrain of hope, opportunity and controversy for gay men. Of course, modern gay life certainly pre-dates the Internet, and understanding how gay men connected without the help of browsers, high speed connections and other trappings of technology provides some insight into why the explosion of the world wide web in the mid-1990s was so critical in the lives of gay men. The development of the Internet ushered in the ability to connect historically isolated geographical gay communities, bring together a global population of sexual minorities into a common conversation, explore non-heterosexual identities and organise disparate social and civil movements. At least, this was the *promise* of the Internet in its infancy. While gay men have proven to be early adopters of new media technologies, exactly how these technologies and the online environment have served to unite them online is in reality far more complicated than these earliest utopian visions suggest.

This chapter explores how gay men use new media technologies and how these emergent media have, in turn, helped shape the contours of the gay community. By providing a historical overview of online spaces that have attracted gay audiences, this article traces the changing uses of digital technologies including the Internet and social media apps to both challenge and recreate notions of gay community in the offline environment. Suggesting that the widespread adoption of online technologies by gay audiences has significant effects for how we conceptualise offline gay communities and social movements, focussing on one very contemporary case study over the struggle for the top-level domain.gay.

Before moving on through the good, the bad and the in between of gay men and the Internet, I want to add a few cautionary words about scope. Specifically, due to space constraints and the onslaught of information found throughout this volume, this particular chapter is about gay men. While bisexuals, lesbian women, transgender individuals, intersexed individuals, the questioning and many other variants of 'sexual minorities' all have their own unique relationship with the Internet, this chapter specifically focuses on gay men because all of these histories and relationships while interrelated are, in fact, ultimately unique. While many are fond of grouping these histories and relationships together (just think of the many permutations of LGBTQIA) this is not unlike a trip to a Las Vegas buffet – you get a taste of everything, but nothing is particularly good.

A brief history of gay life offline and online

How the Internet changed gay culture is best explained by remembering gay life before the Internet. Though popular narratives often situate the Stonewall rebellion of 1969 as the moment when modern gay life emerged from the metaphorical closet, gay men have long found ways to connect and network with other gay men. Chauncey (1994, p. 4) details, as one example, how gay men in New York City before the World War II

> [d]eveloped a highly sophisticated system of subcultural codes – codes of dress, speech and style – that enabled them to recognise one another on the streets, at work, and at parties and bars, and to carry on intricate conversations whose coded meaning was unintelligible to possibly hostile people around them.

Even earlier, Humphreys (1970) shows how an elaborate system of gestures and codes allowed gay men to seek out sexual partners in public spaces before a concrete gay identity even existed. This offline networking was crucial in forming a community of like-minded men who are rarely born into gay families, grow up in gay neighbourhoods or have any meaningful contact with other gay men during their own adolescence. Of course, a gay community did develop before the Internet, but forming that community came at a steep price: gay bars were raided, discrimination was rampant and the simple act of picking up a gay periodical or book in public was an exercise in bravery.

Throughout much of the twentieth century, the first other gay men that many gays would 'meet' would be fictional characters in film or television

(Gross, 2001). These representations were typically dire – flamboyant stereotypes, menacing villains and tragic victims. This 'symbolic annihilation' of gays in mass media was partially corrected by the turn of the last century, though Gross (2007, p. 267) cautions, "[d]espite the dramatic increase in the public visibility of gays found in nearly all domains of public culture, most lesbian, gay, bisexual, and transgender youths still find themselves isolated and vulnerable". Gross holds out hope that newer forms of digital media may avoid some of the pitfalls of older media adding that "[t]he Internet is a godsend, and thousands are using computer networks to declare their homosexuality, meet, and seek support from other gay youths" (2007, p. 267).

The Internet, with its decentralised content creation model and more democratic gatekeeping mechanisms, provided clear opportunities for gay men who previously had very little access to information about any sort of gay community. Writing in *Wired* in 1994 in the very early days of browsers accessible to recreational users, Silberman (1994) recognised the inherent potential of the web to connect a younger generation of gay men. He says, "[j]ust 10 years ago, most queer teens hid behind a self-imposed don't ask don't tell policy until they shipped out to Oberlin or San Francisco, but the Net has given even closeted kids a place to conspire" (1994, p. 1).

Unlike traditional media that was controlled by a handful of companies and beholden to mass (mainly heterosexual) audiences, the Internet was portrayed by commentators early on as a space where the most marginal members of society could access a more level playing field (Gross and Woods, 1999). One of the key differences of the Internet in comparison with traditional media like film and television is that the decentralised nature of the Internet allowed for the creation of content about gay men by gay men intended for gay men (Alexander, 2002; Christian, 2010; Mitra, 2004). These seemingly more authentic depictions of gay sexuality proliferated early in the history of the Internet and have maintained relevance from MySpace and YouTube to SnapChat and Periscope. This seemingly symbiotic connection between gay men and the Internet was recognised early on by even the mainstream media. The Associated Press in 1996 said, "[i]t's the unspoken secret of the online world that gay men and lesbians are among the most avid, loyal and plentiful commercial users of the Internet" (quoted in Gross and Woods, 1999, p. 528). The article continued to note the specific utility of the Internet as a gathering point for those "who may be reluctant to associate in public" (Gross and Woods, 1999, p. 528).

The Internet did much more than just erase the stigma from walking into a local bookstore to pick up a gay periodical (or a gay man). Instead, the Internet created a space where gay men could communicate, connect and organise. Scholars recognised the web as a place where individuals could try on new identities and experiment with sexuality without facing the same repercussions they might in the offline world (Drushel, 2010; Turkle, 1995). Part of the utility had to do with the fact that the Internet is a place where users can maintain a sense of anonymity and where connections were not limited by physical proximity (Barnhurst, 2007). The ability of the Internet to help facilitate 'coming out' and to connect individuals questioning their sexuality has long been considered a transformational shift within gay culture. Studies of chat rooms, list serves, newsgroups and other online platforms have demonstrated that discussing taboo topics like marginalised sexualities is more plausible online than in traditional face to face settings (Baams *et al.*, 2011; Gray, 2009; McKenna and Bargh, 1998).

The Internet helped usher in dramatic changes to gay culture. Gays were able to come out earlier and experiment with their sexuality even if not out in the offline world. Similarly, the historical reliance on physical gay meeting spaces like bars or bathhouses became less important. With progress comes some setbacks, and research has also shown that while these online spaces have the potential to be a judgment free zone, there is still great importance placed on physical appearance, discrimination based on Human Immuno-Deficiency Virus (HIV) status and other real-life biases that get translated into digital contexts (Bond, 2009; Davison *et al.*, 2000; Hays *et al.*, 1990; Peterson, 2009). Moreover, the possible negative consequences of coming out earlier or the slow loss of gay neighbourhoods and gay spaces in the real world raises contentious questions if the Internet facilitates gay culture or degrades it.

After coming out, we know that the support functions of the Internet become less salient for gay men (Szulc and Dhoest, 2013). While a lot of academic attention has focused on the Internet as a means of support, especially for younger users, it should not be shocking to anyone that the Internet has always been used as well for far more utilitarian purposes – namely pornography, sex-seeking and other romantic and not-so-romantic endeavours. Although a new technology being used to transmit pornographic content is not unique to the Internet, this combination of young people and sexual content was an early and enduring concern about the web. In contrast to early theories that held out hope the Internet would help bring together global gay communities for purposes of support, organisation and advocacy, the ability to connect with other gay people online through dating sites and hook-up apps is used primarily for local instead of global purposes (Gudelunas, 2005). In other words, gay men logged on in order to find someone nearby to get off with, more frequently than they used the net for purposes of global activism.

This ability to quickly locate and cycle through sexual partners spurred concern about the transmission of sexually transmitted diseases (STDs), sexual predators and the reification of culture that privileges perfect bodies (Ashford, 2006; Bauermeister *et al.,* 2010; Brown *et al.*, 2005; Campbell, 2004; Davis, 2009). Scholars have commented on how despite the possibilities of the Internet to erase or mask perceived imperfections, many of our prejudices around race, class, hetero-normative practices and other biases actually became more pronounced online (Baker and Potts, 2013). Consider the number of online profiles that privilege 'straight-acting' and 'whites only'

(Eguchi, 2009). Conversely, some studies of how gay men use the Internet have focused on how niche websites and platforms opened up possibilities for the celebration of non-normative bodies and sexual practices. Sites dedicated to fat bodies, Bondage and Discipline, Dominance and Submission, Sadism and Masochism (BDSM) fetishes and other marginalised practices and identities were able to proliferate online (Adams and Berry, 2013). As the Internet migrated from computers to mobile devices, the ability to use geo-spatial capabilities to literally locate sexual partners within close proximity resulted in a far different sort of connection than first envisioned by scholars thinking about the possibility of the web (Gudelunas, 2012).

After more than two decades of widespread access to the Internet, the relationship between gay men and the not-so-new technology is at best a mixed bag. The early hopes of the Internet providing a space for the global gay community to congregate virtually and produce its own representations today feels like a distant utopian dream. One of the more interesting recent developments to at least partially re-capture this dream is reflected in the on-going struggle over the top-level domain .gay.

Does community matter? ICANN and global recognition of gay community

Since its inception in the 1960s, governance of the Internet has been anything but logical (Mueller and Woo, 2004; Richards and Calvert, 2011). Most governance has been dominated by the US through *ad-hoc* bodies from the private sector (Atkinson, 2006; King, 2004). Since 1998, the Internet Corporation for Assigned Names and Numbers (ICANN) has served as a private, not-for-profit organisation subcontracted by the US government that has managed most aspects of Internet governance (Christou and Simpson, 2007). This complex network of stakeholders is further complicated by ICANN's current plans to unveil thousands of new generic top-level domains (gTLDs) (these are the commonly known.com,.biz. edu, and others). The reasons for this rapid expansion range from the logistical – the dual need for non-Latin extensions and for increased domain space as more of the world's population heads online, to the cynical – the need for ICANN and dependent organisations to generate revenue quickly ("Do brands need a Chinese-language address on web?", 2013; Greeley, 2014).

The development of a community based .gay application as it moved through the Community Priority Evaluation (CPE) process put in place by ICANN is a fascinating story about legitimacy and an attempt to operationalise many of the ideals that dominated early theories about the Internet and its impact on gay users. Four different groups ultimately pursued the top-level domain .gay. Three of the four groups were commercial enterprises vying for control of multiple domains beyond .gay, and one was a California Corporation that applied under ICANN's Community Priority Evaluation Guidelines. DotGay LLC, the company behind the only community based application for .gay, presented an application to ICANN that promised to redirect 67% of all profits generated by domain sales back to not-for profits to the queer community through an independent board.

As a story that develops in the quasi-public (and often performative) space of ICANN and its various subcommittees, the struggle over .gay attracted a significant amount of popular and niche media attention, not to mention global advocacy from individuals and coalitions across various social media platforms. While it should not be surprising that Internet activists were particularly adept at using new media channels to rally support, just how many competing players entered into the debate over .gay is rather unique. While some Middle Eastern nations were objecting on religious grounds to a gTLD based on sexual orientation, various members of the so-called 'gay community', including trans and intersexed individuals, were leveraging campaigns against gay men (it should be noted here that the DotGay LLC application for the .gay domain was made in the name of the entire queer community and not solely gay men despite the use of the word 'gay').

In November 2013, there were 22 gTLDs (.com.biz,.name and others) as well as country (.uk,.fr,.us) top-level domains. While ICANN has historically been slow to release new top-level domains, a new wave of releases is expected to expand the number to around 1,400. While anyone who can afford the 185,000 United States Dollars (USD) application fee through ICANN can apply for a new generic top-level domain, multiple applicants for the same string would go into a bidding war for the right to control a new gTLD. For many companies and individuals, this rapid expansion of domains presents a challenge to protecting trademarks and brand names (Del Rey, 2012). Similarly, for not-for-profit organisations, the cost to pre-emptively protect a name or recover a name from a cyber squatter can be prohibitively expensive. ICANN built in a mechanism whereby existing communities not necessarily defined by geography could secure a top-level domain outside of the commercial application process. The development of this CPE process, however, was riddled with bureaucratic problems that many critics argued favoured commercial as opposed to community interests (Naimark, 2013).

One coalition that attempted to win community approval through ICANN was DotGay LLC. On its website, the company states,

> [o]ur position is that .gay cannot be operated as just a 'marketing platform' or a piece of real estate to be subdivided based solely on economic imperatives [...].gay can become empowering space that recognise and celebrates diversity, while also serving as a rallying point for an entire community.
>
> ("Dotgay.com", 2014)

Part of the proposal included DotGay LLC holding onto lucrative 'root' or 'second level' domains like pride.gay or hotels.gay that would be generic enough to serve as a type of meta index of all gay pride celebrations around the globe or all gay owned and operated hotels. This was an attempt to limit cybersquatting and profit gouging for lucrative .gay domains (Fisher, 2014; King, 2000). The application also specifically stated that hate-domains would not be sold (e.g. dyke.gay), and that individuals or companies wanting to purchase a .gay domain would first have to be 'authenticated' through one of the company's 'authentication partners'. These partners were essentially not-for-profit groups that span a wide range of the global queer community.

Essentially, in order to ensure that members of the gay community were able to participate in this domain, a business, organisation or individual would first have to be vetted by a designated not-for-profit organisation as queer or queer-friendly. In other words, a company like IBM would have to receive a code from the National Gay and Lesbian Chamber of Commerce or the Human Rights Campaign in order to be able to register IBM.gay. A company like IBM could also not buy technology .gay as that would be held as a second-level domain to index all the globally 'approved' queer-friendly technology related businesses, and would serve as a master directory of sorts.

DotGay LLC's plan to run the gTLD.gay as a partnership between a privately held company and a global community of sexual minorities, however, may only ever exist in planning documents. In early October 2014, DotGay LLC learned that their application for community priority status was rejected by ICANN and the Economist Intelligence Unit contracted by ICANN to evaluate community applications. Interestingly, the part of the CPE process that caused the application to fail on a complicated scoring rubric was the connection between the string (.gay) and the community as defined by DotGay LLC. In other words, in the opinion of ICANN, 'gay' did not connect to a pre-existing global community. ICANN's decision means that .gay will go up for bidding and will most likely be controlled by a conglomerate that runs multiple TLDs.

The announcement was, perhaps expectedly, met with an outcry from queer activists and critics of ICANN's regulatory practices (Naimark, 2014). One close watchdog of the process explained in *Slate*, "[t]he process has been confusing at best, scandalous at worst, with ICANN making up rules as it goes along and clearly not really understanding what it thinks a 'community' must be [...]" (Naimark, 2014). On one of the other (many) sides of this multi-faceted debate, critics faulted DotGay LLC for claiming everyone and essentially creating a community where there is none: "What DotGay tried to do with its .gay application was to define its community as basically everyone. I don't think I would call it gaming, but I might call it a failure to follow the community rules closely enough" (quoted in Murphy, 2014). What is undeniable, however, is the irony that a gay community that was shaped and arguably recreated by the Internet in its infancy was unable to be recognised as a community by ICANN just two decades later.

At the intersections of global queer activism and Internet policy, this case study of .gay is not about a domain, it is instead about the identity and the legitimacy of both a community of sexual minorities and ICANN as a regulatory body that oversees not just the Internet, but also the identities of those individuals that connect and coalesce online. It is also about one potential use of the Internet that returns to early notions of a safe space where the global gay community can come together for support, advocacy and community building.

While it is virtually impossible to predict what the next 20 years of gay life online will look like, it is obvious that meaningful engagement with digital technologies will be necessary in order to ensure the survival of the gay community. Whether this happens through community-based organising like the model proposed by the DotGay group, or through other initiatives, only time, and a new generation of gay Internet users, will tell.

References

Adams, T. E. and Berry, K. (2013). Size matters: Performing (Il)logical male bodies on FatClub.com. *Text and Performance Quarterly 33*(4), 308–325.

Alexander, J. (2002). Homo-pages and queer sites: Studying the construction and representation of queer identities on the World Wide Web. *International Journal of Sexuality and Gender Studies 7*(2/3), 85–106.

Ashford, C. (2006). The only gay in the village: Sexuality and the net. *Information & Communications Technology Law 15*(3), 275–289.

Atkinson, D. (2006). Catalan on the Internet and the.ct and.cat campaigns. *Journal of Language and Politics 5*(2), 239–249.

Baams, L., Jonas, K., Utz, S., Bos, H. and Van Der Vuurst, L. (2011). Internet use and online social support among same sex attracted individuals of different ages. *Computers in Human Behavior 27*(5), 1820–1827.

Baker, P. and Potts, A. (2013). 'Why do white people have thin lips?' Google and the perpetuation of stereotypes via auto-complete search forms. *Critical Discourse Studie, 10*(2), 187–204.

Barnhurst, K. G. (2007). "Visibility as paradox: Representation and simultaneous contrast". In Barnhurst K. G. (ed.), *Media/Queered: Visibility and its discontents*. New York: Peter Lang.

Bauermeister, J. A., Giguere, R., Carballo-Dieguez, A., Ventuneac, A. and Eisenberg, A. (2010). Perceived risks and protective strategies employed by young men who have sex with men (YMSM) When seeking online sexual partners. *Journal of Health Communication 15*(6), 679–690.

Bond, B. J. (2009). Out online: The content of gay teen chat rooms. *Ohio Communication Journal 47*, 233–245.

Brown, G., Maycock, B. and Burns, S. (2005). Your picture is your bait: Use and meaning of cyberspace among gay men. *Journal of Sex Research 42*(1), 63–73.

Campbell, J. E. (2004). *Getting it on online: Cyberspace, gay male sexuality and emodied identity*. London: Harrington Park.

Chauncey, G. (1994). *Gay New York: Gender, urban culture and the making of the gay world 1890–1940*. New York: Basic Books.

Christian, A. J. (2010). Camp 2.0: A queer performance of the personal. *Communication, Culture & Critique 3*(3), 352–376.

Christou, G. and Simpson, S. (2007). Gaining a stake in global Internet governance. *European Journal of Communication 22*(2), 147–164.

Davis, M. (2009). *Sex, technology and public health*. New York: Palgrave.

Davison, K., Pennebaker, J. and Dickerson, S. (2000). Who talks? The social psychology of illness support groups. *American Psychology 55*, 205–217.

Del Rey, J. (2012). Few brands admit to buying new domains. *Advertising Age 83*(15), 1–59.

Ad Age Staff. (16 December 2013). Do brands need a Chinese-language address on web?). *Advertising Age 84*, 0011, Retrieved 30 June 2016 from the Advertising Age website: http://adage.com/china/article/china-news/do-brands-need-a-chineselanguage-address-on-web/245687/.

Dotgay.com. (2014). *About Dotgay*. Retrieved on 30 June 2016 from the Dotgay website: www.dotgay.com.

Drushel, B. E. (2010). Virtually supportive: Self disclosure of minority sexualities through online social networking sites. In Pullen, C. and Cooper, M. (eds.), *LGBT identity and online new media* (pp. 62–72). New York: Routledge.

Eguchi, S. (2009). Negotiating hegemonic masculinity: The rhetorical strategy of "straight-acting" among gay men. *Journal of Intercultural Communication Research 38*(3), 193–209.

Fisher, D. (27 February 2014). Cybersquatters Rush to Claim Brands in the new GTLD Territories. *Forbes*. Retrieved 26 May 2016 from the Forbes website: https://www.forbes.com/sites/danielfisher/2014/02/27/cybersquatters-rush-to-claim-brands-in-the-new-gtld-territories/#73ba95ea73ba

Gray, M. L. (2009). Negotiating indentites/queering desires: Coming out online and the remediation of the coming-out story. *Journal of Computer Mediated Communication 14*(4), 1162–1189.

Greeley, B. (24 March 2014). Yes, it matters who controls Icann. *Bloomberg Businessweek,* 44+.

Gross, L. (2001). *Up from invisibility: Lesbians, gay men and the media in America.* New York: Columbia University Press.

Gross, L. (2007). "Gideon, who will be Twenty-five in the Year 2012". In Barnhurst, K. G. (ed.), *Media/queered: Visibility and its discontents* (pp. 261–278). New York: Peter Lang.

Gross, L. and Woods, J. D. (1999). "Queers in cyberspace". In Gross, L. and Woods, J. D. (eds.), *The Columbia reader on lesbians and gay men in media, society and politics* (pp. 527–530). New York: Columbia Univerity.

Gudelunas, D. (2005). Online personal ads: Community and sex, virtually. *Journal of Homosexuality 49*(1), 1–33.

Gudelunas, D. (2012). There's an app for that: The uses and gratifications of online social networks for gay men. *Sexuality and Culture 16*(1), 347–365.

Hays, R. B., Chauncey, S. and Tobey, L. A. (1990). The social support networks of gay men with AIDS. *Journal of Community Psychology 18*(4), 374–385.

Humphreys, L. (1970). *Tearoom Trade*. London: Duckworth.

King, S. H. (2000). 'Law that it deems applicable': ICANN, dispute resolution, and the problem of cybersquatting. *Hastings Communications & Entertainment Law Journal (Comm/Ent) 22*(3/4), 453–507.

King, I. (2004). Internationalising Internet governance: Does ICANN have a role to play? *Information & Communications Technology Law 13*(3), 243–258.

McKenna, K. Y. A. and Bargh, J. A. (1998). Coming out in the age of the Internet: Identity "demarginalization" through virtual group participation. *Journal of Personality and Social Psychology 75*(3), 681–694.

Mitra, A. (2004). Voices of the marginalized on the Internet: Examples from a website for women of South Asia. *Journal of Communication 54*(3), 429–510.

Mueller, M. and Woo, J. (2004). Participation in international governance regime by the "Rest of the world": An analysis of ICANN. *Conference Papers–International Communication Association*, 1. Retrieved 26 May 2017 on the All Academic Research website: http://research.allacademic.com/meta/p_mla_apa_research_citation/1/1/2/3/6/p112362_index.html?phpsessid=5565ff06b002613a07c530e62379f9af.

Murphy, K. (2014). Why kicking out the.gay "community"was right. *Domain incite.* Retrieved on 30 June 2016 from the fomainicite website: http://domainincite.com/17516-why-kicking-out-the-gay-community-was-right-comments.

Naimark, M. (2013). How the ICANN Top-Level Domain Scheme Puts LQBTS Organizations at Risk. *Slate.* Retrieved on 30 June 2016 from the Slate website: www.slate.com/blogs/outward/2013/11/20/icann_generic_top_level_domains_the_battle_for_gay_and_lgbt.html.

Naimark, M. (Producer). (10 October 2014). For ICANN, hotels are a community, gays are not. *Slate.* Retrieved on 30 June 2016 from the Slate website: www.slate.com/blogs/outward/2014/10/10/icann_s_new_generic_top_level_domain_process_failed_the_gay_community.html.

Peterson, J. L. (2009). "You have to be positive." Social support processes of an online support group for men living with HIV. *Communication Studies 60*(5), 526–541.

Richards, R. D. and Calvert, C. (2011). Adult websites and the top-level domain debate. *Cardozo Arts & Entertainment Law Journal 29*(3), 527–563.

Silberman, S. (1994). We're Teen, We're Queer, and We've got Email. *Wired* (11/01/1994), 1–4. Retrieved 26 May 2017 from the WIRED website: https://www.wired.com/1994/11/gay-teen/.

Szulc, Ł. and Dhoest, A. (2013). The internet and sexual identity formation: Comparing Internet use before and after coming out. *Communications: The European Journal of Communication Research 38*(4), 347–365. doi:10.1515/commun-2013–0021.

Turkle, S. (1995). *Life on the screen: Identity in the age of the Internet.* New York: Simon and Shuster.

12 Two-faced racism in gay online sex

Preference in the frontstage or racism in the backstage?

Jesus Gregorio Smith

Introduction

Claims of racial progress and racial unity have been plentiful thanks in part to changing technologies and political victories in the US. At the start of the Internet Age, beliefs that the new technology would aid in the breakdown of racial boundaries abounded in part thanks to chat rooms and dating sites where different racial groups were able to interact (Daniels, 2012). With the election of Barack Obama, even more assertions of a post racial future were being espoused by some public figures and intellectuals (Bonilla-Silva, 2010). Despite the declarations of racial progress and the belief that the Internet would exacerbate positive racial relationships, racial identities and racial boundaries have been reconstructed and maintained online in different ways. The reconstruction of racial identities is in the infrastructure of the websites, as well as in the way they depict race online (Nakamura, 2002). Even in chatrooms and different community venues, racist discourse has proliferated and white Supremacist spaces have been maintained (Daniels, 2012).

In reaction to these claims of a post racial society, whites have maintained racism by engaging in racial performances in front of multiracial audiences publicly that appear non-racial or 'colour-blind', in order to not be seen as racist (Bonilla-Silva, 2010). In spaces where whites are more comfortable, like in private spaces with all white friends and family, they are able to and often do express racist beliefs, thoughts and emotions (Picca and Feagin, 2007). In these all white spaces, for example, whites may make racist jokes about people of colour more comfortably than they would around people of colour (Picca and Feagin, 2007). If people are uncomfortable with the jokes, they may lob them up to being nothing more than 'just a joke'. This enactment of 'colour-blindness' in front of people of colour in public and blatant racism behind people of colour's backs in private, is called two-faced racism (Picca and Feagin, 2007, p. 19). There has been little research exploring how two-faced racism is utilised online. To further complicate the matter, race and racism may have more intricate relationships in particular communities and spaces. For example, in the case of online dating and hook-up sites, are racial preferences and racism conflated or distinct? That is, are racial preferences in partners for love or sex, racist? When engaging Internet dating and hookup sites, do users do so because they see them as public spaces that require the observance of certain conventions such as insisting on being colour-blind when it comes to potential partners? Or does the anonymity afforded to individuals online mean they see online dating sites as private spaces where they can express hostile feelings without being disavowed such as in the case of racially rejected partners? If two-faced racism is white behaviour regarding race in multiracial public spaces versus all white private spaces, how does two-faced racism operate in gay spaces where gayness has historically been equated with whiteness (C. Han, 2007; Teunis, 2007)? Since the gay rights movement for freedom to love and have sex with whomever you want is so pivotal to gay men, does this mean partner 'preferences' are understood differently in the context of a gay online hook-up site?

This chapter will attempt to explore and answer these questions by investigating an online hook-up and dating site called adam4adam.com. A4A is a popular American gay hook-up and dating site. It is distinguishable from other sites because it is free to users and pays for itself through online pornography ads that litter the sides of the website when users peruse it, much of which is racialized porn. Here, I ask several men who use the site their thoughts and beliefs regarding race, sexuality, partners and behaviours in order to assess how race and racism materialise online and if this, in fact, is maintained by two-faced racism. The goal is to understand whether racial preferences in lovers and racism are viewed similarly. Past literature regarding two-faced racism in US society is examined concluding with the findings and the implications they may have for understanding racial performances online.

Racial blindness

Colour-blindness and two-faced racism

As more public policy has been passed to counter some structural forms of systemic racism, such as the Voting Rights Act and Affirmative Action, an ideology of colour-blindness has permeated America today (Bonilla-Silva, 2010). As a result, being blatantly racist in public has become seen as a social malady. Regardless of this progress in society, racism is still none the less systemically replicated at both the structural level and within everyday interactions between people that whites often times do not notice or do not want to change (Feagin and Elias, 2012). Instead, whites engage in racist behaviours and actions in spaces with mostly only other whites, where they are more comfortable to do so, or what Picca and Feagin (2007) refer to as two-faced racism. Based on concepts developed by Erving Goffman (1956), two-faced racism argues that whites put up 'fronts' in spaces where they are not sure how their racial performances will be accepted. That is, if it is common to say racist jokes around people they are comfortable with, they will adjust their performance of these jokes in spaces with non-whites (Picca and Feagin, 2007). This does not mean that whites do not engage in racism in the frontstage, but instead that they are more likely to do this in the comfort of the backstage (Picca and Feagin, 2007). This also does not mean that other whites will not express discomfort to this racism, but if they do, they are typically told to stop being politically correct, to learn to take a joke or that it is the truth (Picca and Feagin, 2007). In essence, two-faced racism is about *the right way* to do racism.

Other studies have also explored the way two-faced racism operates in different spaces. For instance, during the context of Halloween, many whites engage in racist performances of blackness by using blackface and other racial or ethnic costumes in order to trivialise racism as well as reinforce racial stereotypes that maintain white Supremacy (Mueller, Dirks and Picca, 2007). Similarly, in the workplace, front and backstage discourses around the intersections of race, class and gender were frequent (Embrick and Henricks, 2015). For instance, the way whites described their sexual disgust for white women dating or having sex with black men echoed the anti-miscegenation laws of the past. Desire for Asian women who were 'trained' to be submissive, reflected a particular racialised history that could be expressed safely around other whites but strategically contradicted in public (Embrick and Henricks, 2015, p. 172). In examining racist language and behaviours in chat rooms, the special boundaries delineated by Picca and Feagin (2007) seem to be blurred in cyberspace. That is, the anonymity provided to people online allows for a sort of backstage setting without the social repercussions of an offline front stage (Steinfeldt *et al.*, 2010). As a result, some might find it even more comforting to say racist things online than in all white spaces offline (Steinfeldt *et al.*, 2010). Even in chat rooms with mixed races, whites expressed racist beliefs, suggesting that cyberspace blurs the boundary between a frontstage and backstage (Steinfeldt *et al.*, 2010). Building on these studies by exploring a specific online gay hook-up site, I examine the role of two-faced racism in racial preferences for gay men.

The Internet is an important space to study such social forces as sexuality, race, racism and sex and dating. Brickell (2012) argued that "sexuality is everywhere on the Internet" (p. 28), with the Internet operating as an "enabler and mediator of sexual relationships in society" (p. 28) through different websites. One of the main functions of these online sites is to allow users to set up personal profiles that enable identity management, allow for online communication with others and find potential mates (Finkel *et al.*, 2012; Heidemann, Klier and Probst, 2012). Ellison, Hancock and Toma (2011) assert that online users draw from their "past, present, and future selves when constructing their profiles", allowing them to accentuate the qualities they may have had, want to have or plan on having (p. 56). The presentation of their online profiles allows users to filter out those who are not desired and filter in those that are desired (Best and Delmege, 2012) by specifying what it is one is looking for. This was done mostly by the use of a profile picture

(Best and Delmege, 2012). Self-presentation in online dating allows individuals to highlight their attractive features while de-emphasizing their negative features in order to present themselves as desirable (Hirschman, 1987; Ellison, Heino and Gibbs, 2006).

The Internet has also impacted the lives of gay men with the creation of websites that allows them more freedom to find other gay men. Bolding and colleagues (Bolding, Davis, Sherr, Hart and Elford, 2004) found that gay men preferred the Internet over bars and other venues to find partners. Building on this, Bull, MacFarlane, Lloyd and Rietmeijer (2004) found that 86% of men used the Internet at least once a week and 97% of men who use the Internet as a way to find partners for sex met someone online. Robinson and Moskowitz (2013) surmised that young men found Internet cruising to be erotic and that they tended to use the Internet to "come out" or acculturate into the mainstream gay culture. As a result, Internet cruising and emailing play a significant role in gay men's search for sexual partners (Paul, Ayala and Choi, 2010). Within their study of Internet sex ads and race based partner criteria, Paul, Ayala and Choi (2010) found that race and ethnicity were frequent criteria for online sexual partner selection and online discourse was blatant in prejudice.

Data and methods

The following section explores the method for data collection and analysis for this study, what measures were taken to collect the data, who is represented in the sample and what methods of analysis were utilised in the interpretation of the data.

Recruitment and sampling

The data was collected along the US-Mexico border town of El Paso, Texas. The demographic makeup of El Paso includes Mexican Americans 82%, African Americans 3% and non-Hispanic whites 14% (US Census Bureau, 2010). Interviews were conducted with 16 men who have sex with men (MSM); the participants reflected the racial demographics of the city.

I sought to interview MSM who used the popular online gay men's dating site, adam4adam.com (A4A). A4A is an American online dating website designed to meet other men for, as it describes on its website, "friendship, romance or a hot hook up" ("Adam4adam.com", n.d.). This purposeful sampling technique lead to 16 in-depth interviews with MSMs. Much like previous studies (C. S. Han, 2008; B. A. Robinson, 2015), the sample size was exceptional but small due in part to the difficulty of capturing hidden populations.

Data collection and respondent demographics

Two research assistants were trained to help collect the data due to concerns over the 'race of the interviewer effects', where the racial identity of the interviewer can influence the results. Hence, the interviewer and respondents were matched by race. The lead author, being a dark skin, mixed race man, conducted interviews with black men and mixed race men (specifically black and Latino MSMs).

The men interviewed reflect the largest racial groups represented in area, specifically, Latinos ($N = 4$), Blacks ($N = 4$), Whites ($N = 4$) and mixed race (Black and Latino and White and Latino, and Black and White) ($N = 4$) (Appendix A). One participant opted to describe himself as American rather than black, although later in the interview he did describe his racial history as black. The participants were between the ages of 20 and 58 (Table 12.1).

Data analyses and interview guide

Interviews lasted approximately an hour, were recorded and transcribed verbatim for the purpose of examining themes that emerged. The transcribed interviews were assigned pseudonyms, coded and analysed through NVivo9 qualitative analysis software. The questionnaire guide was adapted from Plummer's (2007) instrument within her study on sexual racism but was modified with questions regarding the context of the study (i.e. the border) and online profile identity.

The study was approved by the Institutional Review Board (IRB), and written informed consent was required by all participants. Participants were debriefed on the purpose of the study, its importance and how the data would be used.

Results

The utility of two-faced racism can be difficult to understand when considering the context of the Internet, how race operates in gay spaces and how race is seen in terms of partner preference. Through this analysis, I found that two-faced racism is challenged in the context of the online dating site adam4adam.com. Most users saw the website as a hook-up site and therefore everyone had much of the same expectations in terms of sexual desires and partners. This meant what was considered a frontstage and backstage performance of two-faced racism relied heavily on (1) why they were using the website; (2) how they understood race to operate on the website; and (3) whether or not they saw racial preferences in partners as racist. The answer to these questions demonstrated whether or not two-faced racism was utilised in the frontstage, backstage or both, and in some instances, not at all.

Hook-up websites

The reasons why the men use adam4adam.com plays a vital role on whether or not they feel the Internet allots a frontstage or a backstage performance of race. This is made strikingly clear in online dating and

Table 12.1 Frequencies on sample characteristics

Age	f
20–29	5
30–39	4
40–49	4
50–59	3
60–69	0
Occupation	
Professional	8
Service	4
Retail	1
Manual labor	1
Student	2
Racial/ethnic identity	
Black	3
White	4
Latino	4
Black and White	2
Latino and White	1
Black and Latino	1
No answer	1
Sexual identity	
Gay	14
Straight	0
Bisexual	1
No answer	1
Gender identity	
Masculine (masc)	8
Feminine (fem)	0
In between (masc and fem)	5
Both (more fem)	1
Both (more masc)	1
No answer	1
Socio-economic status	
High class	1
High middle	5
Middle	6
Lower middle	1
Working class	3

hook-up sites, where individual actors post images and descriptions of themselves on their profiles in an effort to maximise hits to their profiles. This may suggest a sort of frontstage performance, especially if the user is looking to date and potentially find a long-term partner and wants to put their best appearance forward to look like the greatest potential mate.

Yet, what about if the point is to find a partner for just a one-time tryst or non-committal sexual relationship? If it is just sex, do the expectations change and if so, does the online performance change with it? What does this then say about two-faced racism? To help answer these questions, nineteen-year-old mixed race Claudio explained what his purpose was for using adam4adam.com:

> I would like to find someone that I could be with for the rest of my life however, um, I guess the main purpose of that site is to find someone just to have a quick encounter with or find someone that you have encounters with on a regular basis without the hassles and the strain of a relationship
>
> (Claudio, 6 June 2011)

This in turn fosters an environment where the expectations of profile presentation differ and so what is considered the frontstage and backstage become blurred. If one is looking for a partner to spend the rest of their life with, they may do the opposite of a quick encounter and spend more time getting to know the person, thus presenting a more honest self online. For sex, it may be less about getting to know someone and more about seeing who you will be hooking up with later. This was expanded upon by forty-four-year-old Latino Octavio:

> How do you identify yourself on your online profile?
> OCTAVIO: I put masculine, top only, Latino, uh I list my height, my weight, body type, things like that.
> Do you show pictures of your body or face?
> OCTAVIO: Yes.
> Why do you choose to present yourself in this way?
> OCTAVIO: Hmm…well if I keep with the same thinking that people are coming on the site for sex, I in turn want to be able to see how the eventual hookup will look like. So that's my reasoning. They want to see what I look like and I want to see what they look like.
>
> (Octavio, 25 May 2011)

The emphasis is on the way Octavio presents himself online, from his race and body type, to showing pictures of his face, all for an eventual sexual hook-up. This suggests that physical appearance is the most important aspect to hooking up and that the online profiles in this instance are a front where appearance is negotiated in exchange for eventual sex. Thirty-one-year-old white male Jesse furthers this idea when asked why he uses adam-4adam.com: "It's great. What are you looking for? Yup, well I'm in it for this, this, and this. It's just as easy as ordering a pizza and thirty minutes or less, they're at your door" (26 May 2011). Whereas offline, meeting sexual partners maybe more complicated, online eases the process by providing the avenue for selective sexual partnering. This online 'build your own pizza' world is contrasted with the offline world in so much that online you can be more upfront with what you want and offline you may be forced to acquiesce to social norms about discriminatory behaviour. Thus online profiles may racially exclude more freely than offline. Again, this supports the idea that the Internet is a space for 'slippage' between the backstage, where racism can be more blatant as well as a frontstage where racism is presented as more colour-blind (Picca and Feagin, 2007).

Racial dynamics online

In order to understand how two-faced racism operates online, we must grapple with how race is utilised in these spaces. That is, how is race used in the context of a hook-up website? We can begin to understand more clearly how two-faced racism is used in the frontstage and backstage online. According to participants in the study, many felt race online was explicit because users could vividly express what they wanted. Greg, a twenty-three-year-old mixed race man explained the difference with racial dynamics online:

> No. I feel like online you create like a pseudo person that represents you but isn't really you, and so you get to, if you so choose, be harsher and be stricter on what you're looking for.
>
> (Greg, 7 July 2011)

As Greg describes in his comment, the context of the Internet and the environment of online dating and hook-ups presents a circuitous climate online where the frontstage and backstage mesh. The online environment works as frontstage in the sense that people can use their profiles as 'pseudo' representations of who they are and more vividly express their racial desires in terms of a sexual partner and really speaks to the slippage provided by cyberspace. Online, the virtual frontstage is where an online persona represents the offline person as well as the virtual backstage is where people can be blunter about what they want because of the anonymity of being online. As a result, the online space is both a frontstage and backstage simultaneously. This is further supported by other online users such as twenty-sex-year-old Latino Luis:

> I think they are probably even worse. Like the online world acts like a little mask for you and people feel more empowered to say what they want to say and so people would say things online that they would never say in person.
>
> (Luis, 22 July 2011)

Luis supports Greg's claim that the online world works as a mask. This is important because with two-faced racism, the idea is that whites in the presence of people they do not know or multiracial crowds, engage in colour-blind racism so as to seem not racist. Yet, in the presence of all white family or friends that they are close to, they are more honest with their racial views. As we can see in Luis' comment, the anonymity afforded to whites online allows them to be more explicit with their racial desires in the context of Adam4adam.com. Danny, a thirty-year-old Latino male felt similar:

> Do you think that racial dynamics are the same online?
> DANNY: Yes.
> And can you explain why you think that way?
> DANNY: I think the best reference would be the online hookup web-sites where people more clearly express what they're into and what they're not into. You can see a number of profiles that say 'white only', 'white and Latino only' and 'no black'.

> (Danny, 8 June 2011)

Danny, confirms that online, people again more freely express their preferences in partners. Here, expressing what you are into is usually in the form of a negative 'no blacks' or affirmative 'white only'. In both scenarios, it is exclusionary to blacks as a racial group of potential partners. This seems to suggest that if whites feel compelled to write 'no whites' clearly on their online profiles, there may be a level of comfort that is similar to the backstage, where racism is more blatant. Then again, a profile that says, 'white and Latino only' instead of 'no black', may be an adjustment to the front of profiles so as to not come off as explicitly racist, insinuating that the online space is more of a frontstage. In order to understand which is which, we must understand how individual actors see racial preferences in sex partners. Is it racist to want 'white only' partners if you yourself are white or 'blacks only' if you yourself are black? Understanding racial preferences can help to clarify how two-faced racism operates in an online gay hook-up space.

Just a preference

Finally, how the users of adam4adam.com understood racial preferences online influenced what they deemed as racist or not. For instance, if they saw adam4adam.com as a hook-up site where physical attraction superseded other needs, they might not see racial preferences as racist and willingly expressed their racial desires. Yet if they saw racial preferences as exclusionary, they might see open racial preferences as racist. Who expressed these preferences and was on the receiving end of the preferences played a big role on whether publicly expressing a racial preference in a partner was frontstage racism or backstage. Take the case of twenty-two-year-old black male, Ian, who was asked if his choices in a partner change when it comes to sex:

> I think for casual sex, my preferences would come into play a little more because I think I feel like I'm playing into a fantasy of, like, this is what I want, this is how I like it and if it's just going to be a casual one-time thing, like why not get what I want?
>
> (Ian, 16 June 2011)

Ian certainly expresses the thoughts of many users online when it comes to hook-ups. For him, if it is just casual sex, he is more specific with what he wants. This is because, similar to Jesse, the online world provides a fantasy space where you can have your partner your way instead of going through the hassle of offline dating and having to get to know people. The expediency online for sex specifically suggests that there is a common understanding that people express what they want openly in a partner. This common understand among the gay men suggests again that online works as a backstage where people are more open about what they want. According to twenty-year-old Latino male Juan when asked when it comes to attraction, is finding someone attractive because of their race the same thing as finding them attractive because of other characteristics like body type, or are racial preferences a form of racism? He said:

> Are they the same? I would say yeah; it is the same because your targeting something. So if you have a thing for somebody who has big arms, you're looking for somebody who has big arms. If you're looking for somebody who's Hispanic, you're looking to see if they're Hispanic. I guess race could be a characteristic of an individual so yeah, I would say it is the same.
>
> (Juan, 2 August 2011)

Juan does not perceive racial preferences to be racist and therefore has no problem with profiles that ask for or exclude races. From this perspective, a profile with 'no blacks' is not any more racist than a profile for 'no skinny arms'. On a website intended for casual sex, partner preferences are seen as nothing more than physical requirements from some men. In this case, this would not be the case that two-faced racism is being expressed in the frontstage or backstage. Still, what if you are on the receiving end of the preferences? Twenty-one-year-old black male Demetri explains when asked about racism in the gay community:

> Yes. Well like online profiles that say "no Blacks" or "no Asians" or "I prefer Whites." I would say I see that kind of racism because it's discriminating against someone based on something that they can't control. Like I was born Black, why am I not attractive because of that? It should be based on who I am… and you should look past the surface and see what is inside.
>
> (Demetri, 22 June 2011)

For Demetri, being on the receiving end of racial exclusionary preferences, he sees them certainly as racist and discriminatory. In fact, Demetri explains how being born black should not exclude him from people's desires, being that desire can be much more than what is on the surface. Thus, in this case, racial preferences are racist expressions of desire cloaked in 'preference' in the frontstage of an online profile for black men but understood as racial discrimination in the backstage that is no worse than other forms of discrimination such as body-type for other men.

Conclusion

Two-faced racism centres on the idea that because of blatant racism increasingly becoming socially unacceptable, whites engage in colour-blind racial performances in the frontstage around multiracial audiences and in blatant racist behaviour in the backstage with mostly all whites present. This concept is complicated when it comes to the Internet, gay hook-up sites and what is understood as racist behaviour or not. In this study, I investigated a gay men's hook-up site, adam4adam.com, to see how two-faced racism played out online. Two-faced racism depended on why the men used the website, and what they thought of race within the website. For instance, most users saw the website as a hook-up site where physical preferences in a partner are expected. Thus some men expressed blatantly wanting 'whites only' and 'no blacks' on their profiles. Whether or not these statements were seen as racist depended on if one saw racial preferences as nothing more than physical desire, such as wanting 'big arms' in a partner, or if they saw it as something more. On the opposite end, the men on the receiving end of those preferences, usually black men, saw these expressions as racist. Thus profiles that expressed blatant racial preferences could be seen as expressing them in the frontstage, where 'preference' is used as a front to disguise racist desire in multiracial spaces. It could also be seen as a backstage where everyone is gay and there is a comfort in expressing racial desire because it is presumed everyone sees physical desire the same when it comes to hooking up. Also, what is considered the frontstage and backstage is complicated thanks in part to the Internet. Being online did provide anonymity to users by providing them little masks and pseudo personalities online that represented them but were not really them, thus making it easier for them to be more open with their racial preferences in partners online even though they would not use the same language offline. In sum online, two-faced racism operated in the frontstage and backstage sometimes simultaneously and sometimes not at all, depending on the context. This complicated slippage between the frontstage and backstage may speak to the reality that there is never really a strict binary between a private self-performance and public self-performance. In actuality, there seems to be multiple stages to each person, each with its own frontstage and backstage.

References

Adam4adam.com, Retrieved on 30 January 2012 from the Adam4adam website: www.adam4adam.com/.

Best, K. and Delmege, S. (2012). The filtered encounter: online dating and the problem of filtering through excessive information. *Social Semiotics 22*(3), 237–258.

Bolding, G., Davis, M., Sherr, L., Hart, G. and Elford, J. (2004). Use of gay Internet sites and views about online health promotion among men who have sex with men. *AIDS Care 16*(8), 993–1001.

Bonilla-Silva, E. (2010). *Racism without Racists: Color-Blind Racism and the Persistence of Racial Inequality in the United States.* Lanham: Rowman & Littlefield Publishers.

Brickell, C. (2012). Sexuality, power and the sociology of the internet. *Current Sociology 60*(1), 28–44.

Bull, S. S., McFarlane, M., Lloyd, L. and Rietmeijer, C. (2004). The process of seeking sex partners online and implications for STD/HIV prevention. *AIDS Care 16*(8), 1012–1020.

Daniels, J. (2012). Race and racism in Internet studies: A review and critique. *New Media & Society 15*(5), 695–719.

Ellison, N. B., Hancock, J. T. and Toma, C. L. (2012, first published in 2011). Profile as promise: A framework for conceptualizing veracity in online dating self-presentations. *New Media & Society 14*(1), 45–62.

Ellison, N., Heino, R. and Gibbs, J. (2006). Managing impressions online: Self-presentation processes in the online dating environment. *Journal of Computer-Mediated Communication 11*(2), 415–441.

Embrick, D. G. and Henricks, K. (2015). Two-faced-isms: Racism at work and how race discourse shapes classtalk and gendertalk. *Language Sciences 52.* Elsevier Ltd, Springer Press, 165–175.

Feagin, J. and Elias, S. (2012). Rethinking racial formation theory: A systemic racism critique. *Ethnic and Racial Studies 36*, 1–30.

Finkel, Eli J. *et al.* (2012). Online dating: A critical analysis from the perspective of psychological science. *Psychological Science in the Public Interest 13*(1), 3–66.

Goffman, E. (1956). *The Presentation of Self in Everyday Life.* New York: Anchor Books.

Han, C.S. (2007). They don't want to cruise your type: Gay men of color and the racial politics of exclusion. *Social Identities 13*(1), 51–67.

Han, C.S. (2008). A qualitative exploration of the relationship between racism and unsafe sex among Asian Pacific Islander Gay Men. *Archives of Sexual Behavior 37*(5), 827–837.

Heidemann, J., Klier, M. and Probst, F. (2012). Online social networks: A survey of a global phenomenon. *Computer Networks 56*(18), 3866–3878.

Hirschman, E. C. (1987). People as products: Analysis of a complex marketing exchange. *Journal of Marketing 51*(1), 98–108.

Mueller, J. C., Dirks, D. and Picca, L.H. (2007). Unmasking racism: Halloween costuming and engagement of the racial other. *Qualitative Sociology 30*(3), 315–335.

Nakamura, L. (2002). *Cybertypes: Race, Ethnicity, and Identity on the Internet.* New York: Routledge.

Paul, J. P., Ayala, G. and Choi, K. H. (2010). Internet sex ads for MSM and partner selection criteria: The potency of race/ethnicity online. *Journal of Sex Research* 47(6), 528–538.

Picca, L. H. and Feagin, J. (2007). *Two-Faced Racism: Whites in the Backstage and Frontstage*. New York: Routledge.

Plummer, M. D. (2007). "Sexual racism in gay communities: Negotiating the ethnosexual marketplace." Dissertation, Doctor of Philosophy, University of Washington, available at: https://digital.lib.washington.edu/researchworks/handle/ 1773/9181.

Robinson, B.A. (2015). 'Personal preference' as the new racism: Gay desire and racial cleansing in cyberspace. *Sociology of Race and Ethnicity* 1(2), 317–330.

Robinson, B. A. and Moskowitz, D. A. (2013). The eroticism of internet cruising as a self-contained behaviour: A multivariate analysis of men seeking men demographics and getting off online. *Culture, Health & Sexuality* 15(5), 555–569.

Steinfeldt, J. A., Foltz, B. D., Kaladow, J. K., Carlson, T. N., Pagano, L.A., Benton, E. and Steinfeldt, C.M. (2010). Racism in the electronic age: Role of online forums in expressing racial attitudes about American Indians. *Cultural Diversity and Ethnic Minority Psychology* 16(3), 362–671.

Teunis, N. (2007). Sexual objectification and the construction of whiteness in the Gay Male Community. *Culture, Health & Sexuality* 9(3), 263–75.

US Bureau of Census (2010). *Characteristics of Population* (Vol.1). Washington, DC: US Government Printing Office.

13 Representing bisexuality in the digital age

Nora Madison

Introduction

This chapter will examine the practices and techniques bisexuals employ to represent bisexuality in digitally mediated spaces, and the affordances digital media provide in (re)creating bisexual signifiers. This analysis is drawn from data collected during a three-year ethnographic project examining bisexual-specific spaces, both online and off. Central to this chapter is a discussion of the significance of the efforts to represent bisexuality within a dominant Western system of sexual orientation. The social media platforms, user interfaces and cultural norms of users ideologically shape the intelligibility of representing bisexuality; bisexuality is often misinterpreted or entirely erased when read within the widely adopted dominant binaries of heterosexuality and homosexuality in Western culture. The practices of representing bisexuality in digital spaces include using, manipulating and re-appropriating symbols, images, text and hyperlinks to construct a culturally intelligible notion of a bisexual identity. Participants discuss the complexities of an identity that can appear more visible in digital spaces than it does offline.

This research was conducted as a multi-method, qualitative examination of bisexual spaces. For this study I operationalised the term bisexual space as a semiotic category referring to any social space constructed by bisexuals and designated for bisexuals. I utilised ethnographic participant-observation and social semiotics to provide a comprehensive analysis of the practices of constructing and representing bisexuality within these spaces.

One of the most salient themes to emerge from this research is participants' affective struggles with feeling 'invisible' – both in mainstream straight communities, but also significantly in queer communities, from which many desire recognition. A significant finding from this research is the frequency of discourse specific to invisibility, its expressed negatively associated to experiences and feelings, the public sharing of those reactions among individuals and the ensuing discourse that emerges from those interactions. These include the articulation of 'solutions' to counter perceived invisibility.

Bisexuality

Bisexuality can be defined in a multitude of ways; however, even among self-identified bisexuals there is no one definition that has been adopted by all bisexual-identified people. The culturally popular definition of bisexuality in Western cultures – the romantic attraction, sexual attraction or sexual behaviour towards both males and females – is not fully congruent with the majority of bisexual-identified people. The definition of bisexuality that is most widely adopted by bisexuals today has been put forth by the American national bisexual group, BiNet USA:

> A person whose enduring physical, romantic and/or emotional attraction is to other people of various sexes and/or gender identities. Individuals may experience this attraction in differing ways and degrees over their lifetime.
>
> (BiNet USA, 2014)

Similarly, Robyn Ochs, a prominent bisexual activist and educator, has popularly stated:

> I call myself bisexual because I acknowledge that I have in myself the potential to be attracted – romantically and/or sexually – to people of more than one sex and/or gender, not necessarily at the same time, not necessarily in the same way, and not necessarily to the same degree.
>
> (Robyn Ochs, 2014)

Defined this way, bisexuality is much broader than a binary two-sex system. As one participant on a listserv posted:

> [Listserv] I saw video a couple of months ago that described "bi" as being attracted to "same and different sexed people". I considered my internal debate settled at that point. Yes, it is binary, but only in the broadest sense. Arguing over language has always felt nit-picky and really detracts from real issues faced in the community.
>
> (Jamie, June 2013)

These definitions allow for a broader interpretation of bisexuality as more than just being attracted to males and females; rather, these definitions focus on bisexuality as a non-monosexual identity.

Monosexuality is the romantic or sexual attraction to members of one sex or gender group only. A monosexual person may identify as either heterosexual or homosexual, the key element being that their sexual or romantic attraction remains consistently directed towards one sex or gender group. Congruently, a heterosexual male could be attracted to a transgender woman and remain heterosexual as well as monosexual. Moreover, this shift away from bi as male/female positions bisexuality as the sexual, romantic and/or emotional attraction to peoples who can potentially be the same as or different from the interlocutor's sex or gender, acknowledging that sex and gender are not the same thing and are not expressed in others in a uniform manner. This definition of bisexuality aligns well with the term queer, which I will discuss later. This contemporary definition of bisexuality counters the culturally dominant male/female binary as well as the parallel straight/gay binary.

Inscribing bisexuality

From my collection of data[1] I classified participants' interactions, communications and activities within bisexual spaces into the following five broad categories: (1) sharing coming out and identity narratives; (2) social support; (3) organisational activities; (4) inscribing bisexuality; and (5) social activism. This chapter will focus exclusively on inscribing bisexuality; however, these five categories are not mutually exclusive and activities such as coming out can also be considered a form of inscribing bisexuality, for example. This analysis will emphasise participants' efforts to "appear" visible as a bisexual in digital spaces.

Inscribing more generally means to write on something, and as such connotatively suggests to write or carve, or to dedicate something through signature. In this sense, inscribing bisexuality are the practices of 'marking' oneself as bisexual and can be thought of as the ways bisexuals mark and modify their physical bodies through clothing, fashion, piercings, tattoos and other visible means. But inscribing is not related only to the physical. Inscribing bisexuality in digital spaces are the practices of marking the digital self. This could include profile pictures, the use of graphically rendered symbols, affiliations to organisations and links to other sites through Web 2.0 technology. However, it is not necessary for bisexuals to inscribe themselves in order to be bisexual; bisexuals may choose not to inscribe in the ways I document in this research or simply not inscribe their bisexuality at all. However, what is critical in this account is that bisexuality falls outside of the hegemony of both heterosexuality as well as monosexuality; therefore, in order to be seen as bisexual one must mark oneself as neither straight nor gay. This is a particularly challenging prospect as bisexuals are frequently misread within mono-sexual culture. Consequently, the act of inscribing is a constantly intentional and subversive practice.

Participation in bisexual spaces

An obvious but important mode of inscribing bisexuality is through participation in bisexual spaces. When attending a meetup, a protest event or participating in a digital space, one is inscribing bisexuality through the act of affiliation. Participation in face-to-face (f2f) events is an impermanent form of inscribing. It has strong meaning but low retention. Once the participant leaves, the inscription fades or disappears completely. Inscribing participation through a medium (such as photographs) creates an archive and allows the reading of past inscribing to be recalled. Inscribing though participation in Internet connected digital mediums both creates an archive, and can be accessed globally. Therefore, I argue that participation in digital spaces potentially has lower meaning (because of ease of participation) but high retention. The larger study from which this data is drawn included both digital and f2f spaces; however, this chapter focuses on the specific challenges and affordances of representing bisexuality in digital spaces.

Using symbols

There are four predominant symbols used widely within bisexual spaces. The symbol purported to be the oldest is the Bisexuality Triangles, sometimes called "biangles". These emerged in popular use among bisexual activist groups in the 1980s but their origin is unclear. The use of triangles is clearly borrowed from gay iconology, which is a re-appropriation of the Nazi symbol used to identify homosexuals and perverts. Biangles are two interlocking pink and blue triangles, with a small section of purple where the triangles overlap. Participants in my study who self-identified as bisexual historians claim that the colours pink, blue and purple were established as the bisexual pride colours through the adoption of this symbol in the 80s.

The back-to-back double crescent moon symbol was purportedly created to replace the biangles because of their negative association with Nazi concentration camps. The double moon symbol is most commonly depicted in the same shades of pink, blue and purple, but is sometimes also depicted in all black. When the moons are depicted in pink, blue and purple this version of this image references back to the biangles, making the colours the dominant theme of the symbol.

Another common symbol used within bisexual spaces are the interlocking male and female gender symbols. These symbols are taken from the astrological symbols for Mars and Venus and intertwined to signify men attracted to men, men and women attracted to each other, and women attracted to women. This symbol is frequently shown in black, but is also commonly shown in pink, blue and purple.

By far the most common symbol is the Bi Pride flag. The Bi Pride flag was developed in 1998 by Michael Page. The flag was developed, according to Page, to give bisexuals their own symbol distinctive from the rainbow flag that is used internationally to symbolise diversity and pride for all Lesbian–Gay–Bisexual–Transgender (LGBT) people. The Bi Pride flag is especially used in spaces where the rainbow flag is also used, so as to mark bisexuals as a distinct group. Page designed the flag with the top 40% pink, the middle 20% purple and the bottom 40% blue. Page is quoted as explaining his creative decisions:

> The key to understanding the symbolism of the bi pride flag is to know that the purple pixels of color blend unnoticeably into both the pink and blue, just as in the 'real world', where bi people blend unnoticeably into both the gay/lesbian and straight communities.
>
> (Free Republic, 2002)

Fashion and aesthetics

Objects become bearers of social meaning when they move from being function to becoming, as Roland Barthes (1972) argued, an object of signification (i.e. having a sign value.) The clothes we choose to wear are a form of communication, however it is not an exact form of communication (Barthes 1972). What things signify are not precise and they also vary in time and space. An article of clothing may signify an aspect of an identity in a specific time, specific place and to a specific audience (Feinberg *et al.,* 1992). Given that clothes have always signalled aspects of the bearer the code has 'low semanticity', Fred Davis (1992) argues that due to the inexactness of the signifiers clothes form part of an aesthetic, as opposed to linguistic, code, whose meanings are complex and open to several interpretations. Clothes form part of cultural signifiers, which by their nature are complex and open to several interpretations.

Within bisexual spaces, choices of clothing and accessories are coded as bisexual dominantly through the use of the bisexual pride colours – pink, purple and blue, most often together so as to directly reference the bi pride colours. Examples of inscribing bisexuality in clothing and aesthetics include wearing clothing and accessories with bi pride colours, such as t-shirts, pins and jewellery. Another example wearing clothing and accessories with text that explicitly include bi messages, such as a t-shirt with the text: "Mighty Bi" or a pin that says "We Are Everywhere" in pink, purple and blue font.

Another mode of inscribing bisexuality through fashion and aesthetics is to quite literally write on the body. Tattoos and body modifications are forms of marking the body with specific meaning. As they are very much a part of self-realisation and presentation, clothing, body modification and adornment also are well suited to be interpreted through the lens of performativity. Judith Butler's (1993) work on the performativity of gender deals with the interplay between self, body, gender and dress. In her work she argues that clothing actively signals certain identities to those who can interpret the signals correctly, while also reinforcing the identity of the individual. In this way clothes are "tools for self management" (Craik, 1994) where the individual, using consumer culture, expresses elements of their identity through the choices of goods they consume.

Inscribing 2.0

Our notions of who we are as individuals are developed through our inter-actions with others. How we perceive that others see us, how we internalise others' feedback and how we judge others, all shape how we view ourselves (e.g., Goffman, 1959; Cooley, 1964). In f2f environments, these interactions involve our physical bodily presence, which creates limitations to how many spaces we can participate in at one time. In digital environments, our physical bodies are mediated through technology. This mediation creates an avatar – an icon or figure that represents a particular person. In this research I was not concerned with questions of legitimacy or accuracy of avatar representations, but rather in how representations of bisexuality are created and sustained.

Following this logic, our digital selves are no more or less plural than our corporeal selves. In *The Digital Self: Through the Looking Glass of Tel-ecopresent Others* author Shanyang Zhao points out: "To say that there is a 'digital self' is not to suggest that a person's self is actually split into phys-ical and digital parts, but to acknowledge the salience of the impact of the "E-Audience" on the formation of self in the Internet medium" (Zhao, 2005, p. 395). By examining digital practices for inscribing bisexuality, I address the direct ways that Internet technologies provide multiple platforms for creating a digital self, each one of them potentially separate or linked to each other, and with multiple audiences (e.g., Papacharissi, 2011).

Inscribing bisexuality in digital spaces includes constructing bisexual specific profiles, using iconic bisexual symbols, anchoring those symbols with text, hyperlinking to bisexual specific content as well as hyperlinking to other bisexual spaces and creating original content specific to bisexuality. None of these practices are necessarily unique to online users, nor are bisexuals using these technologies in necessarily innovative ways for the purpose of inscribing. Rather, what is of interest is the affordance of archi-val properties of the Internet. F2f environments, while constantly shaped by cultural histories – and depending on the audience, sometimes personal his-tories, too – are primarily based on the information available in the present: what is being worn at the time, whose company is being seen together in the moment, etc. However, the ability to archive artefacts of our digital selves, paired especially with the potential of linking multiple digital selves across platforms, affords users opportunities for inscribing bisexuality in ways that can potentially circumvent a dominant monosexual interpretation of their sexual orientation. These forms of inscribing include not only current digital presence, but also extant digital accounts, profiles and activities. Examples of this form of inscribing can include accessible older profile pics in publicly available Facebook accounts, cached blogs, searchable comments made on public articles and older posts stored in listservs, for example. The traces of digital selves can afford users opportunities to continually re-inscribe bisexual identities.

Online profiles

Examples of digitally inscribing bisexuality include superimposing the bi pride flag over a picture of oneself or using a graphic with bi specific text as a profile instead of a picture of oneself. Examples of this form of inscribing can include current profiles as well as archived profiles, creating a durable representation with a traceable history. Additional examples include using a bisexual-specific username or handle in digital spaces. Examples of bisexual-specific usernames in my research include "Bi_Mama", "Switch_Hitter", "fencesitter", "ALLBI" and "notgreedy" to name just a few. All of these are forms of inscribing bisexuality through online profiles.

Anchored symbols

Anchored symbols are graphics using bisexual symbols with accompanying text that provides the reader with additional meaning. Most often, this text helps identify the symbol or image as distinctly bisexual in the event that the reader was not familiar with the symbolic meaning of the image as something bisexual. Anchored symbols help audiences interpret the graphic as representing bisexuality and promote greater recognition of the symbol among wider audiences. For example, the term bisexual is sometimes referred to as "bisexuwhale", a play on the phonetic similarity of "ual" and "whale", as well as an appropriation of whales as a symbol for bisexuality. This term is largely used in-group and the anchor on this image helps the reader make the connection between the image and bisexuality. Once that connection is made, the former image helps to anchor the subsequent image of a narwhale with a bi pride horn with the anchoring text "we exist".

Original and hyperlinked content

A common form of inscribing in digital environments is to either create and post original content (narratives, images, videos, etc.) or to create hyperlinks to existing content. A hybrid form of these activities is to embed other peoples' content into original material (blogs, tweets, posts, podcasts, etc.). These three forms of activity are among the most common activities within social media and form the basis for user-generated content. User generated content generally involves some level of creative effort in producing or adapting content (Bruns, 2007; van Dijck, 2009). This concept is used to denote the shift in the user from a passive consumer to a co-contributor of the material that forms the content of the site (Bruns, 2007). By acting as co-creators of bisexual-specific material and posting it in bisexual spaces (or general Internet platforms) I deem bisexual content creation as well as hyperlinked content as practices of inscribing bisexuality.

Through the uses of bisexual-specific symbolism, appropriations of other signs and innovative creation of new sign systems, participants are purposefully attempting to increase the recognition of bisexual representation within mainstream culture. This modification entails an appropriation of the digital space to construct a representation that it may not have been intended for. These practices serve to signify bisexuality to the viewer as well as increase the recognition of bisexual representation within mainstream culture.

The desire for a visible identity

These practices for inscribing bisexuality outlined in this chapter are illustrative of the aspiration to be seen 'as' bisexual. Relatedly, the two most frequently articulated concerns of participants in the spaces I studied were (1) the frustration of not being recognised or seen as bisexual; and (2) how to achieve visibility. Analogous to some of the struggles articulated within the transsexual, pansexual and omnisexual communities, choices of intimate partners challenge the visibility of identity for bisexuals and sways the perceptions of larger social communities.

As frequently articulated among participants, intimate partners in the physical world often render their bisexual identity 'invisible' when read within the culturally dominant binary of monosexuality. Participants discuss the complexities of an identity that appears more visible in online environments than it does elsewhere:

> [Social Media] I feel I'm more out online than offline. That's because, in the offline world there's the whole "social assumptions" issue. My co-workers, friends, etc, know I have a boyfriend, wich [sic] equals "straight" for most ppl out there… Whereas online, my pic at Facebook (and Orkut) is a Bisexual Pride icon. I follow Bi groups on Twitter. I'm a member of bi groups. So, online it's spelled out, while offline ppl usually think me having a bf means I'm straight.
>
> (Alex, 11 February 2013)

Participants in digital spaces grapple with the seeming paradox of one's offline self as the 'avatar' and one's online presence as the more integrated, represented and recognised true self. This concern with visibility – and frustration with feeling invisible – is the most prominent theme among all data I collected across diverse bisexual spaces. This potential of invisibility – sometimes also referred to as 'bisexual erasure' – produces an anxiety among bisexual participants.

Conclusion

The frustration with invisibility is well illustrated in the words of bisexual activist Gigi Raven Wilbur:

The bisexual community also has grown in strength but in many ways we are still invisible. I too have been conditioned by society to automatically label a couple walking hand in hand as either straight or gay, depending upon the perceived gender of each person.

(Wong, 2013)

Tangible examples such as the Bi Pride flag and the annual #Celebrate BisexualityDay – which has been taking place on September 24 since 1999 and gained social media momentum beginning in 2013 – illustrate the frustration felt by the group that both is part of the larger LGBTQIA movement, while still being marginalised and made invisible.

The need for political voice and recognition is fundamental, as the lack of recognition leads to the silencing of the group and in extension the understanding and definition of the self, it is not enough to be recognised, but it is also fundamentally important not to be mislabelled. As philosopher Charles Taylor asserts: "Nonrecognition or misrecognition can inflict harm, can be a form of oppression, imprisoning someone in a false, distorted and reduced mode of being" (1997, p. 25).

A form of bisexual misrecognition occurs when individuals are seen as either being gay or straight and the group as a whole is seen as part of the Lesbian–Gay–Bisexual–Transgender–Queer/Questioning (LGBTQ) community. The argument that bisexuals are represented by this larger group carries with it an ignorance that does not recognise the differences between the different groups behind the acronym. Therefore, the community is not seen and valued for what it really is but, at best whilst not overlooking the political affordances of solidarity between groups, for being part of a larger whole (LGBTQIA), and at worst it is made invisible. While it may seem that the inclusion of bisexuals in the larger LGBTQIA discussion is part recognition of the group's status it is also the negation of the identity of the group as strong and deserving of independence. This inclusion should also be understood as a form of misidentification, and as with many other misidentification of subaltern groups must be seen as a form of social exclusion which negates the ability of the group to participate and leads to a lack of political and social power.

Following Taylor's assertion (1997), non-recognition or misidentification can inflict harm and is therefore a form of oppression. For a society to be just, politics must have as a primary goal to overcome subordination and aid the misidentified groups and individuals be fully functional social members – without discrimination.

The Internet, which was touted early on as a space of great potential for anonymity and exploration where visibility could be masked, here becomes the place where users try to make the perceived invisible 'visible' through digital mediation. Participants discuss the complexities of an identity that appears more visible in online environments than it does offline. Digital spaces provide particularly useful environments for participants to negotiate issues of (in)visibility through digital mediation as they employ 'technologies of visibility' through daily posts, images, videos and discourse in which bisexuality as a subject position is discursively produced.

Importantly, these cultural texts and artefacts do not represent bisexuality, but rather co-produce bisexuality within a dynamic but not limitless system of representations. Bisexual visibility is dependent upon, firstly, having an audience and, secondly, an audience that can correctly interpret the signs to co-produce a meaningful bisexual identity. Bisexual visibility, like all signs, is dependent on cultural intelligibility. As a semiotic marker of a sexual-orientation, it is rendered meaningless when there is no one who 'reads' the markers and interprets them as bisexuality.

Digital mediation, a process of enacting forms of identity – like race, gender and sexual orientation – underscores both the non-essentialism of identity as well as its hybridity and fluidity. Digital technologies contribute to the complex and multidimensional processes that shape subjectivities; they can create or deny opportunities for the articulation of different types of subjects and subject positions, and where users try to make their perceived invisibility 'visible' and culturally intelligible.

Note

1 From November 2011 until December 2014 I collected data from the following spaces: Listservs ($n = 4$), blogs ($n = 7$), organisation web portals and pages ($n = 2$), public group Facebook pages ($n = 22$), as well as face-to-face regional, national and international meetings ($n = 3$).

References

Barthes, R. (1972). *Mythologies*. London: Cape.

BiNet USA (3 March 2014). BiNet USA Bisexual Media Guide. Retrieved on 14 April 2014 from the BiNet USA website: http://binetusa.blogspot.com/2014/03/binet-usa-bisexual-media-guide.html.

Bruns, A. (2007). Produsage: Towards a Broader Framework for User-Led Content Creation. Paper presented at *Creativity and Cognition* 6, Proceedings of the 6th ACM SIGCHI, 13–15 June.

Butler, J. (1993). *Bodies that Matter: On the Discursive Limits of "Sex"*. New York: Routledge.

Cooley, C. (1964). *Human Nature and the Social Order*. New York: Scribner's.

Craik, J. (1994). *The Face of Fashion: Cultural Studies in Fashion*. London: Routledge.

Davis, F. (1992). *Fashion, Culture and Identity*. Chicago, IL: University of Chicago Press.

Djick, van, J. (2009). "Users like you? Theorizing agency in user-generated content." *Media Culture Society 31*(1), 41–58.

Feinberg, R.A., Matero, L. and Burroughs, W.J. (1992). Clothing and social identity. *Clothing and Textiles Research Journal 11*(1), 18–23.

Free Republic (7 June 2002). The History of the Bisexual Pride Flag. Retrieved on 10 December 2013 from the Free Republic website: www.freerepublic.com/focus/f-news/696174/posts.

Goffman, E. (1959). *The Presentation of Self in Everyday Life*. New York: Doubleday.

Ochs, R. (2014). Selected Quotes by Robyn Ochs. Retrieved on 14 April 2014 from the Robyn Ochs website: https://robynochs.com/quotes/.

Papacharissi, Z. (2011). *A Networked Self: Identity, Community, and Culture on Social Network Sites*. New York: Routledge.

Taylor, C. (1997). "The politics of recognition". *New Contexts of Canadian Criticism 98*.

Wong, Curtis (24 September 2013). "'Celebrate Bisexuality Day' Exists Because of These Three LGBT Activists". *Huffingtonpost.com*. Retrieved on 8 October 2016 from the Huffington Post website: www.huffingtonpost.com/2013/09/24/celebrate-bisexuality-day_n_3977289.html.

Zhao, S. (2005). The digital self: through the looking glass of telecopresent others. *Symbolic Interaction 28*(3), 387–405.

14 Exploring polyamory online

Ethics, relationships and understanding

Abbi Bloedel and Jimmie Manning

In this chapter, we explore how online interaction has the potential to provide both education and potential relationships for those interested in polyamory. From our viewpoints – Abbi as an activist and campaigner for polyamory recognition and rights, Jimmie as a sex researcher who often studies online interaction – we believe it is important that this chapter address three particular aspects of how polyamory might be experienced online. First, polyamory is often confused with other similar and not-so-similar ideas related to relationships and sexuality. Thus, we begin by providing a basic review of terms and consider how they might be misunderstood. Second, because we know that polyamory is often stigmatised by many people and cultures, we consider how online spaces have the potential to provide a private, non-threatening way to explore one's relational and sexual desires. Finally, we consider how future research about polyamory can examine online interaction.

As our brief review shows, many researchers have started to re-explore polyamory in the past decade, but in general these studies are still limited in approach and are not examining entry points into learning about how people come to know what polyamory means and how they seek polyamorous relationships. To that end, we offer a research agenda related to online explorations of polyamory that we hope will contribute to the continuously expanding and increasingly robust discussion of non-normative sexuality (see also, Manning, 2013; Manning, 2014; Manning, 2015).

Characterising polyamory

Similar to many words, phrases, concepts or identities related to sexuality and gender, *polyamory* is a contested term. The nuances of its meaning largely depend on who is using it as well as the particular situation and culture in which the utterance is embedded. In her review of polyamory literature, Dixon (2016) defines polyamory as "the ideology and/or practice of maintaining multiple romantic and/or sexual relationships with consenting partners" (p. 143). For some who identify as polyamorous, both romantic and sexual attraction (sometimes referred to as sexualove) would be required for the relationship to be polyamorous; others believe that sex and roman-tic love can easily be compartmentalised and separately explored (Anapol, 2010). Many, including the authors, believe it is important that terms such as *honesty* and *integrity* should be part of the definition to help highlight the distinct philosophies that often undergird polyamory.

Those who embrace or practice polyamory will often identify as *polyam-orous* or *poly* (e.g., "I'm poly" or "My girlfriends and I are in a poly re-lationship"). That identification alone could mean many different things. Some might confuse or conflate polyamory with the term *open relationships* because both reject monogamy. Yet, in many open relationships – where two people are dating and there is an agreement that at least one of the relational partners can have sex with other people – the understanding is often that while sex is allowed outside of the relationship, romance or in-tense emotional connection is not. Others see or recognise polyamory as a *type of* open relationship. For example, Dixon (2016) pointed out that open relationships were those that involved more than one partner, and that pol-yamory was a particular subset of open relationships guided by specific re-lational philosophies.

A relationship that is only open for one relational partner would not be considered as polyamorous by some poly communities, especially if they had a don't ask/don't tell arrangement (see Fierman and Poulson, 2011). This rejection would be especially likely if both partners wanted to be with other people (e.g., "I know you don't mind that I see other people, but if I were to see you do that it would make me too jealous"). Other poly commu-nities or individuals might reject do not ask/do not tell arrangements as not being in the open, honest spirit they see as characterising poly relationships, especially if guidelines and boundaries are not negotiated (Anapol, 2010).

Debates that examine nuances such as these can be found on a variety of online forums where polyamory is discussed. For example, the online message board reddit features many discussions about polyamory, with one of the most frequent questions asked involving how poly relationships differ from swinging. As those message boards (and discussion on other online forums) indicate, two of the key differences many poly people see be-tween them and swingers involve 'sexualove'. First, they argue poly people generally espouse the values of sexual and emotional connection, whereas swingers are simply seeking sex. Second, they characterise swinging as less dialogic and more about one partner setting or pushing a sexual agenda whereas polyamory is characterised as being more open to both or all part-ners' needs.

Even though polyamory involves openness that does not mean that peo-ple in polyamorous relationships do not have agreements about what is acceptable or unacceptable when it comes to interacting with other part-ners. Most poly relationships – similar to monogamous relationships – have rules. In monogamous romantic relationships, these rules are often implicit and unspoken until someone breaks or encroaches upon breaking the rule

(Roggensack and Sillars, 2014). However, it is common in polyamorous relationships that explicit agreements are made that include details such as what sex acts are or are not permissible with whom, what safer sex practices should be used, how much time and resources can be invested in relationships with others, which relationships take priority and when and how new relational partners are introduced to the current relationship (Anapol, 2010).

Because so much care and consideration often goes into exploring poly partners' needs, desires and comfort levels, many who are part of poly relationships take exception to the characterisation that people in polyamorous relationships are cheating on each other (Dixon, 2016). Rather, those in poly relationships are consenting to their partners exploring their social, romantic and sexual desires in agreed-upon ways. That means that people in poly relationships can also cheat if they go beyond the established rules and betray a partner or partners' trust. In addition to rules and trust, consent is another key concern for those in poly relationships. Polyamory philosophies are frequently grounded in the idea that people are in charge of their own bodies and what they do with them (Wosick-Correa, 2010). Of course, even if people love and are sexually attracted to more than one person that does not automatically mean that equal commitment can be made to all partners. Commitment takes resources, time and energy; and part of being polyamorous involves understanding that people you are in a relationship with might have stronger connections with another partner (Dixon, 2016). To honour these concerns, and to assist with the pragmatics of everyday life, some poly relationships involve one primary partner and one or more secondary partners. In such relationships, the primary partners look out for each other's wants and needs before accommodating any secondary partners (Anapol, 2010).

Even from our small overview alone it is apparent that the concept of polyamory is fluid. No universal rules regarding polyamory exist. People do polyamory in different ways, even if there is some convergence of meaning about what a polyamory philosophy entails and what is accepted or rejected as fitting under the polyamory umbrella. This umbrella, whether named or not, has long been a part of relational practices even if it was not explicitly recognised (Klesse, 2006). Yet, it was only in the late 1980s that the movement was named and recognised. As Anapol (2010) described, many advances in awareness and education were a result of the Internet.

Learning about polyamory online

Although Morning Glory and Oberon Zell came up with the word polyamory in the late 1980s using the Greek root *poly* (many) and the Latin root *amory* (love) (Anapol, 2010), it was not until the early 1990s when it gained widespread prominence through two synergistic occurrences. First, in 1992 Jennifer L. Wesp created a Usenet group *alt.polyamory* for people to discuss polyamory on the nascent Internet (Frequently Asked Questions, 2014).

Second, Morning Glory Zell-Ravenheart authored the article "A Bouquet of Lovers" for *Green Egg Magazine* that explained polyamory and its ethics. That meant that both new and traditional media were simultaneously making the idea of polyamory known and allowing people to both learn about it and potentially identify with the readings.

Soon, as Internet use increased and the number of polyamory-oriented print resources expanded, it became possible for more people than ever to learn that what they were doing was not necessarily unique or unusual; that a whole community of people were exploring polyamory. Academic literature about polyamory or other similar practices was practically non-existent until Deborah Anapol wrote an academically-informed and highly personal guide in 1992: *Love without Limits: The Quest for Sustainable Relationships – Responsible Nonmonogamy.* First sold via mail order and later being picked up by a publishing house and subsequently supported for a second edition in 1997. First published in 1997, Easton and Liszt's *The Ethical Slut: A Guide to Infinite Sexual Possibilities* also went into a second printing in 2009 – then with Liszt dropping her pen name and using her birth name, Janet W. Hardy.

Hardy's concerns about anonymity were justified. Even today, when queer rights are more prominent than ever before in an increasing number of countries, to say that one practices any form of open relationship opens the risk for being stigmatised (Matsick, Conley, Ziegler, Moors and Rubin, 2014). One of the key advantages of exploring polyamory online back then, as it is now, is the potential for privacy and comfort. Both webpages dedicated to polyamory as well as online forums allow those interested in polyamory to obtain information and support.

Privacy and anonymity

An on-going cultural dialogue regarding digital media – especially social media – involves the blurring of boundaries between public and private selves. Such discussions often note how much people share on social media and question whether such representation into one's inner life is healthy, even though little research suggests that using social media has detrimental effects for most people (see Baym, 2015, for a fuller discussion). However, the notion that digital media allow for a sense of privacy – especially for exploration of personal identity – are often ignored. For topics that might cause someone embarrassment if they were to ask others face-to-face, check out a book from the library or purchase materials from a store, Internet access can allow such exploration without fear of face threat or word spreading that such materials were accessed or purchased.

The web is rich with resources for those who wish to explore polyamory, often written with care and passion by activists. For example, a number of online blogs and webpages offer information about polyamory. As one example, Laurie Ellington's *Poly Coach* blog features a number of entries about common questions and experiences people might have about poly-amory. She offers such articles to build her expertise and to encourage people to seek out her coaching services even though the blog materials are free. Ellington's blog features a clear disclaimer that she has no official training, but rather writes from her own experiences of being polyamorous and from her experiences of working with other poly people.

Whereas *Poly Coach* is more information-oriented and reads more like a conversational textbook, other blogs can be highly personal and not centered specifically on polyamory even though they represent the lives of poly people. One such blog, *Journals of a Polyamorous Triad*, features entries about being a gamer geek, having a scar or the life of Amelia Earhart in addition to entries explicitly about poly relationships or politics. These blogs can allow people to see and understand the lives of polyamorous people outside of their sexualities. Other blogs use novel or artistic approaches when engaging readers. One of these, Kimchi Cuddles, is described as a "webcomic spreading awareness about poly, queer, and genderqueer issues in the most hilarious way possible" (Kimchi Cuddles, 2016). Its creator, Tikva Wolf, is polyamorous and the comic is based on her own experiences. The blog even features an illustration, charmingly titled the "Character Poly-cule", that allows readers both a sense of who the characters are, how they are connected and all of their different forms of identities and relationships.

The interactive aspects of online communication can also be a resource for learning and exploring identity. A number of discussion forums exist for those who are interested in polyamorous relationships, although it is important to read the description for each to understand who is or is not welcome in a given space as well as the purpose for the particular forum. As is the case with many forums where privacy, sensitivity or respect might be an issue, a number of poly discussion forums request that anyone who is part of them – including lurkers – make at least a brief introduction. Even though the idea of introducing one's self to a group of strangers might seem intimidating, especially because that information will remain in place for others to read, some anonymity is still possible. Most online profiles request minimal or select personal information, and with the right forum someone can interact with others while not fully revealing their identity. It is important to read the rules and frequently asked questions associated with a forum to learn what kind of information is required as well as what kind of information is not allowed to be asked of others in a web space. In many cases, people are allowed to use screen names or handles without listing their real name or any other personal information.

Ample evidence shows that many online communities are formed with genuine, even caring, online interactants about a variety of topics that they otherwise might not pursue (Barak, Boniel-Nissim and Suler, 2008). Actually, empirical studies suggest that people are more likely to be themselves online. Coined by Joseph Walther as the hyperpersonal effect of computer-mediated communication, people often feel less threatened revealing more about themselves and their desires when interacting online – especially with text-based platforms – than in face-to-face conversations (Walther, 2007). Thus, engaging in online communication can actually be beneficial for openness and expression. However, it is also important to consider that virtually anything posted online is traceable, sometimes quite easily. When interacting in an online forum, it is good to be cautious about what is revealed.

Support

The ability to be more open with others online can also lead to forms of support that might not be as readily available in face-to-face contexts (Wright, Banas, Bessarabova and Bernard, 2010; Wright and Miller, 2010). For example, many polyamory discussion forums have threads where people talk about how they deal with jealousy in their relationships. Jealousy is noted as one of the most difficult aspects of poly relationships for some to deal with (Easton, 2010). Ideally, people will feel more compersion – a sense of satisfaction or joy related to a partner connecting with someone else sexually and romantically (Deri, 2015) – even though jealousy is often normal, too. Online forums provide a space where jealousy and other emotional issues can be discussed with people who have likely faced similar issues themselves.

Online support might be especially beneficial for someone who is new to polyamory or who might be questioning whether or not they have a poly identity. As studies regarding coming out illustrate, the hardest aspect of many coming out conversations is the actual disclosure itself (Manning, 2016). The hyperpersonal aspects of computer-mediated communication can make it easier for someone to come out to another person online, or even to express curiosities about polyamory or a variety of other sexual or romantic desires or needs.

Other forms of online support can be more pragmatic in nature. Many institutions and social systems were created with the assumption that romantic relationships involve two people (Kipnis, 2001). Navigating processes that are already complex – such as purchasing a home, completing insurance paperwork or filing taxes – can become even more so when they involve poly relationships, especially when cohabitating (Anapol, 2010). Many online forums have discussions that address these issues allowing people to vent as well as receive emotional and instrumental support. One area of discussion that is especially popular is how poly families handle responsibilities related to children as well as how those responsibilities and other relational aspects are presented to others outside of the relationship. How romantic and family relationships are presented publicly causes anxieties for almost anyone (Duck, 2011), and so it makes sense that presenting a non-normative relationship to others would be difficult.

As these examples suggest, support for poly people can reach across the lifespan and can be offered for a variety of experiences. These include ending relationships, growing old and dealing with particular health issues or how to handle multiple people in the home post-retirement, and even the death of a partner or partners. As these topics indicate, many forums involve highly personal information that is shared among people who have formed clear on-line communities. When participating in these communities, as when partic-ipating in any web community, it is important to consider one's place in that community and for participants to consider whether or not they truly have the expertise to share the information being requested (Schon, Ristić and Manning, 2015). Online interaction – similar to any other information source – allows the potential for someone to be misinformed through low-quality or false information or even misled by both well-meaning and nefarious people. It is also important to consider that just because support is requested does not mean it will be received. Still, for those who feel isolated or who simply prefer online social interaction, online forums can provide respite.

Extending the conversation: continued exploration of polyamory and digital terrains

In this chapter, we have provided a basic introduction to polyamorous relationships and a largely descriptive explanation of how people can learn about polyamory online. In preparing this chapter it became evident that little research exists about how polyamory is represented, performed and understood in digital worlds. Moreover – and as has been noted by a vari-ety of researchers (e.g., Barker and Langdridge, 2010; Dixon, 2016; Matsick *et al.*, 2014) – polyamory itself has been grossly understudied both as a sin-gular concept and in larger literatures related to identities, sexualities and relationships. As Noël (2006) has noted, what is there is often permeated by an overwhelming sense of whiteness and an ignorance of diverse poly com-munities. With this lack of research in mind, we conclude this chapter by making a call for three areas of exploration related to polyamory and digital terrains that would make valuable contributions to the scholarly literature.

First, it is apparent that many people who visit online communities are either struggling with their poly identity, either personally or with how they present that identity to others. In many ways, being polyamorous is an ori-entation similar to being gay, lesbian or bisexual. It is not uncommon to see or hear poly people espouse that being polyamorous is a part of who they are and how they love. Moreover, polyamorous-oriented people choose to practice polyamory because it allows them to live with integrity while be-ing true to themselves. To live as monogamous would force them to deny parts of themselves or to break their relationship agreements. It would make sense, then, that more studies examine the poly closet and what it means to come out of it. Future research should examine how online information and interaction is a part of this coming out.

The constitutive model of coming out (Manning, 2016) posits that com-ing out happens on three different levels: cognitively, as a person begins to realise a sexual identity; relationally, as they share that identity with others;

and culturally, as they both use a cultural lens to make that identity intelligible and to discern how accepted (or unaccepted) the identity is. Although all levels should be explored more through research, online communication provides a good sense of both the cultural level (How is poly culture being constituted or constructed online?) and the relational level (How do poly folk interact via online spaces?). Those who study poly coming out and how people come to terms with poly identity on a psychological level should also consider what messages people recall receiving at the cultural level and how/ if online communication was beneficial to their construction of polyamory.

Second, it is also apparent that many of the online discourses make assumptions about who poly people are and do not recognise the diversity of who may or may not be poly. To that end, future research should heed the call of Noël (2006) and expand poly studies and writings beyond "white, middle-class, able-bodied, educated, American people" (p. 602) and, we believe, into intersectional domains. As many researchers note about non-normative sexualities, it can be difficult to locate diverse research participants; and when seeking to represent a fuller spectrum of identities, researchers must be cognisant of ethics regarding using or appropriating participants for their own gain or demanding too much of people who are frequently called upon to represent a particular demographic (Taylor, 2009). That is where digital technologies can again be of assistance. Online interviewing, web surveys or other forms of long-distance online research approaches (see Markham and Baym, 2008) can allow insights into wider spectra of identities and diversify research beyond the same group of people or allow for people to opt in with less face to face threat.

Finally, it is important that the research is diverse in terms of method or tradition, too. It is apparent from our review and those of others (e.g., Barker and Langdridge, 2010; Dixon, 2016; Noël, 2006) that many of the studies being conducted about polyamory either involve critical approaches related to identity or socio-psychological studies related to opinions, perceptions and cognitive processes. Although this work has been solid, examining polyamory from other social scientific and humanistic traditions could be beneficial, too. For example, one might take a cybernetic or information-oriented approach to studying online polyamory, meaning that topics such as information quality or availability might be considered. Alternately, scholars might use a sociocultural approach to consider how online poly communities are forming and how they interact. Yet still a phenomenological approach might be adopted, one where the marginalisation of poly people and communities might examine how poly rules and boundaries are negotiated among partners.

These different research traditions could then coalesce to develop a well-rounded, constitutive sense of polyamory. Moreover, this generative approach could allow for a larger research body that could contribute to both general cultural literacy about polyamory, as well as important answers for poly people, their families and their cultures.

References

Anapol, D. (2010). *Polyamory in the 21st century: Love and intimacy with multiple partners*. Lanham: Rowman & Littlefield.

Barak, A., Boniel-Nissim, M. and Suler, J. (2008). Fostering empowerment in online support groups. *Computers in Human Behavior 24*(5), 1867–1883.

Barker, M., and Langdridge, D. (2010). Whatever happened to non-monogamies? Critical reflections on recent research and theory. *Sexualities 13*(6), 748–772.

Baym, N. K. (2015). *Personal connections in the digital age* (2nd ed.). Malden: Polity.

Deri, J. (2015). *Love's refraction: Jealousy and compersion in queer women's polyamorous relationships*. Toronto: University of Toronto.

Dixon, J. (2016). 'Polyamory, sex, and the communication of commitment'. In Manning, J. and Noland, C. (eds.), *Contemporary studies of sexuality & communication: Theoretical and applied perspectives* (pp. 143–151). Dubuque: Kendall Hunt.

Duck, S. (2011). *Rethinking relationships*. Thousand Oaks, CA: Sage.

Easton, D. (2010). 'Making friends with jealousy: Therapy with polyamorous clients'. In Barker, M. and Langdridge, D. (eds.), *Understanding non-monogamies* (pp. 207–211). New York: Routledge.

Fierman, D. A. and Poulson S. S. (2011). Open relationships: A culturally and clinically sensitive approach. *American Family Therapy Association Monograph Series 7*, 16–24. Retrieved on 8 October 2016 from the Tigris Institute website: https://afta.org/wp-content/uploads/2016/05/AFTA-Monograph-Spring-2011.pdf.

Frequently Asked Questions. (2014, March 27). Section – 1). What's alt.polyamory? *alt.polyamory Frequently Asked Questions (FAQ)*. Retrieved on 8 October 2016 from the FAQ website: www.faqs.org/faqs/polyamory/faq/section-1.html.

Kimchi Cuddles. (18 April 2016). Home. *Kimchi Cuddles*. Retrieved on 8 October 2016 from the Kimchi Cuddles website: http://kimchicuddles.com.

Kipnis, L. (14 October 2001). A treatise on the tyranny of two. *The New York Times Magazine*. Retrieved on 8 October 2016 from the NY Times website: www.nytimes.com/2001/10/14/magazine/14AGAINSTLOVE.html.

Klesse, C. (2006). Polyamory and its 'others': Contesting the terms of non-monogamy. *Sexualities 9*(5), 565–583.

Manning, J. (2013). Interpretive theorizing in the seductive world of sexuality and interpersonal communication: Getting guerilla with studies of sexting and purity rings. *International Journal of Communication 7*, 2507–2520.

Manning, J. (2014). Construction of values in online and offline dating discourses: Comparing presentational and articulated rhetorics of relationship seeking. *Journal of Computer-Mediated Communication 19*(3), 309–324.

Manning, J. (2015). 'Ipsedixitism, ipseity, and ipsilateral identity: The fear of finding ourselves in the fissures between phishing and *Catfish*'. In Herbig, A., Herrmann, A. and Tyma, A. (eds.), *Beyond new media: Discourse and critique in a polymediated age* (pp. 83–107). Lanham: Lexington Books.

Manning, J. (2016). 'A constitutive model of coming out'. In Manning, J. and Noland, C. (eds.), *Contemporary studies of sexuality & communication: Theoretical and applied perspectives* (pp. 93–108). Dubuque: Kendall Hunt.

Markham, A. N. and Baym, N. K. (eds.). (2008). *Internet inquiry: Conversations about method*. Thousand Oaks, CA: Sage.

Matsick, J. L., Conley, T. D., Ziegler, A., Moors, A. C. and Rubin, J. D. (2014). Love and sex: Polyamorous relationships are perceived more favourably than swinging and open relationships. *Psychology & Sexuality 5*(4), 339–348.

Noël, M. J. (2006). Progressive polyamory: Considering issues of diversity. *Sexualities 9*(5), 602–620.

Roggensack, K. E. and Sillars, A. (2014). Agreement and understanding about honesty and deception rules in romantic relationships. *Journal of Social and Personal Relationships 31*(2), 178–199.

Schon, J., Ristić, I. and Manning, J. (2015). 'When the Internet becomes the doctor: Seeking health information online'. In Brann, M. (ed.), *Contemporary case studies in health communication* (2nd ed., pp. 311–322). Dubuque: Kendall Hunt.

Taylor, H. A. (2009). Inclusion of women, minorities, and children in clinical trials: opinions of research ethics board administrators. *Journal of Empirical Research on Human Research Ethics 4*(2), 65–73.

Walther, J. B. (2007). Selective self-presentation in computer mediated communication: Hyperpersonal dimensions of technology, language and cognition. *Computers in Human Behavior 23*, 2538–2557.

Wosick-Correa, K. (2010). Agreements, rules, and agentic fidelity in polyamorous relationships. *Psychology & Sexuality 1*(1), 44–61.

Wright, K. B., Banas, J. A., Bessarabova, E. and Bernard, D. R. (2010). A communication competence approach to examining health care social support, stress, and job burnout. *Health Communication 25*(4), 375–382.

Wright, K. B. and Miller, C. H. (2010). A measure of weak-tie/strong-tie support network preference. *Communication Monographs 77*(4), 500–517.

15 Becoming BDSM in an online environment

Rebecca S. Randall and Alan McKee

This chapter presents the voices of five young Bondage and Discpline, Dominance and Submission, Sadism and Masochism (BDSM) practitioners discussing the development of their identities and the role of online pornography – and other texts – in that process.

There exists a lot of research into young people and BDSM online – although little of it is frank about its object of study. It is part of a longstanding tradition of research into the relationship between young people, online pornography and violence (see e.g. Bhuller, Havnes, Leuven and Mogstad, 2013; Lam and Chan, 2007; Peter and Valkenburg, 2009; Wallmyr and Welin, 2006), for it is notable that most of this research does not distinguish between 'violent' sexual materials and consensual BDSM (McKee, 2015). Instead, much of this work deliberately confuses consensual and non-consensual sex acts, so that the majority of the material being studied under the rubric of 'violence' is in fact consensual kink and BDSM material (see e.g. Bridges, Wosnitzer, Scharrer, Sun and Liberman, 2010). Concerns about whether exposure to 'violent' pornography makes young people sexually aggressive often turn out to be concerns about whether exposure to consensual kink turns people into consensual BDSM practitioners. That is to say – as we explain in this chapter-research into young people, pornography, the Internet and violence often turns out to be – at least implicitly – work on the development of BDSM identities.

The heteronormative brain that changes itself

In his influential book *The Brain That Changes Itself*, Norman Doidge offers a possible model of how the Internet pushes consumers to embrace a BDSM identity:

> [I]n 2001, shortly after he first went online, [Thomas] got curious about the porn everyone said was taking over the Internet [...] galleries of naked girls, of common types of sexual fantasies [...]. Then one day he came across a site that featured spanking images. To his surprise he got intensely excited [...]. 'This was the moment', he writes 'that the real

addiction set in [...]. What other kinks was I harbouring? What other secret and rewarding corners lurked in my sexuality that I would now be able to investigate [...]. Plenty as it turned out [...]'. Until he happened upon the spanking pictures, which presumably tapped into some child- hood experience or fantasy about being punished, the images he saw interested him but didn't compel him.

(Doidge, 2007, pp. 109–110)

Using terminology from neuroscience, Doidge explains how he believes that everyone who encounters images of BDSM is at risk of being infected by this 'perversion' (Doidge, 2007, p. 102):

[T]he plastic influence of pornography on adults can also be profound, and those who use it have no sense of the extent to which their brains are reshaped by it [...]. The content of what they [porn consumers] found exciting changed as the Web sites introduced themes and scripts that altered their brains without their awareness. Because plasticity is com- petitive, the brain maps for new, exciting [ie, BDSM] images increased at the expense of what had previously attracted them.

(Doidge, 2007, pp. 103, 109)

Doidge is not alone in this belief. The model of BDSM as caused by ex- posure to dangerous images underlies much academic writing about the dangers of pornography, often expressed through slippery-slope language of 'graduation' (Zillmann and Bryant, 1986, p. 574), 'desensitisation' (Seigfried-Spellar and Rogers, 2013, p. 1997) or 'escalation' (D'Orlando, 2011, p. 59). People start looking at images of vanilla sexuality, these academics argue, but when consumers become bored with these (as they as- suredly will, in this model), they respond not by switching off the Internet and going to do something more interesting instead but rather – inevitably, these researchers claim – by becoming interested in more 'exciting' (to use Doidge's term) BDSM images.

It is worth stating explicitly that, despite the popularity of this model, there is no evidence to suggest that sexual identities – whether BDSM, va- nilla, heterosexual or homosexual – are so plastic that they can be caught from exposure to images. It is true that the research tradition exploring how people form BDSM identities is not so well developed as the litera- ture on, for example, the development of gay and lesbian identities. There exists less of a tradition arguing over whether BDSM is natural or cultural (Kruse, 1985) and there are fewer sophisticated arguments about whether such binaries are in themselves cultural constructions (Sedgewick, 1991, pp. 26–27). This chapter does not engage with these considerations, although they are important. Rather, it presents some data from the perspective of young BDSM practitioners on their experiences of becoming BDSM and the role of online media in that process. The chapter makes no claims about the nature or stability of BDSM, its root in nature or culture or its status as an identity. But it does offer young people's insights into the role of online materials in the formation of their BDSM identities.

Listening to young BDSM practitioners

Five practitioners under the age of 30 were recruited in Brisbane, Australia, in 2011 – Participant 1 (female, age 26), Participant 2 (female, age 20), Participant 3 (female, age 21), Participant 4 (male, age 29) and Participant 5 (male, age 21). The group met for a focus group and individual follow up interviews.

In asking about the role specifically of online materials in the development of BDSM identities it is useful to know whether BDSM attractions predate the consumption of Internet content. We found it interesting that several of the participants recalled incidents from their childhoods that they see as part of their developing BDSM identities. These occurred before they encountered BDSM materials on the Internet. In some cases there were no immediately identifiable texts involved in the memories: Participant 1 talked about a powerful sex dream when she was four. She vividly recalled being tied up by a woman with a penis, who did things that "felt naughty, but... felt so good at the same time" (20 July 2011). Similarly, a recurring theme in Participant 3's childhood was an affinity for animal personas. Her biting, scratching and miaowing practices saw her suspended from school several times at the age of ten. She now identifies this as a part of her developing BDSM identity. Participant 4's key point in his sexual development did not occur until he was 14:

> My first blow job was also my first orgasm and, was in front of 20 people. I was at a party and didn't understand the power of drinking vodka straight out of the bottle. [...]. I've always had kinks from there, I started off with exhibitionism [...]. I was 16 when I started swinging [...].
>
> (Participant 4, 20 July 2011)

In these memories we see a very different account of the evolution of BDSM identity from that claimed by writers like Doidge. In these cases, even before exposure to explicitly BDSM identified texts the participants had an evolving identity. The memories also point to the complexity of BDSM identity, including elements such as animal roleplay – a more sophisticated understanding of the identity than just the 'spanking' that Doidge (2007) identifies as a potential trigger for becoming BDSM.

For other participants early exposure to non-explicit materials about BDSM resonated with them. Participant 2 remembered being approximately eight or nine years old, and watching a video at her grandmother's house. It was a children's movie that had been recorded from the television, so when she went to fast forward the advertisements, she accidentally pressed stop:

[...] and what was playing on the TV was an [Australian multicultural channel] SBS special on Japanese rope bondage (...) I remember thinking about that for, years to come. That would always be at the [back] of my mind, going... 'What is this? What is that?', because I could see the bruising, and I could see the marks that these ropes were leaving on this girl, but she looked...so ecstatic...that it was fascinating to me.

(Participant 2, 20 July 2011)

None of the participants identified any sexual abuse and they expressed no regret for their actions or shame related to their key events.

At the time these incidents occurred the participants did not have BDSM identities and did not understand these events in relation to BDSM. But in retrospect they claim them as part of their sexual development. For example, Participant 1 now recognises the woman from her dream as transgendered. It was incidents such as these that inspired the participants to start to 'research' (as Participant 3 puts it) BDSM online as they grew older.

Seeking out material

Participants 1, 2, 3 and 4 had key events in their lives prior to their online learning processes about BDSM. Participant 5's story is different in that he spoke about a significant event online when he was 13. He mentioned a pornographic banner advertisement that he saw while viewing a game site aimed at young males. He clicked the ad, which took him to a BDSM site that asked for a credit card number. The image on the page still resonates with him today: "There were clothes pegs involved", he says (20 July 2011). He still remembers this image; it was all he could access without a credit card. Participant 1 said she could relate to Participant 5's story of only having the one image to 'inspire' her and that she understood the difficulty of being a minor (with no credit card) and having to rely on erotic images on the sign-in pages to fuel masturbatory fantasies.

However, as adolescents the participants had many ways of finding pornographic material. Participant 1's first sex search online occurred at age twelve, after her parents left her to babysit her brother:

[imitating her parents] *'Now, you can go on the computer but don't do anything stupid like type in SEX into the search engine.' I hadn't even had the idea in my head until [my mum] said it... I was just like '...I wonder what would happen?'.*

(Participant 1, 20 July 2011)

Participant 1's first Google Images search for sex proved it to be an easy-to-obtain source of erotic imagery and her age was not a problem in accessing this material. In Participant 5's follow up interview (26 July 2011), he said that age restrictions on pornographic websites were 'pretty irrelevant', in particular highlighting the ease with which a 14-year old could tick 'Yes I am over 18' on the website's opening page. Participant 2 however had to go to a lot of effort to circumvent her high school's Internet filter:

> [...] I had to pay $5 and my [snack] bar to... [another child], so he would fix my Internet filter on my computer at school, so that I could access all of the naughty things that I wanted ... Because his dad worked for the IT department in the school so he knew how to get around the little Internet filter.
>
> (Participant 2, 20 July 2011)

Participant 2 did not give her age at the time of this event, but she indicated that she did not have access to a home computer until she was 14. Participant 2 wanted to access these 'naughty things' so badly that she was willing to do this in the only public places where she had Internet access; the public library (where she hid her computer screen as she searched) and the high school.

In contrast to the idea that young people are accidentally finding pornography, the participants' stories emphasise their agency. They were choosing to access online materials to answer personal questions and to arouse themselves.

Building relationships online and offline

The participants were not just looking for pornography online. Participant 4 "went through a phase where [he] thought cybersex was a great idea" (29 July 2011). In retrospect he considers his actions as an adolescent as 'irresponsible' – although he thinks they did contribute to his sexual identity development. He was already participating in offline swinger events, but was having additional experiences online by roleplaying sexual scenarios with a range of different people. His choice to stop using the Internet for cybersex came about as he grew older and this transition coincides with his involvement in the Brisbane BDSM community. In addition, the new people coming into the local scene were closer to him in age than his previous connections in the scene.

Participant 3 also explored relationships and identities online. She met a person online when she was 14 and she recognised it as her first experience with learning the master-slave dynamic. This allowed her to test things that she had not had a chance to experience in the real world with someone who had the "same sort of curiosities" (28 July 2011) as herself. Later, as an 18-year old she could finally practice BDSM in the bedroom with her then-boyfriend. What is apparent for both participants is that online resources played a part in the way they formed relationships with other people.

Participant 2 also explored her BDSM identity through online relationships. Like Participant 3 she was able to use the Internet to test out "this whole other life" (30 July 2011). She spoke of a profile she signed up for on

VampireFreaks.com, a profile that was "entirely based on who I wanted to be rather than who I was" (30 July 2011). As a 13-year old on this Gothic themed website she could tell people that she liked handcuffs and power control, and not have to admit that she had never tried them. The quality she appreciated most from this group of people was the support and the community's validation of her new identities was reinforcement of her desires. But she was disappointed at the lack of knowledge in this 'juvenile' community. This search for information led her to Alt.com, another place where she could be "really honest" (30 July 2011) about what she wanted and who she wanted to be. When she was 17 a man in Sydney made contact with her through Alt.com. While she acknowledges that their relationship could have "led to a very dangerous situation" (20 July 2011) (discussed below), she also saw the positives. Her social skills developed through the long-term interaction with this man, and importantly she began to accept that it was a real part of her personality, and something that she no longer wanted to keep as a 'dirty little secret'.

For Participant 1, online support was important not so much for allowing her to discover her BDSM identity as for helping her to stay in the community. While serving as a submissive in an offline relationship, she was not allowed to voice an opinion on BDSM websites without the permission of her dominant. The pair shared a joint profile on Collarme.com, and Participant 1 asked for permission to start forming online friends. This request would prove beneficial when the relationship fell apart:

> [M]y only real experience with it had been this one person who was all kinds of messed up in the head [...] if I was just going to go off that then I would have written it off completely but, through the online friends that I'd made and counselling with them they've gone 'No, it's... like, he's the kooky and crazy one, not you, it's okay'.
>
> (Participant 1, 20 July 2011)

Participant 5's lack of offline support was for different reasons. Growing up in a strict Catholic household, he wanted to know if he was a normal 13-year old for his kinky proclivities. Despite being straight like his peers, he still had no one to discuss his BDSM interests with in the offline world or test out BDSM relationships with. This all came when he turned 18. Participant 5 identifies himself as someone who likes to take what he has learned online and apply it in the real world.

For these young BDSM practitioners, using BDSM pornography to achieve arousal was only one part of their use of online materials. Participant 5 and Participant 1 gained their first exposure to bondage and dominance fantasies online and their preferences developed as they explored the available materials. Trying on different identities online proved useful to Participants 4, 3 and 2. This afforded them opportunities to simulate sexual practices, BDSM etiquette and get closer to being the people that they wanted to become. Once Participants 2 and 1 came closer to whom they wanted to be, the online support networks they had formed for themselves proved essential to reaffirming their identity politics and beliefs. All of this would go on to shape their experiences online as they took the next steps towards being BDSM practitioners both on-and offline.

It is notable that even at a young age these BDSM practitioners had a sense that they were developing an identity that marked them out as different from their peers. Friends the same age were exploring the Internet in the same way and being exposed to similar images – the banner ad involving clothes pegs was visible to anybody clicking through to that site. But for these young people these images resonated in a particular way.

Using online resources today

The participants in this study still regularly use online resources, but now for a different purpose. The online experiences we have discussed so far have been about the identity construction process, and started before the participants turned 18. Now as adults the Internet continues to contribute to their identities. They talked collectively about getting into the offline scene in Brisbane. When asked how she coordinated her social calendar, Participant 2 noted that she regularly takes advantage of Fetlife's Facebook-style layout for events and connecting people. Whether it is munches (social events including food), sexual play parties or other events, Participant 2 has a potential interest in up to thirty events on any given week. Of those, she usually chooses about three to attend. Participant 1 also enjoys the Fetlife social experience, referring to the discovery of Fetlife being akin to the opening of Pandora's box.

Participant 4's experience with the Brisbane scene 'before Fetlife' emphasises the importance of this online resource:

> [B]efore Fetlife, [the] Brisbane scene was run out of Yahoo! Groups and to become a member of the Yahoo! Group you had to know somebody in the Yahoo! Group who would vouch for you and before you could go to a party, you had to know someone willing to vouch for you, and the only way to meet people was to go to the party.
>
> (Participant 4, 20 July 2011)

In the interview on 29 July 2011, Participant 4 called himself an 'early adopter' of Fetlife, having signed up for a profile when the site first opened in 2008. He talked with pride and at length about how a Fetlife member can determine which number their membership carries. His own membership number is "in the 2000 range", and he also has "the dubious honour of owning Group #69" on the website.

The accounts from Participants 1, 2 and 4 paint a picture of a BDSM scene that is more accessible than it used to be. It is also important to appreciate the different viewpoint that Participant 4 comes from. He faces the puzzling situation of still being a young BDSM practitioner, but being considered part of the old BDSM scene. He fought hard to find his identity in a scene that did not support his choice to be a young dominant, and he is even "a little jealous" (29 July 2011) of the young practitioners coming through in the last five years.

Online resources are still a major part of how young practitioners in Brisbane participate in the scene and there is a blend of online and offline interaction. This merging of the two spheres is also prominent in issues of safety.

Safety first

Safety is paramount in BDSM practice (Langdridge and Barker, 2007) and this raises important issues in relation to the use of online resources by young BDSM practitioners. When it comes to BDSM safety online there are two elements: (1) physical safety when practicing BDSM related techniques; and (2) personal safety when choosing who to meet offline. Trust is key in both of these elements. Lack of supervision or experience has led to a number of deaths in the BDSM community, most commonly in the case of auto-erotic asphyxiates (Downing, 2007). The issue of trust and safety came up in the discussion when Participant 5 said that "the anonymity [of the Internet] works two ways"; in that "it's a great way of putting yourself forward" (20 July 2011) but the predators and the 'creeps' can also come out. Participant 4's response to this covers the importance of trust between play partners and some of the safety issues of the Internet:

> If you're at a rock climbing club and somebody introduces themselves and says that they're a rock climbing instructor and gives you a whole bunch of advice ... [but] if they don't know what they're talking about you're going to fall and die. And most people aren't quite that irresponsible. In BDSM lots of people think that because they watched some porn, or been on Second Life, that they're perfectly qualified to give you rock climbing advice [...].
>
> (Participant 4, 20 July 2011)

Misrepresentation of expertise is a recognised problem online (Morpheous, 2008, p. 52). Participant 4's rock climbing analogy is a confirmation of this problem in the Brisbane BDSM scene. Participant 2 knows first-hand that there are people online who can take advantage of the young and vulnerable. The man she met on Alt.com was an example of this kind of person and even as a 17-year old she realised that it was a dangerous situation. In the end, it was her self-preservation mechanism that prevented her from flying to meet the man in Sydney. Participant 3 also admitted that as a 15-year old, she knew very little about the truth of her online chat partner.

Having said this, all of the female participants said that they have created their own safety filters as part of developing their sexual identities. For some this is their own judgement. For others, as in Participant 1's case, it is 'good close friends' that she relies on to serve as her 'safety filter'. Both Participants 1 and 2 refuse to give out contact information on the BDSM social networking sites, but are happy to meet people at public fetish parties such as Hellfire. Participant 3 suggested that in developing their safety filters Fetlife's social networking structure has played an important role. There is a strong reliance on a 'six degrees' style approach to trusting people online. Knowing someone who can vouch for you makes you more appealing to practitioners such as Participants 1, 2 and 3. This recalls Participant 4's comments about old Yahoo! Groups for BDSM in Brisbane where you had to know someone personally to be invited. This is similar to offline groups such as Club Libertine.

Conclusion

The dominant model in academic research for thinking about the relationship between young people and online BDSM materials is the slippery slope argument, powerfully articulated by Zillmann and given new life for the Internet by writers like Doidge. In this model, young people who might otherwise happily repress their 'perversions' are contaminated by visual materials and become BDSM – at least for as long as those materials are available to them. Such approaches display little interest in the experiences or arguments of BDSM practitioners – indeed, writers such as Doidge explicitly argue that we should not listen to such practitioners, whose very happiness with their identity proves their 'perversion'.

This chapter takes a different approach. As we comment above, researchers have noted that young members of minority sexual groups grow up in cultures where they are unlikely to receive supportive or accurate information about their sexual identities from parents, schools or the mainstream media, and that for such youth the Internet can play an important role in providing materials for identity formation. This study suggests that the same is true for young BDSM practitioners. Several of the participants in this study recalled feeling in childhood that they were different, and described actively seeking out material to help them make sense of that difference. There was agreement across participants that online materials were an important part of this process. The uses made of online materials by LGBTQIA youth identified by previous researchers were all mentioned by participants in this research – gathering information, validating their identities, participating in communities and forming relationships. In addition these participants identified a further use of online materials which specifically relates to BDSM identities – the promotion of safety. The participants stated that taking up a healthy BDSM identity involves learning to understand the risks involved and appropriate strategies to manage them. Online materials were identified as an important part of this process.

The evidence provided in this chapter makes clear that the young people who embraced a BDSM identity did so with a clear sense of agency that is missing from the voices of the sad young men reported second-hand by writers like Doidge, who feel powerless in the grip of Internet pornography and are so grateful to be rescued by him from its clutches. The participants in this study have used cultural resources – both offline and online – to build for themselves identities, relationships and safe communities which remain an important and satisfying part of their lives.

In this chapter we have not proposed a mechanism for becoming BDSM. This is not only because a sample size of five young people is not suitable for making such claims. More than this, we accept the arguments of researchers like Kath Albury that teleological accounts of how one takes up a settled sexual identity do not well serve BDSM (Albury, 2015). The scope of this chapter is more modest – to carve out some space for BDSM identities away from the model of BDSM as the necessary endpoint of viewing pornography, and to return some sense of agency to young people who enjoy consensual BDSM practice.

References

Albury, K. (2015). Identity plus? Bi-curiosity, sexual adventurism and the boundaries of "straight" sexual practices and identities. *Sexualities 18*(5–6), 649–664.

Bhuller, M., Havnes, T., Leuven, E. and Mogstad, M. (2013). Broadband internet: an information superhighway to sex crime? *The Review of Economic Studies 80*(4), 1237–1266.

Bridges, A. J., Wosnitzer, R., Scharrer, E., Sun, C. and Liberman, R. (2010). Aggression and sexual behavior in best-selling pornography videos: a content analysis update. *Violence against Women 16*(10), 1065–1085.

Doidge, N. (2007). *The Brain that Changes Itself: Stories of Personal Triumph from the Frontiers of Brain Science*. New York: Viking.

D'Orlando, F. (2011). The demand for pornography. *Journal of Happiness Studies 12*(1), 51–75.

Downing, L. (2007). "Beyond safety: erotic asphyxiation and the limits of SM discourse". In Langdridge, D. and Barker, M. (eds.), *Safe, Sane and Consensual: Contemporary Perspectives on Sadomasochism* (pp. 119–132). Hampshire: Palgrave Macmillan.

Kruse, M. (1985). Nature/nurture. *Journal of Homosexuality 10*(3–4), 141–152.

Lam, C. B. and Chan, D., K-S. (2007). The use of cyberpornography by young men in Hong Kong: Some psychological correlates. *Archives of Sexual Behavior 36*(4), 588–598.

Langdridge, D. and Barker, M. (eds.). (2007). *Safe, Sane and Consensual: Contemporary Perspectives on Sadomasochism*. Hampshire: Palgrave Macmillan.

McKee, A. (2015). Methodological issues in defining aggression for content analyses of sexually explicit material. *Archives of Sexual Behavior 44*(1), 81–87.

Morpheous. (2008). *How to Be Kinky: A Beginner's Guide to BDSM*. n.p.: Green Candy Press.

Peter, J. and Valkenburg, P. M. (2009). Adolescents' exposure to sexually explicit Internet material and notions of women as sex objects: assessing causality and underlying processes. *Journal of Communication 59*(3), 407–407.

Sedgewick, E. (1991). How to bring your kids up gay. *Social Text* (29), 18–27.

Seigfried-Spellar, K. and Rogers, M. K. (2013). Does deviant pornography use follow a Guttman-like progression? *Computers in Human Behavior 29*(5), 1997–2003.

Wallmyr, G. and Welin, C. (2006). Young people, pornography and sexuality: sources and attitudes. *The Journal of School Nursing 22*(5), 290–295.

Zillmann, D. and Bryant, J. (1986). Shifting preferences in pornography consumption. *Communication Research 13*(4), 560–578.

16 Negotiations of identity, pleasure and health in women's online sex work advertisements

Alexandra Marcotte and Justin R. Garcia

Despite evidence that increasing numbers of sex workers are marketing themselves on the Internet (Parsons, Bimbi and Halkitis, 2001; Phua and Caras, 2008), the ways in which women sex workers self-advertise online is not well understood. Existing research on women engaging in sex work is often focused on the various risks and outcomes associated with their labour. Sexual health, drug use and safety are common areas of analysis (e.g., Farley and Barkan, 1998; Tyler, 2009; Hubbard and Prior, 2013), as well as the motivations and circumstances for participating in the sex work industry (e.g. Simons and Whitbeck, 1991; Widom and Kuhns, 1996; Wilson and Widom, 2010). Although sex work is generally presumed to be more regularly done by women with men as clients, the majority of research on sex workers' self-marketing has focused on male sex workers. This chapter examines women sex workers' online advertisements in major US cities, exploring the various gendered and racialised implications of their marketing, particularly in relation to identity, pleasure and sexual health.

Few published studies explicitly examine sex workers' self-marketing techniques, despite increased use of the Internet for social, sexual and commercial exchange. Phua and Caras (2008) explored the online marketing strategies used by Brazilian male sex workers in comparison to white American male sex workers, to understand the extent to which ethnicity factors into personal branding. They found that Brazilian sex workers often highlighted their ethnicity when advertising themselves, but determined that "the decision to employ such a strategy depends on the extent to which sex workers view their ethnic, racial, or national sexual stereotypes as advantageous" (p. 240). Pruitt (2005) also examined online sex work advertisements posted by men. Pruitt's findings were similar to those of Phua and Caras – putatively positive factors (including large penis size and younger age) are included with higher frequency in sex worker advertisements than neutral or negative factors. While these studies offer insights into the presentation of sex work on the Internet, and perhaps into some of the factors involved in recapitulating sex work itself, scholarship suggests that male sex work is quite a different gendered enterprise than women's sex work (Agresti, 2009). Gay male sex workers, for example, face homophobia much more frequently.

Although sex work for both men and women is illegal in many parts of the world, male sex work has historically been more clandestine than female sex work, due to the fact that the majority of male sex workers have male clients (Minichiello and Scott, 2014).

Although not specifically focused on advertisements, Sanders (2005) found that female sex workers often shape their work identities to match normative expectations of particular bodies. Relying on ethnographic data, Sanders and colleagues contend that sex workers emphasise aspects of themselves that are commonly fetishised, such as ethnicity. The findings on sex work advertisements by Sanders (2005), Pruitt (2005) and Phua and Caras (2008), also present similarities to research on personal (dating) advertisements. There have been several studies on personal/dating advertisements, which have found that both men and women emphasise what they believe to be their positive personality and physical features and downplay perceived negative characteristics (e.g. Phua and Kaufman, 2003; Dawson and McIntosh, 2006). Research suggests that such patterns also hold for the advertisements of online sex workers and that the presentation of those traits generally presumed desirable is associated with relatively greater financial costs charged for sexual services (Saad, 2008; Capiola *et al.*, 2014). Although there are clear differences in personal ads and in sex worker ads, in terms of goals and desirable features (sexual fetishes, for example, might be a desirable aspect of a sex worker's ad for potential clients, but generally not for those seeking a romantic dating partner), findings from personal advertisements help inform the process of voluntary self-marketing in an online socio-sexual context.

Drawing on existing research on both sex worker and personal advertisements, this study analyses marketing techniques used by sex workers on the open-access website Backpage.com and examines the ways in which women's self-described attributes are used to increase clientele interest and income. Of particular interest to this study are included discussions of gender, race, age, health and pleasure.

Sex work and the Internet

The Internet is increasingly popular among sex workers because it provides an inexpensive and relatively anonymous space to advertise to potential clients while also being somewhat safer than 'street prostitution' (Phua and Caras, 2008). Several recent studies have examined demographic differences among Internet-based sex workers and outdoor or street sex workers. Cunningham and Kendall (2011) note that male sex workers who use the Internet face fewer negative health, safety and legal consequences than street-based sex workers. Mimiaga *et al.* (2008) report similar findings and also find that drug use among male sex workers who advertise on the Internet is lower than among street-based sex workers. While both of these studies examine male sex work, parallel results have been reported in research on female sex work both inside and outside of the US (Cunningham and Kendall, 2010; Wong *et al.,* 2011).

The demographic differences between Internet-based sex workers and street-based sex workers have also been studied. Numerous studies show that the use of the Internet among sex workers is tied to younger age groups, higher socioeconomic status and higher educational status (Mimiaga *et al.,* 2008; Cunningham and Kendall, 2011; Wells *et al.,* 2011). These findings are not surprising in light of the costs associated with owning a computer or phone with Internet access, along with the technological skill needed to post advertisements.

Public classifieds sites like Craigslist.org and Backpage.com are among the most popular websites in the US for sex worker advertisements because they are easily accessible and simple to browse. Although Craigslist is still used with some frequency among sex workers, its 'Adult Services' section was officially and permanently removed in 2010 in an attempt to limit the number of prostitution advertisements posted to the site (Miller, 2010). As a result, Backpage.com, a lesser-known public classifieds site, became one of the most popular websites among sex workers (Cunningham and Kendall, 2011). Backpage's 'Adult' section has always been somewhat unregulated; and, as demonstrated by the numerous legislative attempts across the US in the years since 2010 to prohibit websites like Backpage from displaying prostitution advertisements, Backpage is well known as a place to solicit sex. Most major cities and towns across the country have a dedicated Backpage sub-site (e.g., atlanta.backpage.com) and across the country there are thousands of new 'escort' advertisements posted every day. Women who post 'escort' ads on Backpage must pay a small fee per advertisement. The fee amount varies across cities and ranges from $1 in smaller cities to $17 USD in larger cities. Charging for advertisements also allows Backpage access to personal information in the form of names, billing addresses and credit card numbers. Obtaining this personal information provides a way for Backpage, and potentially law enforcement, to link advertisements to particular women. Potential clients, however, do not have to pay to contact posters, including sex workers – all they must do is respond with a valid email address. In this way, Backpage provides more anonymity to potential clients than to sex workers, and thus like many other venues for sex work creates an imbalance in legal risk.

An important component of Backpage is that women create and post advertisements for themselves. Therefore, in the current study we remain focused on how women are marketing themselves to clients (typically men). Unlike examining pornography or brothel advertisements in which women have little control over how their sexualised images are used, Backpage provides a rare space where women choose how they are portrayed to a large audience.

Note on language

Throughout this chapter, women who post ads on Backpage are referred to as sex workers rather than prostitutes. The term 'sex worker' denotes that they are performing labour, which is often overlooked in discussions about sex work. While their labour is sexualised, we reject the tendency to exceptionalise sex work, as doing so renders invisible the everyday experience of sex workers and in turn prevents their labour from being considered in discussions of labour reform. The most frequent debate in the feminist literature on sex work focuses on the issue of consent (see MacKinnon, 2006). Although discussions of voluntary and involuntary sex work are undoubtedly important, heavily focusing on consent to the exclusion of the everyday experiences of women involved in sex work can shift attention away from the fact that sex work is a form of work. Further, although there are many forms of sex work (e.g. stripping and pornography), the term 'sex work' in the current study applies specifically to prostitution (i.e. the practice of engaging in sexual activity with someone for payment). Finally, the term 'escort', often used as a euphemism for a sex worker (particularly on the Internet) to suggest a consumer is only purchasing time together and not explicitly sexual activity together (rendering the latter but not necessarily the former explicitly illegal), is used on occasion to mirror Backpage's language.

Methodology

Data were drawn from womens' Backpage.com sex work advertisements (Backpage → 'Adult' → 'Escorts') in the top ten Metropolitan Statistical Areas (MSAs) as indicated at the time of data collection. A MSA is defined as a geographical region with a high population density, containing a core urban area with a population of 50,000 or more people. Ten MSAs across the country were chosen in an effort to include as much demographic diversity as possible, while also serving to neutralise the effect of specific single-city locations in the data. In Miami, for example, most of the ads we observed are of Latina or white women and there are relatively few of other racial groups. Similarly, although a single-city regional analysis of sex work advertisements has utility, it would be challenging to make inferences about place and specific regional customs as an undetermined number of women do not live in cities where they are posting ads. As evidenced by the number of postings with titles like 'Here for one day only' or 'New in town', it is clear that many of these women travel for business. Despite being in different cities on different days, the advertisements often remain the same. A woman might post an advertisement in Atlanta one day and then post a very similar ad in Miami two days later, for example. This makes regional analysis difficult to perform and unlikely to yield useful regionally-specific information.

Two dates (a Monday and a Saturday in February 2014) were selected for days of data collection, and for each of the ten MSAs the first fifteen advertisements posted on each of those two days were recorded and saved for analysis. The resulting 300 advertisements were then coded for the following categories: age, race and ethnicity, health status, how health status was discussed, mention of safe sex practices, requirements of clients, body characteristics and measurements, intent to provide pleasure and use of words such as 'discreet' and 'classy'. Characterisations were made using the typology developed and using the content available from the written text in the advertisements, the written title of the advertisement and presence of photos. The first author coded all advertisements. A sub-section was randomly chosen and also coded by the second author to test for inter-rater reliability. There was over a 95% inter-rater reliability across scoring of all pre-determined typology categories.

Results and discussion

A total of 300 Backpage.com advertisements were coded. In addition to the title listings, most Backpage advertisements contain a few sentences to a paragraph of information about the sex workers. This information typically includes ways to contact the women, location, prices, body and personality descriptors and/or images of the women. The current study looked at the frequency with which certain key descriptors – age, race and ethnicity, health, pleasure and requirements of clients – were used.

The content that women include in their sex work advertisements is strategic and aimed at increasing their clientele (Pruitt, 2005; Phua and Caras, 2008). Sex workers' decisions about including their breast sizes or race(s) in their advertisements, for example, are based on the extent to which they understand these features to be marketable. As Phua and Caras (2008) argue, "[l]ike any other type of business advertising, sex workers highlight their strengths and downplay their less marketable characteristics" (p. 239). Therefore, we infer that the ways in which female sex workers on Backpage. com discuss identity, pleasure and sexual health are not accidental.

Age

Backpage requires women to report their age when posting and this information is displayed next to the title of the advertisement. Anyone posting in a Backpage classifieds category outside of 'Adult Services', such as 'Electronics' or 'Furniture' for example, is required to include a title for their advertisement as well as a price for the object they are selling. Someone browsing the website for an item such as a couch would see the price in the same place on the screen that someone browsing the escort section would see a woman's age. Thus, because of the way in which Backpage is structured, a woman's age becomes a signifier of value.

As the findings show, the highest reported age was 44 years and the lowest was 18 years. Although prostitution is illegal for women of all ages in the US (aside from some regulated forms of sex work in Nevada), clients who solicit sex from women under the age of 18 years face much harsher legal penalties, if caught, than those who solicit from adult women. Additionally, under the US Victims of Trafficking and Violence Protection Act, any sex worker under the age of 18 years is automatically classified as a victim of human trafficking (H.R. 3244). Although the age of sexual consent varies from state to state, the minimum age of consent is 18 years, so federal laws typically adhere to the strictest state standard. As a result of this clause of the Victims of Trafficking and Violence Protection Act, Backpage automatically removes all advertisements posted by women reporting to be 17 years of age and younger so as not to be held liable for promoting human trafficking. If women under 18 advertise on Backpage, they would have to report being at least 18 years of age.

Further, while the minimum reported age must be at least 18, the data show that there appears to be an unspoken maximum age as well. Although there is no way to know the exact ages of the women who posted advertisements, it is unlikely that almost all are between the ages of 18 and 29. The average reported age of posters was 23 years, with 44 years being the oldest reported age and 18 years being the youngest. Only 15 women (5%) reported being 30 years or over, with nine of the 15 listing their ages as between 30 and 34 years. The fact that women are predominantly reporting their ages to be between 18 and 29 years suggests that younger women are more valuable in the sex trade – or younger ages are more valuable at least among those who advertise, and conversely those who seek services, on the Internet.

Race

Of the 300 advertisements analysed, 39% (116 advertisements) mentioned race and/or ethnicity. Of those, 78% included race/ethnicity in the title of the posting. Since titles encompass the first pieces of information that potential clients encounter, the content that women choose to include in the titles of their advertisements is therefore important in terms of marketing. Our finding that 78% of women that mention race include it in the title of their posting suggests that race and ethnicity are more primarily used as marketing tools rather than simply as descriptors. The choice to include race in the title likely indicates that it is intended to direct and entice clients. This further suggests that race is being eroticised and perhaps fetishised, insofar as clients browsing for women can scan the advertisement titles, and in some ways cannot really avoid scanning for particular races/ethnicities while browsing.

The majority of women who mention race and/or ethnicity either in the title or body of their advertisements (or both) are non-white. Among these women, however, there is no noticeable difference between racial groups in terms of how often they disclose their non-white race/ethnicity. While some women use ambiguous racial descriptors such as 'caramel' or 'mixed', others are more detailed about their ethnic backgrounds. One woman from Boston, for example, described herself as 'Czech and Sicilian' and another woman from Philadelphia writes that she is 'Puerto Rican and Italian'. The choice between ambiguity and specificity is most likely connected to whether or not and how these women think of their races/ethnicities as marketable.

Additionally, many of the body type descriptors were often racialised. For example, women who self-identified as black (coded as those who identified their race as 'black', 'chocolate' or 'ebony', among others) commonly used phrases like 'thick', 'curvy' and 'big booty'. In contrast, women who self-report as white or as an ethnicity frequently understood as white in the context of the US (such as French), frequently use descriptors like 'petite' or 'busty'.

The finding that women of colour, particularly black women, were much more likely to use terms like 'juicy' or 'bootylicious' than white women is not surprising given the nearly incessant hyper-sexualisation of black bodies throughout Western history (see McClintock, 1995). Wendy Burns-Ardolino (2009) echoes this when she asserts that "[...] it is important to recognise the ways that the female big butt becomes at once a symbol of empowerment and an object of ridicule as it is racialised, sexualised, and classified" (p. 271). Women who market themselves as 'bootylicious' and so on are thus fetishising and racialising themselves, but it is done in service of increasing their sex work financial standing. Perhaps, then, this is precisely a moment in which these women are empowering themselves while simultaneously re-inscribing norms of race, bodies and gender.

Health

The shift to online advertising has also changed the way that sex workers communicate concerns of sexual health and safety. As such, the frequency with which sexual health was mentioned in the advertisements on Backpage as well as the ways in which this topic was discussed were both important to note. Of the advertisements analysed, 9% mentioned safe sex practices. Phrases such as 'provide your own supplies' or '100% safe' are common to these 26 advertisements. Rarely, however, do the advertisements specifically and unambiguously discuss safe sex practices. Although '100% safe' most likely indicates that condoms will be used and/or other sexual protective measures will be taken (i.e. no unprotected oral sex, no insertion of potentially unclean fingers or objects), given the context in which these women are advertising, it is possible that '100% safe' refers to the safety and security of the meeting location, for example.

The issue of sexually transmitted infections (STIs) was raised by 17% of the advertisements. Common descriptors here include 'clean' and 'disease free'. Terms such as 'clean' are ambiguous and could refer to a clean meeting location or suggest that hygiene is an important consideration, rather than disease status per se. This ambiguity is most likely intentional on the part of the women posting. If potential clients are looking to have safe sex, they are expected to infer that from these advertisements. However, much like other venues wherein one notes their status as STI-free without actually having been tested or expecting others to simply take them at their word, this is not a particularly effective strategy for ensuring sexual health and STI risk reduction.

Pleasure

Discussions of pleasure were common and as one might expect, 79% of the postings included some mention of the intent to provide pleasure to customers. For example, a woman in Atlanta writes, "[...] I'm ready to cater to your wants and needs. You deserve the best baby [...]". Another in Washington DC says "[...] I would love to show you an unforgettable experience". What is interesting about the inclusion of such statements is that they convey a promise of sexual pleasure without a direct discussion of sex. With the exception of a few advertisements in which women promise to cater to fetishes and sexual fantasies, most of the advertisements that discuss clients' pleasure do so without explicitly promising sexual pleasure or particular sexual behaviours/acts. Although sex is certainly a large part of the business, there are several diverse reasons why people might solicit these women – including sexual and nonsexual intimacy, girlfriend experiences and so on.

Women promising pleasure to their clients is to be expected in Backpage advertisements; however, a finding that was unexpected was how frequently these women discussed their own pleasures and desires. Although not a majority, nearly a quarter of the advertisements included mention of the poster's pleasure. For example, a woman in Boston writes that she is 'PlayfulandBorn to pls(it turns me on!)' and an advertisement in Miami includes, 'I Love what I do and so will YOU!!!'.

The decision to engage in sex work is often covered in the research literature in terms of necessity – usually economic necessity or through force, fraud or coercion – rather than in terms of pleasure. However, if a significant portion of women include their own pleasure in their advertisements, as these findings suggest, then perhaps the paradigm through which sex work is considered in the academic literature needs to be expanded to allow for the possibility that some sex workers enjoy their labour and or believe their enjoyment to be a marketable inducement for the purchaser (see Chateauvert, 2014, for more about sex workers' pleasure). Further, the majority of the advertisements that included information about women's sexual pleasure, client pleasure and poster pleasure are often included in the same sentence. This suggests that whether or not women enjoy the encounters, or seem to enjoy it, has an impact on clients' pleasure. This issue of mutual pleasure also raises the possibility that women's comments about their own pleasure are serving to attract clients who can be led to believe that the client will be able to provide sexual fulfilment to a partner, regardless of whether they actually do, and despite the sex worker-client relationship. This would play on a masculine psychology concerned with being a sexually capable man who provides pleasure to partners.

Requirements of clients

More than half of advertisements (53%) include information about 'acceptable' and 'unacceptable' clients. The majority of these are about behaviour – no texting or crude language, for example – but a significant number also include age and/or race restrictions. For instance, a woman from Atlanta writes, "No men under 30 years of age. I prefer upscale clients. White men". A woman from Chicago requires that "no African American men" contact her. Interestingly, several of the women with race restrictions (almost all of which indicated being pro-white men as clients and anti-black men as clients) are women of colour. Although there are several ways to analyse this data, one interpretation is that this information is written for the benefit of white men rather than to benefit the sex workers. That women on Backpage often require their clients to be white or not black, depending on the advertisement, might be a way of attracting men who do not want to solicit sex from women who have also had a sexual encounter with black men. Here, we are reminded of the historical legacies of black male sexuality that understand black men to be dangerous and sexually deviant. Whether the women posting the advertisements are knowingly and purposefully engaging with this rhetoric is unclear through content analysis alone, but the implications should not be overlooked. From the advertisements examined in this study, it appears that women sex workers on Backpage are frequently re-inscribing stereotyped expectations of sexuality while concurrently engaging in sexual practices that are outside of normative sexuality (i.e. prostitution) (Table 16.1 and Figure 16.1).

Table 16.1 Percent of total advertisements ($n = 300$) containing information on descriptors

Age	Race/ethnicity	Sexual health	Pleasure	Requirements of clients
100%*	39%	9% safe sex practices/17% mention STIs	79%	53%

*Backpage requires that advertisers include their age.

Limitations and future directions

These online sex work advertisements are representations of sexuality and a particular aspect of sexuality in the form of sexual labour in exchange for financial compensation. By studying these advertisements, we are better able

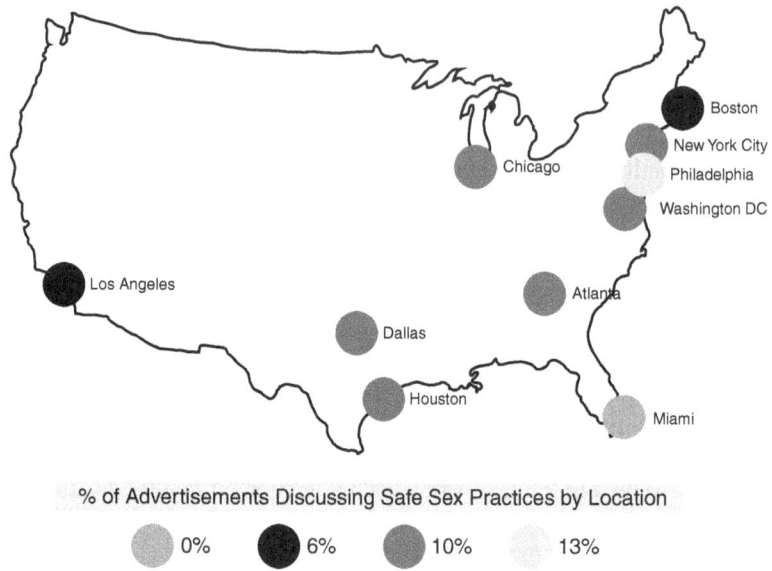

Figure 16.1 Safe Sex Discussions by Location.

to understand how sex workers are using the Internet to market themselves, and what forms of sexualised information are being discussed in order to attract clients and communicate the norms of illegal sex work throughout the US today.

Although outside the scope of the current study, an examination of the images posted to Backpage.com could further our understanding of women's self-marketing techniques. There is one such study that focuses on men's sex work advertisements (Tyler, 2014), but the implications and histories of particular poses and clothing choices do not function the same between men and women. A study that looked at the way women dress in their advertisements, how much nudity they choose to display and their poses would strengthen the existing body of knowledge on contemporary sex work.

Conclusion

The results of this study suggest that descriptors such as age, race and body type are deliberately used as marketing tools by women sex workers in their online advertising. Age appears to be an important factor in attracting clients; however, it is unclear how often and how specifically sex workers would report age if it were not required to by Backpage. Race and ethnicity are clearly highlighted by a high percentage of sex workers while safe sex practices and disease status are mentioned by surprisingly few. All of these factors have broad implications for how we understand sexuality and are important directions for further research both on sex work and on the intersections of sex and technology.

References

Agresti, B.T. (2009). *E-prostitution: A content analysis of Internet escort websites* (Unpublished master's thesis). The George Washington University, Washington DC.

Backpage. Escorts. Retrieved on 14 September 2016 from the Backpage website: www.backpage.com.

Burns-Ardolino, W. (2009). "Jiggle in my walk: The iconic power of the big butt in American popular culture". In Rothblum E., Solovayand S. and Wann M. (eds.), *Fat studies reader* (pp. 271–279). New York: New York University Press.

Capiola, A., Griffith, J.D., Balotti, B., Turner, R and Sharrah, M. (2014). Online escorts: The influence of advertised sexual orientation. *Journal of Bisexuality 14*(2), 222–235.

Chateauvert, M. (2014). *Sex workers unite: A history of the movement from Stonewall to SlutWalk*. Boston: Beacon Press.

Cunningham, S. and Kendall, T.D. (2010). Risk behaviors among internet-facilitated sex workers: Evidence from two new datasets. *Sexually Transmitted Infections 86*(3), 100–105.

Cunningham, S. and Kendall, T.D. (2011). Prostitution 2.0: The changing face of sex work. *Journal of Urban Economics 69*(3), 273–287.

Dawson, B.L. and McIntosh, W.D. (2006). Sexual strategies theory and Internet personal advertisements. *Cyberpsychology and Behavior 9*(5), 614–617.

Farley, M. and Barkan, H. (1998). Prostitution, violence, and posttraumatic stress disorder. *Women's Health 27*(3), 37–49.

Hubbard, P. and Prior, J. (2013). Out of sight, out of mind? Prostitution policy and the health, well-being and safety of home-based sex workers. *Critical Social Policy 33*(1), 140–159.

MacKinnon, C.A. (2006). *Are women human? And other international dialogues*. Cambridge, MA: Harvard University Press.

McClintock, A. (1995). *Imperial leather: Race, gender, and sexuality in the colonial contest*. New York: Routledge.

Miller, C.C. (5 September 2010). Some see a ploy as craigslist blocks sex ads. *New York Times*.

Mimiaga, M.J., Reisner, S.L., Tinsley, J.P., Mayer K.H and Safren, S.A. (2008). Street workers and internet escorts: Contextual and psychosocial factors surrounding HIV risk behavior among men who engage in sex work with other men. *Journal of Urban Health 86*(1), 54–66.

Minichiello, V. and Scott, J. (2014). *Male sex work and society*. New York: Harrington Park Press.

Parsons, J.T., Bimbi, D. and Halkitis P.N. (2001). Sexual compulsivity among gay/bisexual male escorts who advertise on the Internet. *Sexual Addiction & Compulsivity 8*, 101–112.

Phua, V.C. and Caras, A. (2008). Personal brand in online advertisements: Comparing white and Brazilian male sex workers. *Sociological Focus 41*(3), 238–255.

Phua, V.C. and Kaufman, G. (2003). The crossroads of race and sexuality: Date selection among men in Internet "personal" ads. *Journal of Family Issues 24*(8), 981–994.

Pruitt, M.V. (2005). Online boys: Male-for-male Internet escorts. *Sociological Focus 38*(3), 189–203.

Saad, G. (2008). Advertised waist-to-hip ratios of online female escorts: An evolutionary perspective. *International Journal of e-Collaboration 4*(3), 40–50.

Sanders, T. (2005). 'It's just acting': Sex workers' strategies for capitalizing on sexuality. *Gender, Work and Organization 12*(4), 319–342.

Simons, R.L. and Whitbeck, L.B. (1991). Sexual abuse as a precursor to prostitution and victimization among adolescent and adult homeless women. *Journal of Family Issues 12*(3), 361–379.

Tyler, K.A. (2009). Risk factors for trading sex among homeless young adults. *Archives of Sexual Behavior 38*, 290–297.

Tyler, A. (2014). "Advertising male sexual services". In Minichiello, V. and Scott, J. (eds.), *Male sex work and society* (pp. 82–105). New York: Harrington Park Press.

Wells, M., Mitchell, K.J., and Ji, K. (2011). Exploring the role of the Internet in juvenile prostitution cases coming to the attention of law enforcement. *Journal of Child Sexual Abuse 21*, 327–342.

Widom, C.S. and Kuhns, J.B. (1996). Childhood victimization and subsequent risk for promiscuity, prostitution, and teenage pregnancy: A prospective study. *American Journal of Public Health 86*, 1607–1612.

Wilson, H.W. and Widom, C.S. (2010). The role of youth problem behaviors in the path from child abuse and neglect to prostitution: A prospective examination. *Journal of Research on Adolescence 20*, 210–236.

Wong, W.C., Holroyd, E. and Bingham, A. (2011). Stigma and sex work from the perspective of female sex workers in Hong Kong. *Sociology of health and illness 33*(1), 50–65.

106th Congress (1999–2000), Victims of Trafficking and Violence Protection Act of 2000, H.R. 3244.

17 Gaming and sex

Ashley ML Brown and Rob Gallagher

Introduction

The intersection between sexuality and games can be observed across both analogue and digital media. Some scholars have remarked on a seemingly natural connection between sex and playful behaviour that has meant games, even in early Olympic competitions, have flirted with sexual content (Harviainen, Brown and Suominen, 2016). Likewise, as Lauteria and Wysocki (2015) have pointed out, the language we use to discuss sexual activity in English is peppered with ludic terminology. We 'play' with ourselves, reach 'bases' of sexual intimacy and equate marriage with 'game over' or an end to 'playing the field'. While sex and play have, then, long been linguistically and culturally intertwined, our focus in this chapter is on how sexualities are experienced and expressed through digital games. Rather than attempting a chronological overview of the intersections between sex and games, we will address three key areas of research relating to sex and games: (1) sex-as-mechanic; (2) cybersex and erotic role play; and (3) sex and the single player.

The sex-as-mechanic section looks at how sex has been designed into games. Addressing the (over)use of sex as a reward mechanic (Kelly, 2015), it also considers alternate ways sex has been included in games' economies or gameplay. The following section discusses cybersex and erotic role-play, looking at how groups of players use digital games to play with sexuality and sexual themes and topics (Brown, 2015) and at past research, which has conceptualised the ways in which games lend themselves to pushing sexuality to the 'brink' of social acceptability (Poremba, 2007). The final section addresses the representation of sex in both commercial and experimental single player games.

Sex-as-mechanic

The primary way in which games are different to other digital media is through gameplay mechanics. Broadly speaking, a gameplay mechanic "[...] is a rule of a game" and specifically in terms of sexual video games, "[...] particularly those in the hardcore market, sex is a mechanic" (Brathwaite,

2013, p. 12). Mechanics limit what players can and cannot do within a game-world and also dictate win and loss conditions. Games do not have to be sexually explicit to feature mechanical instantiations of sex: for example, in the family friendly simulation *RollerCoaster Tycoon 3: Platinum Edition* (2004) there is a mission to breed lions in captivity with the ultimate aim of releasing cubs into the wild. In this all-ages game players must buy a male and female lion, make zoo enclosure conditions comfortable enough for them to mate, then wait the appropriate in-game gestation period for the cubs to be born. Whilst the mating and birth are not explicitly animated (the player is informed of their success at animal husbandry via pop-up notification) the mechanics to achieve the win condition of releasing new lions into the wild is still predicated upon whether or not players have achieved the conditions necessary for lions to mate.

In the *RollerCoaster Tycoon 3* example, sex can be said to be a passive mechanic. As game designer Brenda Brathwaite (now Brenda Romero) notes,

> [w]hen sex is used as a mechanic, it can be employed actively or passively. An active sex mechanic allows the players to directly control the action [...]. By contrast, a passive sex mechanic puts the game in control of the actual sexual content.
>
> (Brathwaite, 2013, p. 13)

So whilst players might be responsible for ensuring the conditions within the lion's enclosure are conducive to mating, they do not have an active role in the act of mating itself.

Games with an active and explicit sex mechanic are rare, at least in contemporary Europe and America. Japan, the other major producer of digital games, however, has a sizable erotic games industry (for details of which see Pelletier-Gagnon and Picard, 2015; Ruggill and McAllister, 2015) and, as Bogost notes, "there was once a place for sexually off-colour games" in the US market (2011, p. 103). Today, however, Western games seldom represent sex. This is in part because many people still associate gaming with children, making the inclusion of sexual content in even 18-rated games potentially controversial (Brathwaite, 2013, pp. 144–145). The introduction of regulatory boards responsible for rating games in the 1990s, and the refusal of certain retailers to stock games that are rated 'Adults Only' by such boards, has helped to maintain this reticence regarding sex (see Brathwaite, 2013, pp. 155–156; Ruggill and McAllister, 2015; Wysocki, 2015).

The controversial Hot Coffee Mod for *Grand Theft Auto: San Andreas* (Rockstar North, 2004) is one of few mainstream examples where in players take an explicit, and animated role in on-screen sex (Brathwaite, 2013; Wysocki, 2015). In the gameplay, players must press buttons on the game controller in response to on-screen prompts in order to synchronise their avatar's thrusts and achieve orgasm – a system reminiscent of 'rhythm action' titles and the 'quick time events' incorporated into many action games. A similar approach is used in the *God of War* games (Sony Interactive Entertainment Santa Monica, 2005–2015), though here the sexual act itself occurs off-screen, with the camera, in a nod to Hays Code-era Hollywood, zooming into innocuous articles of set-dressing when things begin to heat up.

More common than this type of explicit sex mechanic is the 'sex-as-reward' or 'sex-as-achievement' approach, whereby games "make sexual content available to the player as a result of his or her actions [...] as a reward" (Brathwaite, 2013, p. 13). Just as the winner of a game of strip poker has the pleasure of viewing the losing players take off an article of clothing, so too do some games make sexual or sexualised content available as a reward for successful gameplay. Although there are many examples of the sex-as-reward mechanic throughout video-gaming history, we will concentrate here on one example: *Dragon Age II* (BioWare, 2011), a single player roleplaying game in which players can romance non-player characters (NPCs) and ultimately have sex with them. In between missions and combat, players may chat to NPCs of different genders and sexual orientations to find out more about their backstories, develop friendships, make enemies or create romance through the selection of various dialogue options and gifts. Once the appropriate dialogue options have been selected and the appropriate gifts given, the NPC may invite the player character to have sex with them and the player is rewarded with a cut-scene of their sexual encounter. While these scenes are tastefully suggestive rather than explicitly pornographic, the handling of sex in *Dragon Age 2* has been criticised by scholars who argue it reduces interpersonal relationships to a mathematical equation: dialogue option A + gift B = sex. For these critics, the game's linear progression to sexual intercourse fails to represent the role of romance, chemistry and complexity in human sexuality and reinforces the kinds of crudely masculinist framings of sexual relationships propagated by pick-up artists (Kelly, 2015; Khandaker-Kokoris, 2015; Ware, 2015). However, some research has compared the process of restrained dialogue and gift giving to Victorian and Edwardian courtship practices and noted that whilst this clashes with contemporary perceptions of dating, it may have been a reality in the past (Kelly, 2015).

In *Dragon Age 2*, sex is a literal reward, which can be compared to a game of strip poker: by fulfilling the win condition (e.g. giving the correct gifts to flatter the NPC), the player gains access to a glimpse of sexualised nudity. However, there are other games in which sex is a mechanic resulting in a separate reward. In the game *Mass Effect* (BioWare, 2007), players are given an achievement trophy when they successfully have sex with a character. More than just a pat on the back, the trophy is displayed visibly online to other players and has an impact on the player's overall online ranking (Hart, 2015). In the *Fable* games (Lionhead Studios, 2004–2014), in-game sex with NPCs also results in achievements. In addition to trophies similar to the *Mass Effect* (BioWare, 2007) example, *Fable III* (Lionhead Studios, 2010) "reimagined the sexual reward dynamic by offering players

'Legendary Weapons' that could only be brought to full strength by committing sexual or intrinsically objectifying acts" (Hart, 2015, p. 155). Examples of such acts include having sex with multiple in-game characters, having multiple spouses or even killing your spouse. We can see, then, that sex has been incorporated into the gameplay of mainstream, contemporary digital titles in a variety of ways. Sex can be either an active or passive part of gameplay and it can additionally be used as a way to reward players through cut-scenes or items. The next section will look at how sex has been incorporated into online virtual worlds through a discussion of cybersex and erotic role-play.

Cybersex and erotic role-play

Within online games and virtual worlds, cybersex and erotic role-play are ways to experience digital sexuality, even if the activity is not provided or endorsed by the creators of the online space. Sometimes referred to as 'emergent' sexual content (Brathwaite, 2013), TinySex or virtual sex (Turkle, 1995), sex in virtual spaces (Boellstorff, 2008), cybersex and erotic role-play emerge out of player-to-player interactions in virtual worlds. These virtual worlds might be fully rendered three dimensional (3D) environments in massive multiplayer online games like *World of Warcraft* (Blizzard, 2004), or in text-based multi-user dungeons. Whether the location has a visual component or not, the practice is largely the same.

Similar to other forms of digital sex, such as webcams or televideo sex, the practice always takes place in online spaces. At its most basic, cybersex can be described as "[...] a form of co-authored interactive erotica" (Reid, 1994, cited in Waskul, 2003, p. 79) which occurs online and in real-time. However, it should be noted that not all cybersex might be considered a part of gameplay. In common parlance, the term is used casually to reference sexual activity as it occurs in any online space – including gameworlds. Academically, cybersex is considered too generic a term to reference ludic or playful sexuality (c.f. Brown, 2015). What this means is that practitioners of cybersex describe themselves in real life for the purposes of arousal or fun, and because this is true to life, there is no element of gameplay present. If there were an element of gameplay present, for example pretending to be a *Second Life* (Linden Lab, 2003) avatar or *World of Warcraft* (Blizzard, 2004) character via roleplaying, then the practice would be considered erotic role-play. Of course this attempted separation between cybersex and erotic role-play is problematic, as it is dubious that every person engaging in cybersex faithfully represents him/herself online. For this reason, both terms are included in this chapter, though the primary focus will be on digital sex as it happens in games. In this case, the practice may be defined as "two or more players typing descriptions of physical actions, verbal statements, and emotional reactions for characters" (Turkle, 1995, p. 223) within a sexualised scenario.

Although the practice takes place in a virtual space with virtual avatars and characters, it has real implications for the lives of participants and virtual worlds research. Importantly, the existence of sexuality in online games counters the popular and persistent idea that now more than ever people are giving up active, healthy, real-world social lives for an isolated existence online. As Tom Boellstorff notes in his research on *Second Life*, "[...] virtual worlds can not only transform actual-world intimacy but create real forms of online intimacy" (Boellstorff, 2008, p. 156). For Boellstorff's participants, online intimacy usually took the form of friendships developed through communicating in the virtual space of *Second Life*, but occasionally this included sexual activity. In terms of prevalence of sexual activity in the virtual space, he writes,

> [f]or some residents, sex was the main reason they logged on, others engage in sexual activity only on occasion or not at all-seeing it as being 'like licking honey through the glass', or viewing *Second Life* as a place for creativity and friendship, but not sexual expression.
>
> (Boellstorff, 2008, p. 160)

In the above example, the type of intimacy experienced in virtual worlds was sharply delineated between friendship and sexual relationship. Other research has found this not to be the case. In a study on erotic role-players in *World of Warcraft*, Brown (2015) found that players would often develop a friendship as their characters developed romantic relationships. For this group, the delineation between friendship and romance happened between characters and players, which is to say that whilst characters might develop romantic feelings through the course of role-play, players would usually develop friendships with each other. The separation occurred and was maintained through separate chat channels, which delineated when a character was speaking or acting versus when actions or emotions were expressed on the part of the player.

This section described how sexual content emerges in online virtual worlds through a discussion of cybersex and erotic role-play. Although the terms are often used interchangeably, it was noted that they do not signify the same activity. Digital sexuality is experienced through fictional, role-played characters in the case of erotic role-play, which is arguably more game-like in form than experiencing digital sexuality through an 'authentic' self in cybersex. Whilst this section focused on multiplayer online experiences, the next section will illustrate that sex can also be experienced in single player games.

Sex and the single player

There remains a widespread misapprehension that the appeal of single player games lies in giving players free rein to act out primal fantasies, whether of violent domination, sexual conquest or both, on a cast of docile NPCs. Such assumptions were made manifest in Fox News' notorious coverage of *Mass Effect*, which saw pundits mistakenly claiming that the game "contained full frontal nudity and pornographic scenes", granting players full control over a range of graphic sex acts (Ferguson, 2010, p. 70). While these claims were false, they stemmed from misconceptions that are more understandable if we take into account the 'hypersexualised' characters who populate many games (Downs and Smith, 2010) and the way that advertisers portray gaming technologies as means of 'immersing' ourselves in unprecedentedly realistic dream worlds. Factor in a long-standing tendency to associate gaming with thwarted masculinity, 'social isolation and addiction', and it makes sense that non-gamers would be willing to believe there were single player games based on choreographing sex acts (Kirkpatrick, 2012). In actuality, however, few single player games feature sex in any form, and almost none let players stage sexual encounters of the kind Fox invited viewers to imagine. This section addresses the forms sex does take in such games, focusing particularly on independent and experimental projects that depart from the model of cut-scenes presented as a reward for successful play.

Nowadays it is not uncommon for mainstream game series like *Assassin's Creed* (Ubisoft, 2007–2015) and *The Witcher* (CD Projekt RED, 2007–2016) to feature non-interactive sex scenes. Such scenes can help to establish the personalities and motivations of the characters, enabling players to invest emotionally in – or even fall in love with – NPCs (Waern, 2015). However, they often seem more focused on providing titillation while reassuring players that games can tell stories just as 'mature' as Hollywood films or Home Box Office (HBO) series, serving as evidence of gaming's on-going tendency toward 'cinema-envy' (Zimmerman, 2002). If designers have struggled with the question of how to incorporate intercourse into actual gameplay, this is in part because, in reality, the appeal of single player gaming has less to do with letting players act out power fantasies or transporting them to fully-realised virtual words than it does what Juul calls the 'paradox of failure', whereby players willingly subject themselves to frustrating and humiliating experiences of defeat in the knowledge that victory will be all the sweeter when they finally attain it (2013, p. 2). Games that offer no resistance are no fun and, as Brathwaite argues, the few games that have attempted to fulfil players' sexual desires offer so little challenge that they can barely be called games at all (2013, p. 7).

Such 'games' forget that, as Navarro-Remesal and Garcia-Catalan remind us, single player games grant "freedom and power" only within "strict limits" (2015, p. 120). For them the resulting tension between "freedom and control" may, in fact, be the sexiest thing about gaming (Navarro-Remesal and Garcia-Catalan, 2015, p. 130); citing games like *Bind Her!* (Arnott, 2012), they argue that the player/game relationship can be viewed as akin to the master/slave dynamic in sadomasochistic sex. Philosopher Bernard Suits was already making somewhat similar claims in the 1970s, arguing that while "the sexual act [cannot] be considered a type of game", gameplay and sex both involve using perversely inefficient means to attain ends that are tantalisingly deferred (1978, p. 80).

Perhaps it should not surprise us, then, that sex often figures in single player games as a reward. If we have already addressed the ethical and political issues that framing sex in this way presents, critics also argue that the lack of randomness in traditional romance/relationship systems makes for boring gameplay – something that Khandaker-Kokoris' *Redshirt* (The Tiniest Shark, 2013), as we shall see, attempts to rectify. Other designers have sought to render single player sex more engaging by experimenting with different interface technologies. After all, if the gleefully juvenile treatment of sex in *God of War* and 'Hot Coffee' extends to control schemes, which reduce it to a matter of rhythmically jabbing the right buttons, perhaps new interfaces might facilitate a more nuanced treatment of the subject? The 'Move Edition' of Quantic Dream's *Heavy Rain* (2010) is notable both for attempting to incorporate interactive sex scenes into an straight-faced thriller and for implementing a gesture-based interface via Sony's Wii-style Move controller. In practice, however, the experience of ushering the protagonists through their sexual encounter proves eerily ridiculous rather than moving or arousing, suggesting that games might be better suited to comic treatments of sex. This, certainly, is the approach favoured by the Wii game *No More Heroes* (Grasshopper Manufacture, 2007), which satirises gaming culture's awkwardly adolescent handling of sex by making players mime male masturbation in order to recharge their avatar's 'beam sword', a weapon very much framed as a phallic substitute (Gallagher, 2013).

That said, more abstract and experimental treatments of sex have also been successful. Tale of Tales' *Luxuria Superbia* (2013) borrows from 'tube shooters' like *Tempest* (Theurer, 1981). Here, though, we zoom through labile tunnels reminiscent of Rorschach blots or Georgia O'Keefe canvases, rubbing, swiping and tracing circles with the mouse to infuse them with colour. A similar system underpins the touchscreen-based *La Petite Mort* (Lovable Hat Cult, 2016), in which players encounter abstractly rendered vulvas each of which likes to be touched in a different way. Some versions of the psychedelic cyberpunk shooter *Rez* (United Game Artists, 2001) came with a 'trance vibrator' that (while the developers' insisted this was not its intended purpose) doubled as a sex toy (Bogost, 2011, p. 82). Rather than ape filmic sex scenes, such games exploit the medium's ability to engage players through gesture and texture, rhythm and kinaesthetics.

Single player games have also focused on other dimensions of sexuality and sexual experience. The 'newsgame' *The Oldest Game* (Lynch and Gabrielle, 2015) addresses the legal and economic factors shaping sex work in Canada; Anna Anthropy's *Triad* (2013), meanwhile, opens in the wake of a *ménage a trois* and tasks players with configuring the bodies of the three participants so that nobody falls out of bed. Essentially a digital jigsaw, *Triad* riffs on the difficulty of finding a place for alternative sexualities in a world designed to fit heterosexual pairs. Such games support Lauteria's argument that games already contain systems and mechanics that designers can adapt to talk about sex (2011, p. 6).

Single player games have also addressed sex in relation to heredity and genetics: in *Tokyo Jungle* (Crispy's, 2012) our animal avatar must secure a mate to prolong their bloodline, while in the strategy simulation *Crusader Kings II* (Paradox Interactive, 2012) players arrange marriages, groom heirs and disinherit bastards, becoming entangled in positively Shakespearean conflicts over mortality, lineage, identity and ambition. The Role Playing Game (RPG) *Oreshika: Tainted Bloodlines* (Alfa System, 2013) sees players controlling a clan of warriors who breed with the gods, investing traditional RPG progress mechanics with overtones of eugenics – a subject also tackled in Tom McHenry's bleak cyberpunk text adventure *Horse Master* (2013). Then there are the numerous independent games that, pertinently for this collection, address the influence of digital media on sex. Robert Yang's *Cobra Club* (2015) raises questions of privacy and consent by putting us in the skin of a naked man trading explicit selfies online, before revealing that our images are being stolen and stored by the National Security Agency; the aforementioned *Redshirt* (The Tiniest Shark, 2013), a satirical sci-fi adventure game played via a Facebook-style interface, allows us to sleep our way to the top of a space station's social hierarchy, introducing more randomness into romance than traditional RPGs and dating games. Kara Stone's interactive fiction *Sext Adventure* (2014), meanwhile, sketches a future where artificial intelligences are trained to swap come-ons and nude photos with users.

Conclusion

As this chapter has shown, the treatment of sex in digital games can still be juvenile and primitive, with regressively masculinist attitudes on display and crude mechanics and interfaces used to model sexual interaction. There is, however, more to video game sexuality than smut and sexism. Multiplayer games are providing new contexts for expressing sexuality, attesting to the ingenuity of player communities. There are also numerous single player games that explore the new modes of dramatising sexual issues and experiences that games make possible. With more people playing digital games than ever before, and as new distribution and design solutions continue to challenge the dominance of traditional publishers and retailers, there is every reason to expect such experimentation will continue.

References

Alfa Systems. (2013). *Oreshika: Tainted Bloodlines*. Sony Computer Entertainment.
Anthropy, A. (2013). *Triad*. Self-published.
Arnott, L. (2012). *Bind Her!* Self-published.
Atari. (2004). *RollerCoaster Tycoon 3: Platinum Edition*. Frontier Developments.
BioWare. (2007). *Mass Effect*. Microsoft Game Studios.
BioWare. (2011). *Dragon Age II*. Electronic Arts.
Blizzard. (2004). *World of Warcraft*. Blizzard Activision.

Boellstorff, T. (2008). *Coming of Age in Second Life: An Anthropologist Explores the Virtually Human*. Princeton, NJ: Princeton University Press.

Bogost, I. (2011). *How to Do Things with Video Games*. Minneapolis: University of Minnesota Press.

Brathwaite, B. (2013). *Sex in Video Games*. Self-published.

Brown, A.M.L. (2015). *Sexuality in Role-Playing Games*. London: Routledge.

CD Projekt RED. (2007–2016). *The Witcher series*. CD Projekt.

Crispy's. (2012). *Tokyo Jungle*. Sony Computer Entertainment.

Downs, E. and Smith, S.L. (2010). Keeping Abreast of Hypersexuality: A Video Game Character Content Analysis. *Sex Roles 62*(11), 721–733.

Ferguson, C. (2010). Blazing Angels or Resident Evil? Can Violent Video Games be a Force for Good? *Review of General Psychology 14*(2), 68–81.

Gallagher, R. (2013). No Sex Please, We're Finite State Machines: On the Melancholy Sexlessness of the Video Game. *Games and Culture 7*(6).

Grasshopper Manufacture. (2007). *No More Heroes*. Marvellous Entertainment/ Ubisoft/Rising Star Games.

Hart, C. (2015). "Sexual Favors: Using Casual Sex as Currency within Video Games". In Wysocki, M. and Lauteria, E. (eds.). *Rated M for Mature: Sex and Sexuality in Video Games* (pp. 145–160). London: Bloomsbury.

Harviainen, J., Brown, A.M.L. and Suominen, J. (2016) Three Waves of Awkwardness: A Meta-Analysis of Sex in Game Studies, *Games and Culture 11*(3).

Juul, J. (2013). *The Art of Failure*. Cambridge, MA: MIT Press.

Kelly, P. (2015). "The Digital Courting Process in *Dragon Age 2*". In Enevold, J. and MacCallum-Stewart, E. (eds.). *Game Love: Essays on Play and Affection* (pp. 46–62). Jefferson: McFarland.

Khandaker-Kokoris, M. (2015). "NPCs Need Love Too: Simulating Love and Romance, from a Game Design Perspective" in Enevold, J. and MacCallum-Stewart, E. (eds.). *Game Love: Essays on Play and Affection* (pp. 82–96). Jefferson: McFarland.

Kirkpatrick, G. (2012). Constitutive Tensions of Gaming's Field: UK gaming magazines and the formation of gaming culture 1981–1995, *Game Studies 12*(1).

Lauteria, E. (2011). Procedurally and Fictively Relevant: Exploring the Potential for Queer Content in Video Games. *Berfrois*.

Lauteria, E.W. and Wysocki, M. (2015). "Introduction". In Wysocki, M. and Lauteria, E. (eds.). *Rated M for Mature: Sex and Sexuality in Video Games* (pp. 1–9). London: Bloomsbury.

Linden Lab. (2003). *Second Life*. Linden Lab.

Lionhead Studios. (2004–2014). *Fable Series*. Microsoft Game Studios.

Lionhead Studios. (2010). *Fable III*. Microsoft Game Studios.

Loveable Hat Cult. (2016). *La Petite Mort*. Self-published.

Lynch, L. and Gabriele, S. (2015). *The Oldest Game*. Self-published.

McHenry, T. (2013). *Horse Master*. Self-published.

Navarro-Remesal, V. and Garcia-Catalan, S. (2015). "Let's Play Master and Servant: BDSM and Directed Freedom in Game Design". In Wysocki, M. and Lauteria, E. (eds.). *Rated M for Mature: Sex and Sexuality in Video Games* (pp. 119–132). London: Bloomsbury.

Paradox Interactive. (2012). *Crusader Kings II*. Paradox Interactive.

Pelletier-Gagnon, J. and Picard, M. (2015). "Beyond *Rapelay*: Self-Regulation in the Japanese Erotic Video Game Industry". In Wysocki, M. and Lauteria, E. (eds.).

Rated M for Mature: Sex and Sexuality in Video Games (pp. 28–41). London: Bloomsbury.

Poremba, Cindy. (2007). "Critical Potential on the Brink of the Magic Circle". In *Situated Play: Proceedings of the 2007 Annual Digital Games Research Association Conference* (pp. 772–778). University of Tokyo, September 2007.

Quantic Dream. (2010). *Heavy Rain.* Sony Interactive Entertainment.

Rockstar North. (2004). *Grand Theft Auto: San Andreas.* Rockstar Games.

Ruggill, Judd and McAllister, Ken. (2015). "E(SRB) Is for Everyone: Game Ratings and the Practice of Content Evaluation". In Conway, S. and deWinter, J. (eds.). *Video Game Policy: Production, Distribution and Consumption* (pp. 71–84). London: Routledge.

Sony Interactive Entertainment Santa Monica. (2005–2015). *God of War series.* Sony Interactive Entertainment.

Stone, K. (2014). *Sext Adventure.* Self-published.

Suits, B. (1978). *The Grasshoper: Games, Life and Utopia.* Toronto: University of Toronto Press.

Tale of Tales. (2013). *Luxuria Superbia.* Self-published.

The Tiniest Shark. (2013). *Redshirt.* Positech Games.

Theurer, D. (1981). *Tempest.* Atari.

Turkle, S. (1995). *Life on the Screen: Identity in the Age of the Internet.* New York: Simon and Schuster.

Ubisoft. (2007–2015). *Assassin's Creed series.* Ubisoft.

United Game Artists. (2001). *Rez.* Sega.

Waern, Annika. (2015). "'I'm in Love with Someone Who Doesn't Exist!' Bleed in the Context of a Computer Game". In Enevold, J. and MacCallum-Stewart, E. (eds.). *Game Love: Essays on Play and Affection* (pp. 25–45). Jefferson: McFarland.

Ware, N. (2015). "Iterative Romance and Button-Mashing Sex: Gameplay Design and Video Games' Nice Guy Syndrome". In Wysocki, M. and Lauteria, E. (eds.). *Rated M for Mature: Sex and Sexuality in Video Games* (pp. 225–239). London: Bloomsbury.

Waskul, D. (2003). *Self Games and Body-Play: Personhood in Online Chat and Cybersex.* New York: Peter Lang.

Wysocki, Matthew. (2015). "It's Not Just the Coffee That's Hot: Modding Sexual Content in Video Games". In Wysocki, M. and Lauteria, E. (eds.). *Rated M for Mature: Sex and Sexuality in Video Games* (pp. 194–209). London: Bloomsbury.

Yang, R. (2015). *Cobra Club.* Self-published.

Zimmerman, E. (2002). "Do Independent Games Exist?" In King, L. and Bain, C. (eds.). *Game On* (pp. 120–129). London: Barbican.

18 Hell yes!!!!!

Playing away, teledildonics and the future of sex

Paul G Nixon

This chapter examines the path to the mainstream acceptance of sex toys. It then traces the emergent technological developments inherent in teledildonics which are helping us to produce devices which can replicate most if not all sexual functions and "[…] aim at heightened experience of pleasure, an experience that would not be possible without the help of technology" (Ornella, 2015, p. 319). Subsequently it moves on to investigate future notions of post/human sex, which are often characterised as a step too far (Hawkes, 2016). However, due to the pace of technological advances the gap between the present and the future is shrinking and holds tantalising possibilities for sexual fulfilment.

Sex toys

The Oxford English Dictionary defines a sex toy as "[a]n object or device used for sexual stimulation or to enhance sexual pleasure" (OED, 2016). Often seen as an artifice to be used in isolation modern technologies are helping reshape our perceptions of sex toys. At the time of writing sex toys have their own specific search category on major internet porn sites with You Porn offering 16,368 videos under the heading 'Dildos/Toys' illustrating their place in sexual activity today. Each generation feel that they are the ones who have really 'discovered' sex. But, just as each generation did not actually discover sex it also holds true for sex toys. Pleasuring ones' self or others with objects for sexual gratification is not new. With a history that can be traced back through written history to Aristophanes' anti-war play 'Lysistrata' and then beyond, sex toys have evolved from their primitive ancestors. Palaeontologists argue over the purpose of stone carved phalluses discovered to date from the Palaeolithic age. Were they religious artefacts, early sex toys or perhaps both? The evolution of (wo)man has also produced a concomitant evolution of sex toys leading to the present-day information age where information technologies are utilised to enhance or replace sexual experiences.

The development of the vibrators we know today is built upon the emergence of mechanical vibrators which were designed to treat conditions such as pain relief or neuralgia amongst others (Mortimer Granville, 1883). Maines (2001) put forward the theory that vibrators were used in the practice of treating women patients for a condition which was known as 'hysteria'. The treatment involved manual or mechanical stimulation to induce orgasm to address hysteria, reflecting a very androcentric vision of sexuality that prevailed at the time. Though this theory is strongly contested by a number of writers, it is believed that whilst such treatments may have existed they were far from widespread (Hall, n.d.).

When the advent of electricity in the 19th century facilitated the invention of the vibrator notable cost savings were made. These large, unwieldy, electro-mechanical vibrators allowed patients to be treated faster, by practitioners with less technical expertise and experience. Rather than being performed by doctors such treatments were often delegated to nurses and midwives. As the technologies developed updated versions became cheaper, more user friendly and more portable (Maines, 2001).

Despite the stigma attached to such devices and the androcentric denial of women's sexual needs and desires, vibrators were sold in the mid-20th century both by mail order and also by a network of travelling salesmen. Advertising was dualistic with devices being portrayed as overtly nonsexual whilst discretely using imagery to hint at their sexual use and by the sale of phallic, dildo-like attachments (Lieberman, 2016). Later the therapeutic nature of their use was usurped or repositioned by the increasing awareness of sexual pleasure as not just the preserve of the hedonistic, but as a 'right' for all. As the sexual revolution of the 1960s, spread throughout society, sex toys became a more commonplace sign of the diminution of sexual shame and a proclamation of freedom and self-expression. Women increasingly viewed sexual gratification as a right, thereby becoming less inhibited and looking for new experiences (Winks and Semans, 2002, p. 134). Fahs and Swank have noted that "[...] women described vibrators as contributing to intense orgasms and high levels of sexual satisfaction whether alone or with partners" (2013, p. 668).

This sexual revolution was disputed by some feminists who viewed many overt expressions of sexuality, such as pornography and the wider sex industries as being expressions of differing forms of violence against women (Bronstein, 2011; Dworkin, 1981; Dworkin and McKinnon, 1988). However a counter movement of 'sex positive' feminists advocating sexual freedoms, including the freedom to enjoy pornography, particularly female produced pornography as well as opening sex shops to try to nurture a non-threatening arena for sexual consumerism emerged. Such shops were clean, open and welcoming, with staff who were trained and knew their product range which embraced not only heteronormative products but also those aimed at people living other, often fluid, sexual identities and experiences.

Sex toys are much more abundant now. Not only the scope and range of models has increased but the method and physical location of their commodification has also changed. Now to be found openly on sale and display in most major European chemist shops, sex toys are moving out from "shady back street to shiny high streets" (Comella, 2010, p. 296) and are becoming more welcoming (Martin, 2013). Gone are the days when purchasing a sex toy meant entering the male dominated world of seedy sex shops, or buying by mail order, hoping that your purchase would arrive in the promised anonymous brown wrapper so as to not exhibit your 'wantonness' to the mail man and your neighbours; or purchasing your preferred items under the watchful eyes of friends or family members at an Ann Summers party. Such parties which were usually held in someone's home and attended by their (female) friends. They were facilitating spaces where females were free to challenge expectations of sexual stereotypes configured around their own sexual needs and desires (Storr, 2003) and encouraged to expand their sexual satisfaction repertoire via the purchases of sex toys such as vibrators or ben-wah balls. Though, still not everyone is as open about the sale of sex toys as illustrated by parents being upset that vibrating penis rings had been placed for sale next to children's medicines in a supermarket (The Sun, 2016). However, it would seem that sex toys are becoming a fixed part of our sex lives and as sex becomes more of an open topic so too does the use and value of sex toys.

This evolving situation is fuelled by a number of changes in society. Juffer observed the "[...] discussion of the vibrator's reception as a masturbatory aid in the 1970's, many women were reluctant to endorse its use because it represented the 'technologization' of sex, the coming together of the natural and the mechanical" (Juffer, 1998, p. 29). However, aided by the inculcation of gaming into modern living in what Raessens terms the 'ludification of culture' (2006), and the increased adoption of technological devices into many areas of our lives we can see a shift in acceptance which illustrates the changing social and sexual mores. What was once hidden is now mostly socially acceptable, with even a thriving market in the recycling of sex toys emerging (Seale, 2013). These changes are reflected in, or fuelled by, elements of popular culture such as the recent Bondage and Discipline, Dominance and Submission, Sadism and Masochism (BDSM) (lite) inspired book trilogy *Fifty Shades of Grey* which also later transferred to the cinema screen (Heljakka, 2016). This was accompanied by a range of sex toys the likes of which were once considered to be niche apparatus for BDSM aficionados but now became acceptable in the mainstream sex lives of millions of people whereby, as Martin notes, "[...] sexual fantasy itself becomes commodified via the transition of fictional objects in the book into real commodities for sale" (2013, p. 982). This illustrates how porn has to some extent entered the main stream where once sex toys would be marketed via links to the pornography industry, with a relatively low retail price point, cheaply made from plastic and rubber, sold in packaging that was often adorned with the picture of a porn star (more often than not a female one) and featured clear plastic to allow a degree of pre-usage fantasy; thus, emphasising the way in which the marketing of sex toys has often taken account of, and been designed to appeal to, the male gaze.

The perceived role of sex toys in expanding sexual horizons goes beyond the merely sexual and inculcates our behaviour in other social settings and impacts upon the ways in which we view society in a post-industrial, digital age. This ubiquity of purpose is reflected by Smith who notes that "[t]oys are tools for producing orgasm and 'symbolic good', they are signifiers of cultural values" (2007, p. 169). This echoes Bauman's arguments that "the late modern or postmodern rendition of eroticism appears unprecedented [...] it proudly and boldly proclaims itself to be its only, and sufficient, reason and purpose" (Bauman, 1998, p. 21). Smith (2007, p. 171) articulates the battle that sex toys (along with other parts of the sex industries) have been undertaking in order to seek acceptance and validation. Although it is noticeable vibrators are still often marketed as massage tools (Winks and Semans, 2002, p. 275).

As previously noted their appearance in popular cultural settings such as *Fifty Shades of Grey* or in the hit TV series *Sex and the City*, and the ways in which sex toy marketing has also honed in on female consumers has really brought them into the mainstream. Consider the following descriptions of devices all quoted in Rossolatos' (2016) examination of the discursive texts contextualising how such devices are described and marketed:

> Opening the Lelo Pebble feels like unwrapping a luxury box of chocolates. This really is the Rolex of vibrators!
>
> (Lelo Pebble)

> It's like the Swiss army knife of double-ended vibrators.
>
> (Picobong Transformer)

> [T]he vibrating bunny ears are positioned in just the right place to send you straight to orgasmic heaven.
> (Cupids Club Mini Rabbit Vibrator) (in Rossolatos, 2016, pp. 10–11)

Such devices are ushering in an era of conspicuous sexual consumption, which seems to chime well with the sex positive times, ostensibly delivering sexual freedom and satisfaction for all (Watson *et al.*, 2016). Although it must be noted with pricing points that may indicate that these are a socially segmented example of a luxury item, the ownership of which will only be achievable for the higher earners in society, though less sophisticated vibrators and other sex toys are available at quite low prices. Thus, even sex toys are potentially a practical illustration of the gap between the haves and the have nots, a further more intimate example of inequality.

There is a design and technology led revolution in the sex toy industry. These designs have moved away from graphic realism and lifelike contours with an emphasis on, perhaps male, ideas of size and power, towards embracing characteristics of reliability and functionality. Herbenick *et al.* (2015) found that despite the common quest for size often embodied in modern day pornography, most users preferred sex toys that approximated to the mean penis size, although, of course, there were exceptions to this rule. Fan (2015) has shown how the market in terms of user segmentation is relatively underdeveloped and holds great promise for toy developers and marketeers. Utilising new possibilities Smith notes how manufactures have begun to "exploit qualities, new materials, technologies" (2007, p. 147) in their quest to design new sex toys. These new sex toys are not necessarily phallic in the appearance and are often more ergonomically designed to be both practical and, to an extent, *objects d'art*. With companies such as Je Joue, JimmyJane, Lelo, OhMiBod, etc. aiming to create high end sex toys and to raise market thresholds to cater for a market segment that has increasing disposable income and is not afraid to spend to meet their own sexual needs. One such example is the *Womanizer,* which is a device that uses pressure waves to stimulate the clitoris. Let us now move to examine how teledildonic devices are offering new avenues for pleasure.

Teledildonics and the pursuit of pleasure

Not all sex toys have orgasm as their goal. A recent graduate designer, Wan Tseng, has produced a series of wearable technology pieces from silicone which are worn on the body akin to jewellery including necklaces and bracelets (De Zeen, 2016). The items focus on the pleasure of stimulation rather than on an end goal of orgasm. They can, depending upon their placement, give the sensations of touch and breath to the wearer. The pads connection with the skin are not only sensation giving but can, for example by using the function of the bracelet monitor your own response to the sensations experienced via the other devices you may be wearing, or, even, be utilised to send a subtle message to your partner/s regarding the state of your arousal. Another recent invention is the sex toy to aid in artificial insemination. Called the POP it is basically a strap on with a reservoir for sperm which allows the wearer to discharge into the recipient thus inseminating and, hopefully impregnating their partner (Guardian, 2016).

One can see the advent of three dimensional (3D) printing allowing endless customisation and potentially moulding the shape of a vibrator or dildo to match the contours of the body of the owner. One can also clearly see how the meshing together of new technological possibilities and potentialities could lead to what some might view a more virtual form of what Parikka and Sampson called "digital pollution" when referring to the porn industry (2009, p. 3). As examples of how new products are developing consider Svakom's '*Siime*' a combination of a vibrator and a camera which affords the tantalising possibility of being able to watch yourself from the inside as you masturbate and climax achieved via a cabled link to your screen via an app. Should you object to the thought of a cable being attached there is an ever more expensive cordless version '*Siime eye*' which has all the functionality of its namesake but is also equipped with wireless wi-fi allowing you to send the pictures to whomever you wish, adding yet another layer of digitised possibility to the concept of voyeurism. The manufacturers website (Svakom, 2016) testifies that:

> No secrets would be hidden from the the [sic] eye of Siime, not only brings you a feast to the eye, but also make you pay more attention to the health of your private parts whenever you want.
>
> (Siime)

Jannini *et al.* (2012) have reiterated the positive health effects that may stem from the use of sex toys in certain cases for certain people and here yet again we see the revisiting of health as a reason to buy a vibrating sex toy that offers other forms of user involvement than simple sexual pleasure. OhMiBod's *'Lovelife Krush'*, which whilst vibrating inside you also aims to monitor the effectiveness of pelvic floor exercises, aiding kegel exercising. It works via Bluetooth and a smartphone app that displays visual feedback so that you may monitor your progress and adapt your exercise regime accordingly. OhMiBod have also launched a pair of devices called *'Bluemotion Nex 1'* and *'Bluemotion Nex 2'* which allows a vibrator to be controlled from across the room or across the world via a Wi-Fi link and comes complete with an *'Oh-dometer'* which is billed as an orgasm tracker. Thus, again one can see the blurred boundaries of cybersex and teledildonics making it possible to contribute to your partner's orgasm in a much more touch oriented manner than can be achieved by phone sex. Whilst the users are unlikely to directly equate the sensations received from such remotely controlled devices with the actual sensation of touch from their partner/s such stimulation can create a connection engender a feeling of proximity from their shared telepresence.

Mostly we have talked of sex toys predominantly aimed at the female market (Walther and Schouten, 2016). We should also not forget the burgeoning market in sex toys targeting men. Of course many of the toys designed for women's use can be adopted and/or adapted to meet male heterosexual and homosexual needs also. However, there are a range of toys designed specifically for male use. One of the best known is *'Fleshlight'*. This is a masturbatory sleeve moulded in the form of a vagina or mouth (or an anus in the *Fleshjack* which is targeted at men interested in anal sex). It is available in a myriad of different mouldings representing different body shapes and labia lip size, protuberance, colours, etc. You can also pick one modelled on the vagina, mouth or anus of selected adult entertainers should you so wish and it is interesting to note in light of Susanna Paasonen's chapter on monster Toon Porn (see Chapter 1) that there are several 'freak' versions which relate to monsters such as Frankenstein, Dracula and a Cyborg amongst others (Fleshlight, 2016). The sleeves, which have differing contours inside, can be purchased with a number of accoutrements such as vibratory function and lubricants to enhance the experience.

Also, similar to the *Bluemotion Nex*,(OhMiBod, 2016) one can purchase a teledildonic Fleshlight called a '*KIIROO Onyx*' which can, if connected to another *Onyx* or a '*KIIROO Pearl*', a phallic shaped vibrator which, through a series of five capacitive rings, allow your every touch to be transmitted to and experienced by the *Onyk* user and vice versa. Of course, Fleshlight is not the only masturbatory sleeve available and one competitor, Tenga (2016), is as of the date of writing, offering a tailored service where you can enter your penis measurements together with your preferences of how and where you would like the device to concentrate on performing and it will then recommend the most suitable devices for your particular penis. As an aside, for those who masturbate in colder climates, Tenga also offers for sale the delightfully directly named 'hole warmer' to pre-heat your sleeve.

It is interesting to note that while I have postulated above that sex toys are to be found in many high-street stores it must be noted that this same openness often does not necessarily carry through to male sex toys such as sex dolls, or to sex toys for use by the gay community such as anal beads, butt plugs and masturbatory sleeves (Rosenberg *et al.,* 2012). These products are not afforded the same shelf space in prime shopping locations and are somehow seen as if not the unacceptable face of the sex toy industry then certainly the less acceptable face. In fact, in the case of sex dolls, they are often the most ridiculed of sex toys. Will the combination of more lifelike dolls with haptic technologies change this impression? Or will we go even further in the future?

The future of sex

Howard Rheingold, writing in 1991, posited that it would be 30 years before "[...] most people will use them [teledildonics] to have sexual experiences with other people, at a distance, in combinations and configurations undreamed of by pre-cybernetic voluptuaries" (Rheingold, 1991, p. 346). Well, as we have seen above, some people are already doing just as Rheingold predicted, however the practices are far from ubiquitous. Will they become so?

We will no doubt encounter ethical issues but are there also legal issues to be dealt with? A recent case highlighted a manufacturer being successfully sued for damages in Canada after it transpired that they had sold vibrators which, via an app, transmitted data, relating to the use of the vibrator, to the manufacturer without the knowledge or consent of the user (Hern, 2017).

Another of the negative consequences of teleldildonics is the fear of hacking of one's device. Just as in all other sectors of activity it is possible for a Wi-Fi device to be hacked (Copley, 2016). In effect one could envisage a scenario whereby it was the hacker who was the one who was (unbeknown to you) controlling or sharing your sexual experience and not the partner to whom you were expecting and had consented. The question is posed not to negate the damage that such virtual abuse can wreak but to emphasise the potential physical intrusion in such a teledildonic enabled sexual situation and to question the efficacy of existing laws. Does this raise new, as yet unresolved, issues around the concept of a form of improper conduct which could be construed in varying degrees up to a full-blown perception of 'teledildonic rape'? Would one's consent to a teledildonic activity with person A be valid if the person controlling the teledildonic sexual activity was in fact person B pretending to be person A? As the sexual act could occur in a physical sense, though without the physical co presence of the perpetrator, would it be subject the standard laws governing sexual conduct rather than as a technical offence in non-physical cyberspace?

There is an argument that as we embrace new technology the fear and shame of using technology for much more overt purposes will perhaps fall away and teledildonics will avail itself of the ubiquitous status that Rheingold afforded it. But even though there are still five years to wait to see if his prediction comes true it seems unlikely to be fully achieved. Will such technologies be more encompassing? Without a doubt. We can already see the combinations of sex toys with games and pornographic spin offs from major movies, allowing us to project our sexual fantasies and 'involve' celebrities, at least in our mind. So how will sex toys and their use evolve? All the routes that are possible seem to indicate a closer relationship between human and technology, though there are issues to be overcome. Research by Wagner and Broll (2014) indicated that there was a great deal of resistance to technological solutions with, in particular, the male respondents saying that they felt the lack of a full body inherent in most sex toys was in effect a turn off.

Could we be nearing a time when we will accept the notion of sex with more lifelike robotic devices as a way of providing sexual pleasure, perhaps even as a way of preventing abuse in the prostitution industry? Whilst Richardson (2015, p. 292) argues that this would be both unsafe and unethical, Stowe Bowd argues that "[...] [r]obotic sex partners will be a commonplace, although the source of scorn and division, the way that critics today bemoan selfies as an indicator of all that's wrong with the world" (quoted in Pew, 2014, pp. 19–20). Though there is the perception that a morphing of robotics and teledildonics could lead us into a world where the recreational function of sex is taken to an extreme in what Barber terms "Massive Open Haptic Online Orgies" (Barber, 2014, p. 5). Or are we about see a more widespread acceptance of post humanist concepts of body augmentation in order to boost our sexual pleasure with "[...] surgeries to heighten sexual experience is becoming more and more popular, such as vaginaplasty, labiaplasty or penis lengthening and widening surgery" (Ornella, 2009, p. 312)? As Hughes notes "[w]hy stop with just a cosmetic enhancement or swapping your genitals for those of another sex, when you could have a penis with the responsiveness of a clitoris, or some entirely new sexual organ?" (Hughes, 2003).

Most of the advances mentioned above refer to the sense of touch, increasingly combined with vision through virtual reality capabilities and to a lesser extent sound. What of taste and smell? Will these be the next areas for development in the sex toy industry? Will digital implants or nano technology morph the sex toy and the body and increase stimulation to our nervous systems? Whilst we can be sure that technologies are advancing and will continue to do so what we cannot yet be sure of is the effects that such technologies will have on us as individuals and for society as a whole. We cannot be sure where these possibilities will lead, but it may well be a pleasurable experience to find out and clearly one that no longer has to be undertaken in isolation but which could potentially lead to a rejection of traditional relationships in favour of relationships and sexual encounters involving non-human alternatives. Or will we have a new form of 'augmented sexual reality' in which technology does not replace but enhances human physical sexual contact?

References

Barber, T. A. (2014). *For the love of artifice.* Paper presented at the AISB 50th Symposium 'Love and Sex with Robots', Goldsmiths University (3 April 2014). Retrieved 12 July 2016, from the University of Portsmouth website: http://eprints.port.ac.uk/18927/1/Trudy_Barber_For_the_love_of_artifice_3_4_2014.pdf.

Bauman, Z. (1998). On postmodern uses of sex. *Theory, Culture & Society 15*(3), 19–33.

Bronstein, C. (2011). *Battling pornography: The American feminist anti-pornography movement, 1976–1986.* Cambridge: Cambridge University Press.

Comella, L. (2010). "Remaking the Sex Industry: The Adult Expo as a Microcosm", in Weitzer, R. (ed.) (2nd ed.) *Sex for Sale: Prostitution, Pornography, and the Sex Industry*, (pp. 285–306), New York: Routledge.

Copley, C. (15 March 2016). 'How to Hack a Sex Toy: tech firms warn public on growing cyber risks'. *Reuters.* Retrieved 11 July 2016 from the Reuters website: www.reuters.com/article/us-germany-cyber-idUSKCN0WH1YU.

De Zeen (2016). Wang Tseng's Wisp Wearables Are an Alternative to "Intense" Sex Toys. Retrieved 11 July 2016 from the de Zeen website: www.dezeen.com/2016/06/27/wisp-collection-wan-ting-tseng-alternative-sex-toy-erotic-device-royal-college-of-art-graduate-2016/.

Dworkin, A. (1981). *Pornography: Men possessing women.* London: London Women's Press.

Dworkin A. and McKinnon C.A., (1988) *Pornography and Civil Rights: A New Day for Women's Equality.* Retrieved 11 July 2016 online at: www.nostatusquo.com/ACLU/dworkin/other/ordinance/newday/TOC.htm.

Fahs, B. and Swank, E. (2013). Adventures with the "plastic man": Sex toys, compulsory heterosexuality, and the politics of women's sexual pleasure. *Sexuality & Culture 17*(4), 666–685.

Fan, L. (2015). International segmentation of the sex toy market. *International Journal of Arts and Commerce 4*, 30–39.

Fleshlight (2016). Retrieved 12 July 2016 on the Fleshlight website: www.fleshlight-international.eu/.

Gibb, R. (23 January 2016). 'A Sex Toy for Women's Health', *Guardian.* Retrieved 11 July 2016 from the Guardian website: www.theguardian.com/society/2016/jan/23/sex-toy-dildo-womens-health-conception-she-convention.

Hall, L. (n.d.) Doctors masturbating women as a cure for hysteria/Victorian vibrators. Retrieved November 2016 www.lesleyahall.net/factoids.htm#hysteria.

Hawkes R., (2016) "Forget Westworld there is a real life campaign against sex robots" The Telegraph 12th October 2016 retrieved November 2016, www.telegraph.co.uk/tv/2016/10/12/forget-westworld-theres-a-real-life-campaign-against-sex-robots/.

Heljakka, K. (2016) Fifty Shades of Toys: Notions of Play and Things for Play in the Fifty Shades of Grey Canon, *Intensities: The Journal of Cult Media* 8, 59–73.

Herbenick, D., Barnhart, K. J., Beavers, K. and Benge, S. (2015). Vibrators and other sex toys are commonly recommended to patients, but does size matter? dimensions of commonly sold products. *The Journal of Sexual Medicine 12*(3), 641–645.

Hern, A. (14 March 2017). 'Vibrator maker ordered to pay out C$4m for tracking users' sexual activity', *Guardian*. Retrieved 14 March 2017 from the Guardian website: www.theguardian.com/technology/2017/mar/14/we-vibe-vibrator-tracking-users-sexual-habits.

Hughes, J. (9 February 2003). The Future of Sex. Retrieved 11 July 2016 from the Institute for Ethics and Emerging Technologies website: http://ieet.org/index.php/IEET/more/hughes20030209.

Jannini, E. A., Limoncin, E., Ciocca, G., Buehler, S. and Krychman, M. (2012). Ethical aspects of sexual medicine. Internet, vibrators, and other sex aids: Toys or therapeutic instruments? *The Journal of Sexual Medicine 9*(12), 2994–3001.

Juffer, J. (1998). *At home with pornography: Women, sex, and everyday life*. New York: NYU Press.

Lieberman, H. (2016). Selling sex toys: Marketing and the meaning of vibrators in early twentieth-century America. *Enterprise & Society 17*(02), 393–433.

Maines, R. P. (2001). *The technology of orgasm: "Hysteria," the vibrator, and women's sexual satisfaction*. Baltimore: JHU Press.

Martin, A. (2013). Fifty shades of sex shop: Sexual fantasy for sale. *Sexualities 16*(8), 980–984.

Mortimer Granville, J. (1883). *Nerve-vibration and excitation as agents in the treatment of functional disorder and organic disease*. Churchill.

Moyes, S. (8 July 2016). Supermarket chain under fire for selling sex toys right next to childrens' medicine. *The Sun*. Retrieved 11 July 2016 from The Sun website: www.thesun.co.uk/news/1415095/supermarket-chain-under-fire-for-selling-sex-toys-right-next-to-childrens-medicine/.

OhMiBod (2016). Blue Motion. Retrieved 11 July 2016 from the OhMiBod website: http://shop.ohmibod.com/Boutique-ohMiBod/blueMotion.

Ornella, A. (2009). Posthuman pleasures: Transcending the human-machine boundary. *Theology & Sexuality 15*(3), 311–328.

Oxford English Dictionary (2016) 'Sex Toy'. Retrieved 11 July 2016 from the OED Online website www.oxforddictionaries.com/definition/english/sex%20toy.

Parikka, J. and Sampson, T. D. (eds.). (2009). *The spam book: on viruses, porn, and other anomalies from the dark side of digital culture*. New York: Hampton Press.

Pew Survey (2014) A.I, Robotics and The Future of Jobs. Retrieved 11 July 2016 from the Pew Internet website: www.pewinternet.org/files/2014/08/Future-of-AI-Robotics-and-Jobs.pdf.

Raessens, J. (2006). Playful identities, or the ludification of culture. *Games and Culture 1*(1), 52–57.

Rheingold, H. (1991). *Virtual reality: Exploring the brave new technologies*. New York: Simon & Schuster Adult Publishing Group.

Richardson, K. (2015). The asymmetrical 'relationship': parallels between prostitution and the development of sex robots. *ACM SIGCAS Computers and Society* *45*(3), 290–293.

Rosenberger, J. G., Schick, V., Herbenick, D., Novak, D. S. and Reece, M. (2012). Sex toy use by gay and bisexual men in the United States. *Archives of Sexual Behaviour 41*(2), 449–458.

Rossolatos, G. (2016). Good vibrations: Charting the dominant and emergent discursive regimes of sex toys. *The Qualitative Report 21*(8), 1475–1494.

Seale, A. (2013). Diverting dildos: A Toronto co-op has started Canada's first sex toy recycling program. *Alternatives Journal 39*(5), 40–42.

Smith, C. (2007). Designed for pleasure style, indulgence and accessorized sex. *European Journal of Cultural Studies 10*(2), 167–184.

Storr, M. (2003). *Latex and lingerie: Shopping for pleasure at Ann Summers parties.* Camden: Bloomsbury Publishing.

Svakom (2016). Retrieved 11 July 2016 from the Svakom website: www.svakom.net/camera-vibator/.

Tenga (2016). Tenga Fitting Device. Retrieved 11 July 2016 from the Tenga website: www.tenga-global.com/fitting/.

Wagner, M. and Broll, W. (2014). *I wish you were here–not! The future of spatially separated sexual intercourse.* Selected Papers, AISB 50th Symposium 'Love and Sex with Robots', Goldsmiths University (3 April 2014), pp. 90–96. Retrieved 12 July 2016 Goldsmiths University website: http://doc.gold.ac.uk/aisb50/AISB50-S16/AISB50-S16-Wagner-paper.pdf.

Walther, L. and Schouten, J. W. (2016). Next stop, pleasure town: Identity transformation and women's erotic consumption. *Journal of Business Research 69*(1), 273–283.

Watson, E. D., Séguin, L. J., Milhausen, R. R. and Murray, S. H. (2016). The Impact of a couple's vibrator on men's perceptions of their own and their partner's sexual pleasure and satisfaction. *Men and Masculinities 19*(4), 370–383.

Winks, C. and Semans, A. (2002). *The Good Vibrations Guide to Sex* (3rd ed.). San Francisco, CA: Cleis Press.

Index